# Cosmic and Universal Laws

Infinite Laws

for a Happy and Prosperous Life

Margo Kirtikar Ph.D.

Order this book online at www.trafford.com/07-3095
or email orders@trafford.com

Most Trafford titles are also available at major online book retailers.

© Copyright 2008 Margo Kirtikar Ph.D.

All rights reserved. No part of this publication may be reproduced, stored in a retrieval system, or transmitted, in any form or by any means, electronic, mechanical, photocopying, recording, or otherwise, without the written prior permission of the author.

Cover Design by: Gabrielle Von Bernstorff

Publishers:
1st Edition 'Flowing with Universal Laws'
Printed 07/05/2002 by (First Books) Author House, USA

2nd re-edited Edition 'Cosmic and Universal Laws'
Printed 2008 by Trafford Puplishing, Victoria B.C Canada.

Note for Librarians: A cataloguing record for this book is available from Library and Archives Canada at www.collectionscanada.ca/amicus/index-e.html

ISBN: 978-1-4251-6669-4

*We at Trafford believe that it is the responsibility of us all, as both individuals and corporations, to make choices that are environmentally and socially sound. You, in turn, are supporting this responsible conduct each time you purchase a Trafford book, or make use of our publishing services. To find out how you are helping, please visit www.trafford.com/responsiblepublishing.html*

*Our mission is to efficiently provide the world's finest, most comprehensive book publishing service, enabling every author to experience success. To find out how to publish your book, your way, and have it available worldwide, visit us online at www.trafford.com/10510*

www.trafford.com

North America & international
toll-free: 1 888 232 4444 (USA & Canada)
phone: 250 383 6864 ♦ fax: 250 383 6804
email: info@trafford.com

The United Kingdom & Europe
phone: +44 (0)1865 722 113 ♦ local rate: 0845 230 9601
facsimile: +44 (0)1865 722 868 ♦ email: info.uk@trafford.com

10 9 8 7 6 5 4 3

To my adored grandsons
Rafael and Noah

and

all the Children of the new World

Infinite Laws
that will guide you
to
a Happy and Prosperous Life
In the Golden Age

'We are now in the Satya Yuga
Heaven on Earth
the Golden Age.
It is the time to decide what you want,
to seek divine guidance and the tools to achieve it.

What is possible in Heaven on Earth?
Everything. Limitless. Miraculous. Divine.'

Dattatreya Sivababa

*Introduction*

This book is one of the most comprehensive studies of cosmic and universal laws that exists to date. The general perception is that we are born into life on earth without having any instructions on how to live a productive and happy life. This is of course a gross misconception on our part. Throughout the ages and ever since mankind has existed, infinite universal laws have always existed and they continue to exist for those of us who want to listen, learn and understand. We can look at universal laws as keys that open the mysteries of life itself. The one who holds these keys is able to be in tune with the workings of life and becomes intuitive and inspired. To such a person revelations manifest and his or her language becomes music that inspires others.

There is a wisdom that has been handed down through the ages that can be found in all cultures, in folk tales, in fairy tales, in science, in business practice, and in all spiritual teachings. Some of these laws have been written about extensively and others have been left by the wayside as humanity becomes ever more materialistic.

The Tales of the Arabian Nights, for example, are revelations of divine laws and are much more than folklore for children and adults, when the tales are truly and correctly understood. The inner implications of accomplishments are perfectly possible when one is sincere, worthy and humble enough to be trusted with the power and the truth that they reveal. The great master 'ignorance' and his close friends 'pride, doubt, fear, ridicule, scepticism' and many of such useless parasites, have fastened themselves upon the mentality and feeling of humans making them blind, holding them slaves within their own self imposed limitations. If it were not for these negative traits which act like vampires, humankind would be able to see and to know that within the light that animates the

## Cosmic and Universal Laws

physical body, exists an intelligence and a power that can and will carry out perfectly whatever the mind directs. This can be done when harmony is maintained and all that is thought and aspired for is of a constructive nature.

When we say, 'In Him we live and move and have our Being,' we are referring to the cosmic energy that surrounds us. So we can say that we are living and bathing in God's energy. This field of energy is also known as the Akasha field, the ethereal substance that permeates everything. Cosmic Law rules everything in the cosmos, and Universal Law rules everything on earth. All Cosmic and Universal Laws are spiritual and, therefore, invincible, unchangeable and eternal. These laws manifest themselves through energy, and we humans have been given the freedom, the intelligence and the will power to activate these energies, to make them work for us. But in order to activate these laws, we first need to be aware of them, then, we need to understand them, in order to be in tune with them.

The more we are able to integrate attributes of the universal laws into our daily lives, the more harmony we have in our life, and we experience what we refer to as *going with the flow, when everything seems to flow without extra effort on our part*. When we live, however, against the energies of these laws of nature, we experience a disharmony in our life where everything seems to go wrong for us. We have been given the freedom of choice, to do one or the other, to work with or against these invincible laws. We all know deep inside us of the existence of these spiritual laws, if we would only take a moment to listen, in silence, to the spirit within. It is a life long endeavor to study, to reflect on and to understand the universal laws as good as we can. It is never too late to apply them in our daily life, so that we can make things change for the better in our world. Any moment can be the right moment to begin. The universal laws assure us of that.

Planning is a function of divine intelligence and nothing happens by accident in God's universe. There are planetary influences that we as humans have no control of. Each one of us is an indi-

## Cosmic and Universal Laws

vidual planet and as one planet is related to another, so in the same way all planets are related to mankind. The changing of the condition of a planet, what is produced by it and what effect is produced by the planet have an effect upon a human being's life. Outwardly man is so small as to be a drop in the ocean. If the cosmos with its planets is an ocean then the individual is a drop. But inwardly the planet is a drop in the ocean of the man's heart. A Sufi philosopher once said, when ignorance vanishes, the heart will open and the whole universe will become a bubble in the ocean of the heart. Smallness and imperfections are the outcome of ignorance and relate to limitation. The day the heart is open the whole universe will be in it, and the source of destiny, its secret and its mystery will reveal itself to the man.

The human has two aspects in him. One aspect is that he is a mechanical being where he is but a machine controlled by conditions, his impressions, his actions, by outer and cosmic influences. He is but a tool of influences. The more this aspect is pronounced in man, the less evolved he is. The other aspect in man is his creativity, here he shows the sign of a being representative of the Creator, he shows that he is not only linked with God but is a part of God, i.e. his innermost self is Godly. This Godly spark is within every living soul, it is this Godly power that makes it possible for man to change conditions by his free will, but this can only be when he is aware of his inner Godliness. It is the absence of this awareness that reduces the human being to a machine. With the awareness of and the in-depth knowledge of how the universal laws operate, the human being awakens the Godly Spark within.

This book is but a compilation of universal laws that I have collected so far and expanded upon. I daresay that a book could be written about each of the 269 laws listed here.

# A Personal Note to the Reader

One way to use this book after you have read it completely through at least once to familiarize yourself with the general idea, is to open it any time you feel like it, anywhere, at random and read one universal law. Any law. Read it slowly, get familiar with it, digest it and let the meaning of the law sink in to you. That you do by reflecting on it and thinking about it for one week or longer, any time anywhere. You will find that the more you concentrate on the law and its true meaning, the more it will grow on you and the more you will understand. The next thing to do is to try to integrate the qualities of this law into your lifestyle while observing the law being activated by people around you. Continue to do this for a few weeks and observe how awareness of a particular law affects you and your life. Repeat this any time you feel like it with another law and then integrate that in addition to the first into your life. Repeat again with another law. You will find that if you keep the Noble Eightfold Path of Buddha constantly in your mind you would be activating many of these universal laws automatically.

Another way for you to use this book most effectively is when you are faced with a problem that you cannot solve. Look for one or more laws that relate best to your problem, read them and reflect on the laws and analyze your own thoughts and actions, try to figure out where you might have gone wrong and what you can do to put things right. Your life is guaranteed to take a turn for the better once you have learned to recognize and accept the energies of these universal laws, and then to activate them with full awareness by integrating them in your way of life.

With your understanding of the universal laws you can activate the energies according to your individual experiences and situations. The importance is not the law in its naked version but in its living form. It is something that enables you to enrich yourself rather than impoverish or limit you. It is meant to expand your horizon. Think of universal laws as the elements of rain, vapor, steam, river or spring all of which is water manifesting in different forms with different qualities serving different purposes.

Perhaps now that we have a better understanding of these natural laws we can understand why good ultimately always triumphs over evil. We can understand that any totalitarian regime that limit and reduce its subjects to mechanical robots, robbing them of all their individualism and dignity is inevitably doomed to failure. We can understand that although the selfish and the greedy seem to be winning for a certain time, in the end live to regret and see their deeds boomerang on them in one way or another as are all dictators ultimately doomed to fall.

Humanity in general is becoming more aware. Thanks to modern technology, information and education is reaching out to the far and forgotten corners of the world. In particular we are learning more and more about our origin as humans, we are learning more than ever before about our own make up and our psyche. We also have more knowledge than ever before about our universe and what role our earth and we, the human family, play in this grand symphony of life. As ignorance diminishes along with the old political, educational and religious institutions, there is hope that the younger generations will make this a better world.

This book is not intended as a book of instructions for you to follow blindly, nor do I claim what I have written here to be the ultimate and only truth. My intention is rather to inspire you, to challenge and to activate your mind and imagination, to prompt your own inner personal dialogue, to rouse your curiosity and to intensify your enthusiasm for the joy of life.

I would like to quote the following by C. G. Jung: *'It is always the human being who interprets and gives meaning to any fact. We are susceptible to those suggestions with which we are already secretly in accord. For it all depends on how we look at things and not how things really are in themselves. A certain kind of behavior brings corresponding results, and the subjective understanding of*

## Cosmic and Universal Laws

*these results give rise to the experiences which in turn influence behavior and thus close the circle of an individual's destiny.*

*Whoever protects himself against what is new and strange thereby regresses to the past, falls into the same neurotic conditions as the man who identifies himself with the new and runs away from the past. The only difference is that the one has estranged himself from the past and the other, from the future. In principle both are doing the same thing. They are salvaging a narrow state of consciousness. The alternative is to shatter it with the tension inherent in the play of opposites in the dualistic stage and thereby to build up a state of wider and higher consciousness.'* C.G. Jung, Modern Man in Search of a Soul, p96.

I have used the terms *'man'* and *'his'* etc., throughout the book merely for convenience's sake. Put simply, you see, in Sanskrit, the word 'Manahah' and written as 'Man' means mind, a thinking being, regardless of the gender. So naturally whenever I refer to 'man' I am referring to both male and female.

For the sake of clarity and easy access for the reader to find a specific law, I have listed the laws alphabetically and I have also numbered the laws according to their alphabetical order. Neither the numbers, nor the order of listing the laws, have any specific meaning.

In the first edition of Universal Laws, which was printed in 2002, I had listed a total of 246 laws, in this edition I have a total of 269 laws, that is another 23 universal laws that I have discovered since, while continuing with my studies and research and I am sure that there are many more to discover still. I have the feeling that a book of instructions was given to us mankind after all, but somehow somewhere this was lost and we, humanity, as we evolve collectively, are now in the process of picking up the lost pieces.

# Contents

Introduction ................................................................ *vii*
A Personal Note to the Reader ................................... xi

Who We Are .................................................................. 1
Universal Laws Transcend all Religions ...................... 4
As Above so Below ....................................................... 7
The Constitution of the universe ............................... 10
Universal Laws............................................................ 13

| | | |
|---|---|---|
| 1. | The Law of the Absolute | 21 |
| 2. | The Law of Absorption | 22 |
| 3. | The Law of Abstraction | 23 |
| 4. | The Law of Abundance | 25 |
| 5. | The Law of Acceptance | 28 |
| 6. | The Law of Accommodation | 30 |
| 7. | The Law of Accountability | 31 |
| 8. | The Law of Action | 32 |
| 9. | The Law of Action and Reaction | 34 |
| 10. | The Law of Activity | 36 |
| 11. | The Law of Actuality | 37 |
| 12. | The Law of Adaptation | 38 |
| 13. | The Law of Adjustment | 39 |
| 14. | The Law of Affection | 40 |
| 15. | The Law of Affinity | 41 |
| 16. | The Law of Akasha | 43 |
| 17. | The Law of the Alpha and Omega | 45 |
| 18. | The Law of Analogy | 46 |
| 19. | The Law of Apperception | 48 |

20. The Law of Archetype .................................................49
21. The Law of Ascension .................................................50
22. The Law of Assembly..................................................51
23. The Law of Association ..............................................53
24. The Law of Attitude....................................................54
25. The Law of Attraction.................................................56
26. The law of Attraction and Repulsion...........................58
27. The Law of Authority .................................................62
28. The Law of Averages..................................................63
29. The Law of Avoidance................................................64
30. The Law of Awareness................................................65
31. The Law of Balance....................................................67
32. The Law of Being .......................................................69
33. The Law of Believing and Knowing............................71
34. The Law of Catastrophe .............................................72
35. The Law of Center......................................................73
36. The Law of Challenge ................................................75
37. The Law of Chance....................................................76
38. The Law of Change ...................................................77
39. The Law of Chaos and Order .....................................80
40. The Law of Chemical Affinity....................................82
41. The Law of Choice ....................................................84
42. The Law of Circle/Circulation....................................85
43. The Law of Coalescence.............................................87
44. The Law of Co-creation..............................................88
45. The Law of Cohesion .................................................89
46. The Law of Color ......................................................90
47. The Law of Common Ground ....................................92
48. The Law of Communication.......................................94
49. The Law of Compassion............................................95
50. The Law of Compensation ........................................96
51. The Law of Completion..............................................98
52. The Law of Concentration..........................................99
53. The Law of Condensing Light...................................101
54. The Law of Consciousness.......................................103

| | | |
|---|---|---|
| 55. | The Law of Contact | 105 |
| 56. | The Law of Continuity of Consciousness | 106 |
| 57. | The Law of Correlation | 107 |
| 58. | The Law of Correspondence | 108 |
| 59. | The Law of Cosmic Equation | 110 |
| 60. | The Law of Cosmic Manifestation | 111 |
| 61. | The Law of Cosmic Web | 112 |
| 62. | The Law of Courage | 113 |
| 63. | The Law of Creativity/Creation | 114 |
| 64. | The Law of Credibility | 116 |
| 65. | The Law of Currency Exchange | 117 |
| 66. | The Law of Cycles | 118 |
| 67. | The Law of Cyclic Returns | 120 |
| 68. | The Law of Description | 122 |
| 69. | The Law of Desire | 123 |
| 70. | The Law of Destiny | 124 |
| 71. | The Law of Dharma | 125 |
| 72. | The Law of Differentiation | 126 |
| 73. | The Law of Discipline | 128 |
| 74. | The Law of Disintegration | 130 |
| 75. | The Law of Dissolution | 132 |
| 76. | The Law of Divine Flow | 133 |
| 77. | The Law of Divine Union | 134 |
| 78. | The Law of Drama | 136 |
| 79. | The Law of Duality | 137 |
| 80. | The Law of Duplication | 139 |
| 81. | The Law of Duration and Density | 140 |
| 82. | The Law of Dying | 141 |
| 83. | The Law of the Earth | 142 |
| 84. | The Law of Economy | 144 |
| 85. | The Law of Economy of Force | 145 |
| 86. | The Law of Education | 147 |
| 87. | The Law of Elements | 149 |
| 88. | The Law of Elevation | 150 |
| 89. | The Law of Energy | 151 |

| | | |
|---|---|---|
| 90. | The Law of Enthusiasm | 154 |
| 91. | The Law of Essence | 156 |
| 92. | The Law of Essential Integrity | 157 |
| 93. | The Law of Evolution | 158 |
| 94. | The Law of Example | 160 |
| 95. | The Law of Exclusion | 161 |
| 96. | The Law of Expansion | 162 |
| 97. | The Law of Expectation | 164 |
| 98. | The Law of Faith | 165 |
| 99. | The Law of Fixation | 166 |
| 100. | The Law of Flexibility | 167 |
| 101. | The Law of Forgiveness | 168 |
| 102. | The Law of Freedom | 170 |
| 103. | The Law of Free Will | 172 |
| 104. | The Law of Friction | 174 |
| 105. | The Law of Fulfilment | 175 |
| 106. | The Law of Garment of Light | 176 |
| 107. | The Law of Gender | 177 |
| 108. | The Law of Giving | 178 |
| 109. | The Law of Goodness | 180 |
| 110. | The Law of Goodwill | 181 |
| 111. | The Law of Grace | 183 |
| 112. | The Law of Gratitude | 185 |
| 113. | The Law of Gravitation | 187 |
| 114. | The Law of Group Endeavor | 188 |
| 115. | The Law of Group Life | 189 |
| 116. | The Law of Group Progress | 190 |
| 117. | The Law of Growth | 191 |
| 118. | The Law of Happiness | 192 |
| 119. | The Law of Harmony | 193 |
| 120. | The Law of Healing | 194 |
| 121. | The Law of Higher Will | 196 |
| 122. | The Law of Honesty | 197 |
| 123. | The Law of Honor | 198 |
| 124. | The Law of Humility | 199 |

## Cosmic and Universal Laws

125. The Law of Identity ..................................................200
126. The Law of Impartiality............................................201
127. The Law of Increase ................................................202
128. The Law of Inertia ...................................................204
129. The Law of Infinite Energy......................................205
130. The Law of Infinity..................................................207
131. The Law of Information ..........................................208
132. The Law of Initiation...............................................209
133. The Law of Initiative ...............................................212
134. The Law of Integration ...........................................213
135. The Law of Intelligence...........................................214
136. The Law of Intention ...............................................215
137. The Law of Interdependence ...................................216
138. The Law of Intuition................................................218
139. The Law of Isolation/Limitation..............................219
140. The Law of Inverse Proportions ..............................220
141. The Law of Justice...................................................221
142. The Sirian Law of Karma ........................................223
143. The Law of Knowledge ...........................................226
144. The Law of Least Effort ..........................................228
145. The Law of Leverage...............................................230
146. The Law of Liability................................................231
147. The Law of Liberation .............................................232
148. The Law of Life.......................................................233
149. The Law of Light.....................................................235
150. The Law of Lotus ....................................................237
151. The Law of Love......................................................239
152. The Law of Macrocosm and Microcosm.................242
153. The Law of Magic ...................................................243
154. The Law of Magnetic Control .................................244
155. The Law of Magnetic Impulse.................................245
156. The Law of Magnetism............................................246
157. The Law of Manifestation .......................................247
158. The Law of Mantras ................................................249
159. The Law of Meditation ............................................251

## Cosmic and Universal Laws

| | | |
|---|---|---|
| 160. | The Law of Meekness | 254 |
| 161. | The Law of Mentalism | 255 |
| 162. | The Law of Mercy | 256 |
| 163. | The Law of Miracles | 257 |
| 164. | The Law of Moderation | 258 |
| 165. | The Law of Monadic Return | 259 |
| 166. | The Law of Money | 260 |
| 167. | The Law of Music | 261 |
| 168. | The Law of New Being | 263 |
| 169. | The Law of Non-intervention | 264 |
| 170. | The Law of Non-Judgment | 265 |
| 171. | The Law of Non-Resistance | 266 |
| 172. | The Law of Number Measure and Weight | 268 |
| 173. | The Law of One | 269 |
| 174. | The Law of Opportunity | 271 |
| 175. | The Law of Order and Creation | 272 |
| 176. | The Law of Paradox | 273 |
| 177. | The Law of Patience | 275 |
| 178. | The Law of Patterns | 277 |
| 179. | The Law of Peace | 280 |
| 180. | The Law of Penetration | 282 |
| 181. | The Law of Perception | 283 |
| 182. | The Law of Perfection | 284 |
| 183. | The Law of Periodicity | 286 |
| 184. | The Law of Permanence | 287 |
| 185. | The Law of Perspective | 288 |
| 186. | The Law of Planetary Affinity | 289 |
| 187. | The Law of Planning | 291 |
| 188. | The Law of Polarity | 294 |
| 189. | The Law of Poverty | 296 |
| 190. | The Law of Practice | 298 |
| 191. | The Law of Praise | 300 |
| 192. | The Law of Prayer | 302 |
| 193. | The Law of the Present Moment | 304 |
| 194. | The Law of Privacy | 306 |

| | | |
|---|---|---|
| 195. | The Law of Process | 307 |
| 196. | The Law of Productivity | 309 |
| 197. | The Law of Progress | 310 |
| 198. | The Law of Projection | 312 |
| 199. | The Law of Prophecy | 313 |
| 200. | The Law of Prosperity | 315 |
| 201. | The Law of Purification | 317 |
| 202. | The Law of Radiation | 319 |
| 203. | The Law of Reality | 320 |
| 204. | The Law of Rebirth | 321 |
| 205. | The Law of Rebound | 323 |
| 206. | The Law of Receiving | 324 |
| 207. | The Law of Reconciliation | 326 |
| 208. | The Law of Reflection | 327 |
| 209. | The Law of Reincarnation | 328 |
| 210. | The Law of Relativity | 330 |
| 211. | The Law of Relaxation | 331 |
| 212. | The Law of Release | 332 |
| 213. | The Law of Repetition | 333 |
| 214. | The Law of Repulse | 334 |
| 215. | The Law of Repulsion | 335 |
| 216. | The Law of Respect | 336 |
| 217. | The Law of Respiration | 338 |
| 218. | The Law of Responsibility | 340 |
| 219. | The Law of Revelation | 342 |
| 220. | The Law of Rhythm | 343 |
| 221. | The Law of Right Human Relations | 345 |
| 222. | The Law of Right to One's Space | 347 |
| 223. | The Law of Ritual and Ceremony | 348 |
| 224. | The Law of Sacrifice | 349 |
| 225. | The Law of Sacrifice and Death | 351 |
| 226. | The Law of Schools | 352 |
| 227. | The Law of Seed | 354 |
| 228. | The Law of Service | 356 |
| 229. | The Law of Sex | 358 |

| | | |
|---|---|---|
| 230. | The Law of Silence | 360 |
| 231. | The Law of Simplicity | 362 |
| 232. | The Law of Solar Evolution | 363 |
| 233. | The Law of Solar Union | 364 |
| 234. | The Law of Soul | 365 |
| 235. | The Law of Sound | 367 |
| 236. | The Law of Speech | 370 |
| 237. | The Law of Spiral Movement | 372 |
| 238. | The Law of Spirit | 373 |
| 239. | The Law of Spiritual Approach | 374 |
| 240. | The Law of Spiritual Awakening | 375 |
| 241. | The Law of Spiritual Chemistry | 376 |
| 242. | The Law of Spiritual Non Perfection | 378 |
| 243. | The Law of the Subconscious Mind | 379 |
| 244. | The Law of Substitution | 381 |
| 245. | The Law of Suggestion | 382 |
| 246. | The Law of Summons | 383 |
| 247. | The Law of Supply | 384 |
| 248. | The Law of Surrender | 386 |
| 249. | The Law of Symbols | 388 |
| 250. | The Law of Synthesis | 390 |
| 251. | The Law of Teaching | 391 |
| 252. | The Law of Telepathy | 393 |
| 253. | The Law of Tenfold Return | 395 |
| 254. | The Law of Thought | 396 |
| 255. | The Law of Three | 398 |
| 256. | The Law of Three Requests | 400 |
| 257. | The Law of Time | 401 |
| 258. | The Law of Tolerance | 402 |
| 259. | The Law of Truth | 405 |
| 260. | The Law of Unconditional Love | 406 |
| 261. | The Law of Unfulfillment | 408 |
| 262. | The Law of Unity | 409 |
| 263. | The Law of Unity and Separation | 411 |
| 264. | The Law of Universal Sympathy | 412 |

*Cosmic and Universal Laws*

| | | |
|---|---|---|
| 265. | The Law of Vacuum | 413 |
| 266. | The Law of Vibration | 414 |
| 267. | The Law of Will of God | 416 |
| 268. | The Law of Will Power | 417 |
| 269. | The Law of Wisdom | 419 |

The Soul's Journey ......................................................... 420
Glossary ........................................................................... 423
Bibliography .................................................................... 431

# Who We Are

To truly know who we are we need to understand our complete human identity, our origin, our direction, our purpose, intention and our duty as humans. Through self-knowledge we can create a state of health, in which our spiritual and physical resources are equally active, in balance, working in harmony towards a common goal.

We are created as multi dimensional beings to experience life and to manifest our true nature and essence, the spirit, through a physical form. Our original home is in the spiritual dimension. Our purpose here on earth as we complete our human journey back to the spiritual dimension, is to develop, to strengthen and to refine our human qualities. We are meant to evolve in the physical world because the conditions in the tangible world are non-existent on the spiritual realm. In other words imagine the earth as being our stage and playground, and through each of our earth life, we are going through a specific training in order to evolve. The challenge is for us to progress and to refine our character, while being completely involved in the physical world, using our physical senses. Our challenge is that, as we go through our earth life, we are meant to remember our spiritual identity and origin.

Being the dominant species on earth, we are entrusted with the responsibility of being the guardians of the three lower kingdoms, the mineral, the plant and the animal worlds. Both our internal state of being and our external behavior and actions affect all life on our planet. If our world is out of balance, as we are experiencing now, it is because something has gone wrong within us. We have created a crisis in our relationships with all forms of life on earth and no amount of science or technology can correct this imbalance. Both the problem and the solution relate to our individual and collective state of being. None of what we humanity are experiencing now are acts of nature or done unto us by God. The destruction of our environment, our competitive and materialistic behavior, the poverty, the social injustice, crime, wars, exploitation of natural resources, are all symptoms of the huge imbalance in our own human nature and our development. We humanity, collectively, have no one to blame for all of our misfortunes but ourselves. We are the cause of our misery.

The chaos and the suffering that we presently experience is the terrible price that we must pay for breaking the laws of nature and for neglecting our spiritual faculties causing a disparity within us. Granted we have made gigantic progress in scientific and technological knowledge in the past century but in the meantime, we have sadly also created a chaotic world. The only way to correct this is if we change our individual and collective state of consciousness. To the average human life is an enigma, a deep mystery, a complex and an incomprehensible puzzle. But mystery is only another name for ignorance and everything that is unknown and not understood is a mystery. Once we have understanding, what once appeared to be mysterious is suddenly no mystery any more. Therefore, it is knowledge, plus the understanding, that is the key to the puzzle and the mystery of life.

The human is a creature of constant growth, living in a boundless ocean of progress, to be discovered and conquered by developing and cultivating one's inborn powers. The progress of the individual is mainly determined by the ruling mental powers that regulate one's actions and direction of one's faculties and powers, the sum total of which determine each one's personal fate. The ruling state of mind that is adopted by the individual is in accordance with the experiences and perception of the events in one's life. If one's predominant state of mind and attitudes are broadminded, harmonious, aspiring and positive then all energy will be directed towards constructive channels. If, however, one's disposition is negative, uncontrolled and disharmonious then all forces will be misdirected. Nature has no problems because she is orderly and disciplined and so when we have a problem, it is simply because we are not cooperating with a universal law.

## Cosmic and Universal Laws

Many of us today in the more 'civilized' part of the world suffer from a particular disease, namely an over developed intellect. Our mental activity dominates our inner feelings. While thinking is necessary and valuable to organize, to plan and to structure our life, it is an incomplete way to experience our life because we experience only a part of ourselves and not the whole. Our thoughts must be coordinated with our inner feelings because, it is through our feelings that we identify our human needs and those of other life forms. The other 'malheur' that many of us suffer from is our neglect of the spirit within and this has created a vacuum within our very being. We have managed to fill this vacuum with an over stimulated intellect and we have the tendency to think, rather than feel, our way through life. Unless we can balance our thinking with our feelings, intellect and heart, to be sensitive to our needs and to the needs of others, we reduce ourselves to being materialists, competitive, inconsiderate and egoistic. It is this vacuum that is now actually experienced as a deep empty hole in the chest area. It is this ache that we now desperately try to rid ourselves of, as we turn our attention to find solace in spirituality. We have finally realized that the material world is not the answer to everything and we are beginning to think that there might just be something else out there beyond our physical world.

# Universal Laws transcend all Religions

The nature of spirit is an individual philosophy for each and every one of us. No matter how diverse our beliefs or philosophies are, we in the physical world are all bound together by our thoughts, feelings, dreams, aspirations and actions. Universal laws are the basic principles of life, which transcend the diversity of individual beliefs. These laws apply to whatever our belief system or philosophy is. When applied correctly the universal laws allow us to reach our maximum spiritual potential and greatly enhance the experience of our manifestation in the material world. Understanding, universal laws enables us to review and see why our life is the way it is, if and where we might have gone wrong and how we can amend things.

Various Prophets appeared throughout the ages to all corners of the world to spread God's teachings to people of different cultures and tongues. Each of the Prophets and their disciples, some well known others less known and long forgotten, carried a particular message from the Higher Powers, the Source, The Higher Intelligence, God, suitable to that particular time and in accordance to the needs of the masses. These teachings eventually developed into the many religions and beliefs that are existent today. If we make an in-depth study of the essence of each of these original teachings, however, we would find a great similarity and a common thread running through all the disciplines. In fact we find all religions to be basically the same in essence. The theme of loving and honoring one another is the foundation of all alike. Any differences of opinions found in religions are usually misinterpretations of the truth, and these distortions have been largely imposed and forced upon the minds of the people by ignorant or misguided men with one intention only in mind: to keep the masses under their control through fear.

The essence in all religions talks of non-violence and ethical values, truth and purity, justice, control of the senses, honoring our parents and treating all other living beings as we would treat ourselves. Following are some examples:

'A man should wander about treating all creatures as he himself would be treated.' Jainism. Stutrakritanga 1.11.33.

'Not one of you is a believer until he loves for his brother what he loves for himself.' Islam. Forty Hadith of an-Nawawi 13.

'You shall love thy neighbor as thyself.' Judaism and Christianity Bible, Leviticus 19.18.

'The heart of the person before you is a mirror. See there your own form.' Shintoism from Japan.

'Whatever you wish that men would do to you, do so to them.' Christianity. Bible, Matthew 7.12.

'One should not behave towards others in a way which is disagreeable to oneself. This is the essence of morality. All other activities are due to selfish desire.' Hinduism, Mahabharata, Anusasana Parva, 113.8.

'Try your best to treat others as you would wish to be treated yourself, and you will find that this the shortest way to benevolence.' Chinese. Confucianism. Mencius VII.A.4.

'One who takes a pointed stick to kill a bird should first try it on himself to feel how it hurts.' African Traditional Religion. Proverb Nigeria.

'Whatever affliction may visit you is for what your own hands have earned.' Islam. Qur'an 42.30.

'Suffering is the offspring of violence. Realize this and be watchful.' Jainism. Acarangasutra 3.13.

'Our body in Kali Yuga is a field of action, as man sows, so is his reward. Nothing is determined by empty talk. Anyone swallowing poison must die. Brother, behold the Creator's justice, as are a man's actions, so is his recompense.' Sikhism, Adi Granth, Guri Var, M.4, p.308.

'All who take the sword will perish by the sword.' Christianity, Bible, Matthew 26.52.

'Benevolence, humaneness towards others, honesty, love, trustworthiness' are the highest virtues in Confucianism, China.

'Ashes fly back in the face of him who throws them.' African Traditional Religions. Yoruba Proverb Nigeria.

'Unrighteousness practiced in this world, does not once produce its fruit, but like a cow, advancing slowly, it cuts off the roots of him who committed it.' Hinduism, Law of Manu. 4.172.

'Men who acquire wealth by evil deeds, by adhering to principles which are wrong, fall into the trap of their own passions and fettered with karma they sink further down.' Jainism, Uttaradyayana Sutra 4.2.

'As you plan for somebody so God plans for you.' African Traditional Religions, Igbo Proverb Nigeria.

The following passage is perhaps the most significant because it refers clearly to the energies of Cosmic and Universal Laws that one cannot escape.

'Not in the sky, nor in mid-ocean, nor in a mountain cave, is found that place on earth where abiding one may escape from the consequences of one's evil deed.' Buddhism. Dhammapada 127.

The God Almighty is referred to as *'the all seeing'* that one cannot hide from. Today we have the intelligence and understanding to realize that the 'All Seeing God' and the 'Cosmic and Universal Laws or Energies' are one and the same. We can never hide from *'the all seeing'* because it is there within each and every one of us and *how can we hide from our own selves?*

# As Above so Below

Hermes Trismegistus said: 'That which is below is like to that which is above.' Some people erroneously believe this to mean that what is on earth is the same as it is in Heaven, the macro-micro cosmic relation. In fact, what is actually meant here was that life on earth is subjected to Universal Laws, the same as the Higher Spheres are subjected to Cosmic.

Modern science is well versed in physics and chemistry. However, modern science does not as yet fully accept the existence of spiritual physics or spiritual chemistry, or the psychic world as governed by moral laws. Granted it is not always easy to identify these laws but that is no reason to claim that they do not exist. An invisible world does exist and our whole life, if we really stop to think about it is based on things we cannot see. More and more we are becoming aware of the fact that our inner world is governed by a non-physical world. Even if you do not believe in God you cannot fail to recognize that there is an order in nature and consequently, there must be a 'Higher Intelligence' which created that order.

Initiatic science acknowledges the existence of three worlds:

The divine world which is the level of ideas, the psychic world which is the level of thoughts and feelings, and the physical world, the world of forms and materialism. Just as we earthlings have to obey nature's laws, nature obeys the laws of the spirit and it is spirit that commands nature. The material world in which we live is linked to the 'moral' world, which in turn is linked to the far higher world of ideas. Because these moral laws are not written down on paper, some people think that they have the right to do whatever they want, but ignorance is no defence before the law. Even if we do not know of these unwritten moral laws, those who fail to abide by these laws inevitably pay the high price of remorse, suffering, bitterness, disappointments and sometimes they might even have to pay the price for their folly with money or with their life. More and more we begin to understand that everything in life is connected and related to everything else, so one can never act alone and think it does not concern anyone else. In fact what each one of us thinks and does very much concerns and touches everyone else in some fashion or another, in the short term or the long term.

For us to have a contented and joyful life we must recognize and accept three major laws: Universal Laws, Moral Laws and Human Laws. The same laws are at work on all levels of existence for the Universe is one and on every level and at every stage, the same phenomena can be found, although always in different more subtle forms. Our earth is a living being, it breathes and grows and changes constantly. It is said that nature has a memory and nothing can ever erase what it has once recorded. Whatever we find on earth can be found also in water, and whatever is in water exists in air and in all living things. All four elements of nature obey the same laws with some differences in the way they apply the laws. Some react violently and others rapidly. For instance the human mind is analogous to the element air, and this is expressed in the form of ideas and thoughts. Emotions are analogous to the element water and these can be abysmal, dismal and cumbrous or pure, virtuous and light.

Over and above the physical body, the human has subtle bodies namely: etheric, astral, mental, causal, buddhic and atmic. The tragic reality is that most of us are ignorant of our own structure and composition and of the constant interaction that goes on between human beings and the invisible beings in the other regions of the universe. It is this ignorance that is the cause of all of our misfortunes. It is easy to create the future but it is very difficult to erase the past. Good always produces good and evil always produces evil. Some people might think that if one is too kind one can get hurt or if one is too generous one gets taken advantage of. This is in reality selfish thinking. The truth is we can never be too kind, too generous, too loving or too considerate towards others. The universe created by God is an immense world bursting with treasures in great abundance. How can we go wrong if we live in abundance following the guidance of the Higher Intelligence that has so marvelously ordered and arranged such a miraculous, bounteous, beautiful world.

# The Constitution of the Universe

In recent decades, modern science has systematically revealed deeper layers of order in nature, from the atomic to the nuclear and sub-nuclear level of nature's functioning. This progressive exploration has culminated in the recent discovery of the unified field of all the laws of nature, the ultimate source of order in the universe.

Both modern and ancient understandings, locate the unified source of nature's perfect order in a single, self-interacting field of intelligence at the foundation of all the laws of nature. This field consecutively creates, from within itself, all the diverse laws of nature governing life at every level of the manifest universe. The unified field of natural law inside and its diversified expression outside are completely parallel to each other. The laws governing the self-interacting dynamics of the unified field are the eternal non-changing basis of natural law and the ultimate source of the order and harmony that is displayed throughout creation.

It is written in ancient scriptures that the laws of nature are imposed upon humanity and cannot be avoided. If these laws are broken, infringed or side stepped, they carry their own penalty within themselves, and this nemesis cannot be avoided. This gives us a sense of justice as we create our own heaven or hell right here on earth.

We live in the three worlds, we live in the divine and spiritual world, that of ideas, imagination and creativity; we live in the physical world that of forms and concrete manifestation; and we live in the psychic world, a world of thoughts and feelings. The physical world is linked to the psychic world and that in turn is linked to the divine world. If human beings fail to see this connection it is because they have never observed nor cared to study things with enough care and attention and as long as this deficiency is not corrected, the results will continue to be disastrous. The laws mentioned here are far subtler than physical laws and they are inherent in man's physical body, in his soul and spirit. These laws are not written down anywhere, but people who ignore them and live in the believe that they can do and behave in whatever they please eventually do pay the price of remorse, suffering, bitterness, regrets and loss on every level.

Progress in life is only achieved when we acknowledge and live by these laws. The Cosmic Powers are the law makers, the Intelligences who rule the universe. Initiates understand that if someone wants to become extremely rich, he must never break any laws: not the divine laws, not the moral laws, nor the physical laws and not the laws of man either. Just as we obey the laws of nature, nature itself also has to obey spiritual laws that command it.

Nature has different degrees. On the lowest level is physical nature, above this is a subtler level of nature, which includes thoughts and feelings and above these is the divine world. Nature also has laws to obey, just as we obey the laws of nature, nature obeys the laws of spirit. It is the spirit that commands nature. When a man succeeds in rising above the first two levels of nature, the physical and the psychic level that of feeling and thought, he is then no longer subject to their laws. He is free, he becomes luminous and powerful, in perfect harmony with the spirit, that it is the turn of nature to obey him, and whatever he does it will never be in contradiction to nature. This is the only instance when a man can do whatever he wants and never break a law. There are only a few of such beings on earth, who have always existed, exist now, and will continue to exist as long long mankind exists. These beings are so evolved that they can do whatever they want to, without ever committing a crime or sin, they are so luminous, so filled with pure love and pure light that they can only do good. All that emanates from them is divine hence they are entrusted with the power because this power is safe with them. It is written that no one can attain this height and dwell in the Sephira Kether unless he has been predestined to do so, by the Twenty Four Elders. A

*Cosmic and Universal Laws*

disciple understands that to achieve such a goal certain laws have to be respected.

## About Universal Laws

Universal Laws are unbreakable, unchangeable principles of life that operate inevitably, in all phases of our life and existence, for all human beings and all life, everywhere, all the time. Science attempts to unravel the mysteries of our solar system as it pursues a definite course, operating by a technique of intelligent control for both physical and spiritual forces. This unraveling when clearly understood become laws. To name a few of the laws that we are familiar with— The Law of Gravity, the Laws of Mathematics, the Laws of Physics, the Laws of Chemistry, the Laws of Electricity and the Laws of Thermodynamics. These laws reflect the principles of how the mysteries of physical life unfold. While scientists focus on unravelling physical mysteries, those people who encompass many different belief systems focus on the laws of a spiritual nature.

Universal laws act as guidelines to define the order and structure of creation. They are universal because they apply to all life, any time and any place. Because we all have minds and our minds are designed to work for us, each one of us has the ability to create our heart's desire by cooperating with the universal laws. It does not matter what field of endeavor we pursue, in science, music, media, art, business, religion, politics communication or relationships. Thought control is the key to destiny and in order to learn thought control we have to know and understand these laws.

Universal laws do not discriminate. The same principles work for all alike. These laws can work for you or against you whether you are aware of them or not. You do not have to believe in the laws for them to work. Knowing about and understanding the universal laws and cooperating with them with awareness, however, will make you more effective in all your endeavors. When you comply with universal laws you will be able to create higher and greater achievements while you expend less energy and direct it more efficiently. You will be investing your mental, emotional and physical energy wisely because you will be able to produce what you desire with the minimum of effort.

The universe is an orderly place, in spite of the chaos we observe on earth at times. All forms of life and all actions that occur in the universe are governed by universal laws. Minerals, animals and the vegetative worlds live in accordance with the laws of the Universe. We humans are the only species who are arrogant enough to think that we are clever and powerful enough to override the laws of nature. For our childish foolishness we are presently experiencing the results all around us on every level. Every plant, animal, human and material object have their own needs that must be satisfied if we are all to experience a life of balance and harmony equally. It is our responsibility as the earth's guardians to honor and support these needs. The higher universal laws are laws of transformation. As we apply each of these laws to an aspect of our life, we begin to change the nature of our life from what it is today to what we envision it to be in the future. Sometimes, long struggles and suffering is inevitable to force changes in order to flow with universal laws. It took, for example, struggle, courage, resistance and going against established human laws in order to end slavery and apartheid.

Cosmic and universal laws are described in Holy Scriptures of all religions, in mythology, in fairy tales, in business success literature, and allegories that describe the essence and nature of man. They are natural laws, mental laws, physical laws and spiritual laws all at the same time. They apply to all life forms, all matter and spirit, in all places and at all times. They are the same for all beliefs, all religions, all cultures. Sir Isaac Newton, Albert Einstein and many other famous individuals, who have contributed to mankind, became familiar with some of these eternal truths. We may know some of them as simple truths, eternal principles, philosophies for living and so forth but when we examine them more closely and experience them we will recognize them as divine laws.

## Cosmic and Universal Laws

Everything in the universe is scientific and is mathematically perfect down to the minute detail, there is law and order everywhere and a reason for everything. In everything and in every circumstance is the reign of law. The universal laws rule on every plane of being and grade is under the same laws. The operation of laws can be easily understood. What we absolutely need to understand and remember is that it is we who activate a law of the universe, through our thoughts and actions, individually and collectively. The law does not operate itself. As we have been given the freedom of choice, we can make right or wrong choices. We have at the same time been given the choice to correct our mistakes. When we break one law, therefore, and we repent, we have been given the opportunity to take an alternative action and to put things right again. We do this by activating another law.

The law of the cosmos is one for all and all things are interrelated, nothing, can exist independent of anything else. Matter and spirit, therefore, are interdependent and one cannot exist without the other. The interchange of all creation is infinite, always striving for perfection. All gain nourishment from the one Essence. Cosmic manifestations are limitless and nothing is wasted, everything is correlated. The human being is the highest manifestation of the cosmos and is a co-creator. it is through the psycho dynamic power of spirit that we are able to contact the higher spheres and the golden key is thought control.

The cosmos thrives on boundless opulence and billions of varieties of forms. The cosmos, therefore, does not favor limitations or uniformity and this idea makes us realize just how ludicrous we are when we seek uniformity in our lives, on any level, or when we imagine one to be better than the other because of race, color, shape or size. The whole of human life depends on the cycles of the cosmic rhythm and there are no such things as accidents while we experience the ebb and flow in everything that passes. Above all the beauty of the cosmos is manifested in the language of silence.

It is through expanding our consciousness and intensifying our psychic energy to be in harmony with the cosmic rhythm, that we

## Cosmic and Universal Laws

are able to enter the cosmic silence, gain contact with the creative forces of cosmos and absorb some of the treasures into our consciousness. Every artist, writer, musician, inventor, architect, leader and all creative people in every field on every level, whose work has transformed human consciousness and inspired humanity over a longer period of time, have used this method with or without awareness.

According to ancient teaching there are three fundamental laws of the cosmos of the greater system, recognized by astronomers of which we form a part. Subsidiary to the three major laws are the seven laws of our solar system. An intermediate law known as the Law of Karma is the synthetic law of the system of Sirius.

1) The three cosmic laws are
    - The Law of Synthesis
    - The Law of Attraction and Repulsion
    - The Law of Economy of Force
2) The Sirian Law of Karma
3) The Seven Laws of the Solar System
    - The Law of Vibration
    - The Law of Cohesion
    - The Law of Disintegration
    - The Law of Magnetic Control
    - The Law of Fixation
    - The Law of Love
    - The Law of Sacrifice

The seven laws of the solar system concern the form side of life. These are the basis of all true psychological understanding and when we can comprehend their influence, we will eventually arrive at real self-knowledge.

There are hundreds of subsidiary universal laws and principles, some clear and simple to understand others complex, paradox and oxymoron. It is up to each one of us to gather our own understanding of each law and to apply this according to our own state of mind and state of affairs at any one moment in our life. We need to keep in mind that these laws exist in order for the world to

## Cosmic and Universal Laws

function with efficiency, and that we have been given the privilege of the will to activate these energies, for better or worse with intelligence. The same law might be right in one situation but wrong in another situation. We are given the freedom to discriminate and to make choices. There is a Sufi parable known as the 'Tale of the Sands' that reflects on this issue.

A bubbling stream reached a desert and found it difficult to cross. The water was disappearing into the fine sand faster and faster so the stream spoke to the desert: 'My destiny is to cross this desert but I don't know how to.'

The voice of the desert answered in the hidden tongue of nature and said: 'If the wind crosses the desert so can you.'

'But whenever I try, I am absorbed into the sand and even if I dash myself at the desert, I can go only a little distance.'

The desert voice answered quietly, 'The wind does not dash itself against the desert sand.'

'But the wind can fly and I cannot fly.'

'You are thinking in the wrong way, trying to fly by yourself is absurd. You are water. Allow the wind to carry you over the sand.'

The stream said: 'But how can that happen?'

'Allow yourself to be absorbed in the wind.'

The stream protested that it did not want to lose its individuality in that way. If it did, it might not exist again.

This said the sand, was a form of logic, but it did not refer to reality at all. When the wind absorbs moisture, it carries it over the desert, and then lets it fall again like rain and the rain becomes a river again.

But how, asked the stream, could it know that this was true?

'It is so and you must believe it, or you will simply be sucked down by the sands to form, after several million years a quagmire.

'But if this is so, will I be the same river that I am today?'

## Cosmic and Universal Laws

'You cannot in any case remain the same stream that you are today. The choice is not open to you; it only seems to be open. The wind will carry your essence, the finer part of you. When you become a river again at the mountains beyond the sands, men may call you by a different name; but you yourself, essentially, will know that you are the same. Today you call yourself such and such a river only because you do not know which part of it is even now your essence.'

So the stream crossed the desert by raising itself into the arms of the welcoming wind, which gathered it slowly and carefully upward and then let it down with gentle firmness, atop the mountains of a far off land. 'Now,' said the stream, I have learned my true identity.'

But the stream had a question, which it bubbled up as it sped along: 'Why could I not reason this out on my own? Why did the sands have to tell me? What would have happened if I had not listened to the sands?'

Suddenly a small voice spoke to the stream. It came from a grain of sand. 'Only the sands know, for they have seen it happen; moreover, they extend from the river to the mountain. They form the link and they have their function to perform, as has everything in the universe. The way in which the stream of life is to carry itself on its journey is written in the sands.'

Cosmic Laws

Universal Laws

Subsidiary Laws

# 1

## The Law of the Absolute

The Absolute is the one Reality, the Parabrahm of the Vedantis of India. The Alpha and the Omega of being are but the two facets of the one absolute existence.

Who, where and what is The Absolute, the Almighty, The All-Powerful, nobody really knows. It remains a great mystery to us humans, yet we know it is there, we are aware of its existence. It is intangible, invisible, yet we feel it is there. We feel the energy, the power, a higher intelligence all around us and within every cell of our being. In the realm of the Absolute all is One and all there is LOVE. There is only one Truth.

The Absolute is above all that exists. Universal laws are absolute and non negotiable. No soul stands outside universal law and ignorance of the law is no excuse.

# 2

## The Law of Absorption

All matter in all the universes, regardless of its manifested vibration, absorbs emanations from all other matter and the matter is influenced by this absorption. In other words all things on earth are connected, relate and affect one another.

# 3

## The Law of Abstraction

This law concerns the ability to create through higher abstract thoughts. To arrive to this level we need to master the art of abstract thinking and we need to have gone through the painful lessons of detachment. To achieve the state of detachment, it is necessary to relinquish all attachment to relationships and material forms, and what more it is necessary to do this willingly. Detachment does not mean giving up all the material world of possessions. It merely means not to be a slave to the material world of possessions and a slave to one's emotions. It is through this law of Abstraction that one is lifted, out of the human plane, in an upward drive which all units of life express, in search for identification with the Divine. The entire process of abstraction is involved with pain.

A good place to start is to work with mental power training exercises, 'mind over matter' following the Yoga Sutras of the Indian sage Patanjali. Since the training is quite rigorous it is important to cultivate a happy spirit during the training. Neither loneliness nor depression should bring one down, two qualities that one is sure to experience during the training. One should not dwell on the horrors of the world but meditate instead to convey strength and wisdom. This teaches one to keep the lower emotions in check since spreading emotions such as pity, sadness, criticism and helplessness are negative and detrimental to the spirit and to the world. So by concentrating on the positive such as strength, joy and active intelligence, one spreads these energies into the atmosphere instead.

In order to be a co-creator on a higher level you need to master the ability of abstract thinking. With abstract thought one is able to have a bird's eye view of everything. Imagination and creativity might require some years of practice for some who are better at linear thinking. For others abstract thought, imagination and creativity comes naturally. Do not make the mistake of comparing yourself with others, just follow your own inner prompting and do what seems right for you and appropriate to your circumstances at any one time. Widening one's horizon and mind, changing one's habits and stepping out of one's own limitations, usually involves discomfort and suffering at first, but the transformation in consciousness and the rewards that follow make it worthwhile.

It might be necessary for some to take the radical step of giving up everything that one owns, including relationships, and to go on a spiritual journey, as did the Buddha. This calling to give up everything, however, which manifests as a strong inner prompting, leaving one no choice but to obey, comes to the few only. For the majority, it is very possible to learn the lessons of detachment, without having to actually free oneself of all material belongings or give up personal relationships. How can you know the difference? Simple, if you are taking an action to impress or to please anyone other than yourself, then it is not what you ought to do. Follow your heart and listen to your soul's prompting. With every stage of self-transformation that we go through there is pain involved, because self-transformation involves change and any change is painful. But as you are aware of the transformation and understand that change is necessary, the temporary pain and discomfort involved is easier to bear.

The words to meditate on here are detachment, liberation, rejection, relinquishment, renunciation, withdrawal, negation and abstraction—OM.

See also the law of Creativity.

# 4

# The Law of Abundance

This law is also known as the law of Opulence. God created a world of abundance. This clearly tells us that God loves opulence and variety. If we look around us we see nothing but abundance of everything in our world. Everything comes in a multitude of varieties. Whether we look at colors, animals, fruits, plants, trees, fish, insects or humans, we see a numerousness of varieties and beauty everywhere. No one species exists in just one shape, size or color. There are millions of species and millions of varieties and we are all meant to share in this wondrous world of abundance. Just look at the awesome variety of colors we see in the animal world, birds and fish for example, or the beautiful variety of colors and types of the flower family, the vegetable and fruit world. Every one flower or fruit gives us one or several more seeds to plant even more of the same kind. The human race is no different, we vary in race, color, shapes and sizes and all this was so created with a purpose. Listen to the varieties of music of all cultures and marvel at the fact that all music is based on seven basic major tones.

 We are surrounded by total abundance and wonder, but we have forgotten to enjoy this and to appreciate it. We ought to accept this as a state of affairs and learn to connect to all the natural opulence around us, because we harbor the same abundance in us as well. We can manifest this opulence in our life too, if we are able to learn to escape from our self-imposed limitations. When we humans feel any limitations anywhere, at any time in our life, this is caused usually, through our own blindness, through our own false beliefs and values, through our own fears, selfishness and greed.

We have been given the choice to be co-creators with the Creator of our world. We can also create abundance in our lives by ridding ourselves of our limitations, by believing in ourselves, and then by caring about everything that we love in our life. The key is not to focus on one area only shutting out or neglecting everything else in our life. We need to be aware, at every stage, of all our thoughts and all our multi layered actions. Our mind has the capacity of producing exactly what we expect from it. According to what we think, we can either live in a world of abundance and joy or we can live in a small limited sad world. It is up to us to make the choice, to be happy or to be miserable. We create our world with our mind so if we wish to have an abundance of anything in our lives all we need to do is to change our thoughts.

It is through the trained and well-developed mind that we are able to control and to change our thoughts. Like ebb and flow there is also a time for abundance and a time for holding back, a time for overflow and fullness and a time of emptiness. It is left up to us to be sensitive to our needs, the energies surrounding us, creating the rhythm of our individual lives. When we create an image of abundance in our life, we draw this energy of success and opulence into our reality, and the success and abundance here does not apply to money only. One can have success and abundance in all aspects of one's life, in one's relationships, spirituality, knowledge, communication and above all an abundance of love. Remember you are not the sum total of your possessions.

God meant us to be different and to look different. We were meant to create in our lives the same abundance and beauty that is in the universe. We were meant to enjoy our differences in style of life, art, music, food and cultures. Any limitations on any level, that robs us of our freedom in thought, in deed, in words, in actions, in dress, in behavior, any limitations that keep us confined at any time, go against this law of Abundance.

See also the Law of Order and Creation.

# 5

## The Law of Acceptance

This law is about truth. Because truth is absolute, acceptance of truth is absolute. To resist such a reality will not succeed. To resist is to deny. In a practical way, acceptance of things that we cannot change works to our advantage and makes our life easier to bear.

For example, acceptance of the laws of the universe, acceptance of our birth circumstances, the acceptance of blows that fate dishes out to us over which we have no control. There are many situations in life that are imposed upon us that we have little control of. We cannot change nature and the differences in races, color or culture, therefore, it is wiser to accept the fact that others differ from us and that there is nothing wrong with that. It was meant to be so because we cannot change it. Another example is that we accept the responsibility individually and collectively for our thoughts and actions and that we do not constantly blame others for our own mistakes and shortcomings. Accidents of nature, illness, death, are all situations that are not within our powers to change, so we might as well accept each situation for what it is.

Genuine acceptance of a situation, i.e. practicing non-resistance, is the first step towards finding the solution to turn things around for the better.

This law does not mean you to sit back, to be passive and to allow everything just to happen to you. On the contrary, it requires you to be fully aware, to be able to distinguish between what you cannot change and that which you can change, to see things for

*Cosmic and Universal Laws*

what they are and to accept them. Once you have accepted the situation as it is, you know where you are. Knowing where you are facilitates you taking action in the right direction to change things for the better, for yourself and also for everyone concerned.

See also the law of Attitude.

# 6

## The Law of Accommodation

Accommodation is a direct aspect of love and is mandatory. According to this law failure to accommodate others and ourselves is a violation of the law of Love and this violation sets into motion the universal law of Karma.

Other words for accommodation are, agreement, reconciliation, service, compromise, bargaining, settlement, trade off, concession, give and take, empathy and finding a middle ground.

What this law, therefore, means is that we should be open and willing to find a common ground to meet, for any kind of dispute or disagreement. We should try to see the other person's point of view, standpoint, and always be open to negotiate wherever and whenever possible. If we act stubborn, are fixed in our ideas, forcing our will on others refusing to settle, to finding a common ground that is beneficial to all parties concerned, then we are not only going against the energies of this law but with our refusal we activate the law of Cause and Effect.

# 7

## The Law of Accountability

This law states that you are accountable for what you create at the moment of creation. This accountability occurs on all levels. On the physical level, on the mental and on the spiritual level and once created, it cannot be avoided nor reversed.

This law is also known as the law of Return.

# 8

## The Law of Action

Nothing moves without action taken and as we are each a focal point of energy, it is more desirable and beneficial for us individually and collectively, if we were each a conscious focal point. No matter what we feel or know, no matter what our potential gifts or talents are, no matter what wonderful ideas we have, only our action can bring them to life. Without us taking action to make our dreams come true, without us taking that first step, the second and the third and then more, we will never be able to materialize our visions and achieve our goals.

Without us writing that first page and then with great passion continue to write, the book will never be finished. Without us making an effort to make friends, to make that first contact, to make that call, to accept that invitation or be willing to commit ourselves, we will never have friends. Without that artist actually taking up that brush to apply paint on that canvas there will never be a painting. Without you taking action and practicing diligently, whatever it is you wish to achieve, you will never realize your dream. Without you taking the risk and allowing yourself to fall in love, you will never fall in love and you'll never experience the bliss of loving.

Those of us who think that we understand concepts such as love, compassion, courage and commitment, realize one day that we actually only have this knowingness when we have acted and experienced these traits ourselves; we realize that we cannot experience genuine communion with the Divine in theory no matter how many books we read. We need to meditate to personally experience, to know what genuine communion with the Divine is.

Reading about life, collecting information, knowing things in theory is fine, but not enough. It is only through taking action, through doing and through personal experiencing that we are able to understand life and ourselves. This explains why people who have taken selfless risks in their lives, who have genuinely experienced life fearlessly with all their beings are more open, understanding and compassionate than those who only know life through books and theories.

# 9

# The Law of Action and Reaction

In the chaos that we live in today, it is imperative that we learn to control our emotions in order not to waste our energy. We are expected individually to remember the law of economy of force and not to scatter our energies by reacting, resisting or repelling emotionally to chaotic circumstances. Our efforts should be more focused on keeping our emotions stable and steady and to use our common sense. To say it simply and clearly, mind over lower emotions. What is meant as lower emotions, are all the emotions that throw us out of balance causing chaos and turmoil within us. This does not mean that our lower emotions have to be denied, on the contrary, all our emotions need to be understood and digested. The lower emotions, however such as anger, fear, envy, jealousy, insecurity, worry, depression and doubt need to be guided by the mind. This will allow constructive forces from the Higher Self, such as love, courage, kindness, generosity, and from all those who work for order to pour through the lower self and to radiate out to the surroundings.

To be able to do this we must learn to detach ourselves, to take distance and to discriminate by seeing the true sense of values. In this way we can be separated from the problem and we can act instead of reacting blindly to circumstances. Being detached helps us to stay calm. This in turn will help us to preserve our strength and clear thinking. It will also allow time to be economized and the energies will be wisely distributed instead of being wasted.

When we are able to do this, we become constructive helpers contributing towards the solutions rather than being part of and losing ourselves deeper in the problems.

Simple examples are situations that we are all confronted with every day of our lives. The traffic jam when we are in a hurry, the inquisitive neighbor that gets on our nerves, the waiter that brings us the wrong food, the printer that doesn't work when we need to print something urgently, all of these situations usually make us lose our temper, so much so that we react with hostility, impatience or anger. When angry we can't think clearly or logically, so our being upset does not solve the problem but makes everything worse for all concerned. All these inevitable situations are a part of our daily lives, therefore, by recognizing that and by remaining calm, it is easier to find the solution to each one of these problems.

# 10

## The Law of Activity

The law of Activity represents uninterrupted flow of activity. This law ascertains that with awareness, concentration and focus on a specific goal we can accomplish more with less strain. The more blessing life bestows upon us, the more we are expected to give back to life. This is the way toward gaining illumination. The more we get from life the more we should take responsibility and to give back in kind service in order to keep the balance. Not only the cosmos but also everyone around us will expect that from us.

The law of Activity means that the more active you are, the more energy you will have to do even more. The more you put your talent to good use, the more your talent will grow, the more you do the more you will have to do. Watch nature around you. Nature never stagnates. Nature is always full of activity below and above the earth.

The following might sound familiar to some of you: 'It's not fair, it seems that the more I do, the more everyone expects me to do!' Well this law explains why it is so and why it is fair after all. You are able to do more because you have more blessings, be that wealth, assets, gifts, talents, or energy that enable you to do more, therefore, you are expected to give back more in return. When you think about it and understand this law it does seem to make sense after all.

# 11

## The Law of Actuality

The law of Actuality is a very different idea. It is that law which exists in the mind but not necessarily in the material form. It does not have to have dimension. It does not have to have form. It is what is believed to be.

# 12

# The Law of Adaptation

The law of Adaptation in time and space is the law of economy or the line of least resistance. This line of least resistance is what is sought for and followed on the matter side of existence.

Brahma manifests 'will' because he is purpose and love. In this solar system love is the line of least resistance. Brahma is also activity and intelligence and his main characteristic is adaptability.

This law governs the rotary movement of any atom on every plane and sub plane. To interpret this law in plain words and to make it practical for us, this law represents metamorphosis, conversion, reformation, modification, transformation and major change. The line of least resistance means for us to have the ability to change and to adapt as the circumstances demand of us.

There is a Chinese proverb that says that we should learn to be flexible like a tree that moves, sways and bends with the wind. If we are too inflexible and refuse to adjust to circumstances we would break as the tree would, if it were standing too rigid and unyielding in a storm.

In our solar system love is the line of least resistance. This means that if we can cultivate the feeling of love for life in general, we will have the strength to adapt easily whenever necessary.

# 13

## The Law of Adjustment

This law is also known as the law of Balance. This law is elaboration and continuation of the law of Equalities. The law of Balance is a universal law that supersedes all of man's laws, creating stability for all third dimension manifestation. Each thought must be balanced by who ever creates it. This is divine wisdom.

This law of Adjustment requires us to allow room for all view points without feeling that we must defend our own. Allow no one to tell you what your journey must reflect or what your reality is in life. Do not give your power away easily, but do give your love unconditionally. Any message communicated in love validates equality. Keep in mind that low self-esteem is just as non-productive as a puffed up sense of self-esteem for they both deny equality.

Another manifestation of the imbalance of this law is all kinds of addiction. Any addiction to food, drugs, drink, tobacco, people, work, habit, idea or belief sets to work negative energies that go against this law.

When mind, body and spirit are totally in balance, harmony and peace is flowing and you know that you are applying more and more of the universal laws, there is a fair exchange. All things in nature in all its complexity are always in balance and connected in spite of the differences. This idea is clear enough and needs no elaborating on.

See also the law of Attraction and Repulsion.

# 14

## The Law of Affection

The law of Affection states that affection is a beam of love that may light upon a subject and create an object of adoration. Through this law we can hold someone close to us but at the same time have our arms wide open, wishing to see all creatures as free beings by freeing them from ourselves and from themselves, their fears, guilt, inhibitions and from everything that conceals their preciousness.

The law of Affection possesses not and yet sacrifices nothing of its self, because it gives without expectation even from the joy of giving. As the sun must shine just to be the sun, so must affection be given, if one is to be affectionate. The law of Affection cannot be manipulated or controlled, for its only purpose is to give. You cannot possess or use this law, but if you open your heart it enters and possesses your heart and uses it to shine its warmth of love upon the world. Make a conscious effort to include the feeling of affection for yourself and for others into your life and experience how miraculously your life becomes richer, fuller, bigger and better.

# 15

# The Law of Affinity

The human organism is a microcosm, which exactly reflects the macrocosm the universe. This means that man and the universe are bound together by numerous correspondences. All of esoteric science is based on the law of Correspondences. There is an absolute correspondence between man and the universe. In reality, we humans are children of the cosmos and our organs correspond to energies that fluctuate in the cosmos. According to ancient teachings the subtle worlds of the cosmos create our individual bodies. Each organ of man's body has a special affinity with a specific region of the universe. The organs of the cosmos and ours have something identical in common, and through the law of Affinity, we make contact with the centers and worlds that correspond to certain elements within us. Our bio-energetic system, similar to the universe, consists of seven worlds with seven primary bodies of auric layers that constantly interact with each other. Besides our physical bodies, our individual energy system consists of ether, astral, mental, karmic, intuitive, celestial and absolute subtle energetic bodies, which form the human energy field, our aura. These are subtle energies, difficult to perceive with our normal senses. These bodies consist of the corresponding universal worlds and receive the energetic information from them. All subtle bodies in a human energy system communicate with each other and with the physical body, through the energy transformers known as charkas, centers of different levels of consciousness. It is through the chakras that the cosmic universal life-support energies are transformed into human energy systems. Knowledge of these correspondences opens a whole new world of possibilities for us.

This law is also known as the law of Sympathy or Resonance. Thanks to this universal law we can draw on the immense reservoirs of the universe to obtain all the elements we need as long as we project thoughts and feelings into space of the same sort as those that we want to attract to ourselves. This law is the most important law for us to understand and is worth contemplating on because, when we can really understand the workings of this law, we will have a magic wand in our hands.

Everything in life is connected so you can actually set to work immediately to attract to yourself radiant particles forces of nature that you will begin to improve in every way. As you feel better and better every day, you will radiate this around you to everyone you meet. When those who live and work with you see how happy you are and feel how radiant you are, you will seem more intelligent, stronger and forceful, they will be drawn to you and they will have a better opinion of you. This in turn will make you feel even better about yourself and will change your destiny. Unfortunately, many of us are too busy complaining, are full of fear or are too busy being unhappy, and then we blame everyone but ourselves for our misfortunes. We need to remember that we can determine our own destination by our own inclinations, intentions, tastes and desires.

# 16

## The Law of Akasha

Akasha is a great cosmic law, which is the principle of the intelligence of substance. The Akasha records of all life on earth are found on the etheric level available to see for all those who qualify. Those who qualify are evolved and trained initiates who are able to see the records on the psychic level, invisible for everyone else. Everything in life and everyone in every minute detail is recorded on the Akasha level.

Our planet consists of land and water and above that air. Above the air is ether. Ether is the fifth cosmic element, subtle spiritual essence or a substance that pervades all space. Akasha is a Hindu word for ether. Ether is a subtler state of matter and it is on the etheric plane where all planets are connected on the level of their soul.

Man and woman are considered to be miniature planets and both are more than just their physical bodies. Their beings, emanations and radiation reach out far into space and the action of their aura and magnetic field can be felt at great distances. The human being by means of the subtle bodies can reach out and unite with other souls and with the soul of the universe. This is how prayer and meditation work.

The artist, for example, who wants to create a masterpiece, cannot remain on the level of the five senses. The artist must rise to the higher etheric levels and unite with the Creator, to tap in to the sublime beauty of the Divine, in order to receive some divine

*Cosmic and Universal Laws*

particles, which the artist can then communicate in the work that is being created.

See also the law of Telepathy, the law of Creation, the law of Prayer and the law of Meditation.

# 17

## The Law of the Alpha and Omega

All that is now was then and will be and has always been, so there is nothing new in the Universe.

'I am the Alpha and the Omega, the beginning and the end,' said the Lord, 'which is and which was, and which is to come, The Almighty.' (Revelations 1:8.)

We refer to the Alpha and Omega when we refer to the most important part of something.

# 18

# The Law of Analogy

This law is also known as the law of Correspondence. The human organism infinitely small is a microcosm and an exact replica of the vast universe, the macrocosm. There are points and zones between man and the universe that correspond. All esoteric science is based on this law of Correspondence between the human and the universe. Each organ of the human body has an affinity with a given region of the cosmos. Since we humans have destroyed the original ideal relationship with the macrocosm and the higher powers, our task now is to restore this bond. This we are able to do because when we were created we were given all that we needed to evolve, to develop and in case we got lost, to find out way back home again.

Every spirit that incarnates on this earth possesses all the spiritual faculties that correspond to all the virtues and qualities in the cosmos and so everything is possible. This obviously cannot be done all at once but gradually through learning, training and persistence. If the incarnated soul abides by the laws, the human evolves and eventually learns how to use these inborn faculties.

The cosmic process and the nature of cosmic principles are indicated in the functions, structure and characteristics of a human being, indicated as sign posts not elaborated. The three aspects of man's organism are symbols of the three aspects of being. *(1)* the energy which is the activating principle using the brain as seat—brain, heart, lungs (breath) which equals the spirit. *(2)* the nervous system, the vital energy, and *(3)* the body/flesh, the life and body mass. Understanding and studying the body one can arrive to the activities of God of Nature, spirit/life, soul/consciousness, body/form.

The major linking agent in the universe is the energy of love and wisdom, and the purpose of analogy is to lead the mind back toward the sense of oneness, enlightenement.

See also the law of Affinity.

# 19

## The Law of Apperception

This law states that consciousness of being flows within all entities of the universe. Throughout all eternity, everything has a consciousness and knows its own conscious being. Thought knows it is thought, energy knows it is energy. Every single unit from the great cosmos to the tiniest atom knows what the function of its unit is.

# 20

# The Law of Archetype

The Archetypal law is that law which is the prototype for the echoing reflections of other laws. The law of Archetype is that which serves as the skeleton or framework for other laws.

The first archetypal law is the law of One, the second is the law of Two and the third is the Law of Three. This apparent division is never ending so long as the law of Description is in effect. Concepts and personalities, number, shapes, forms, situations that serve as patterns for others to follow are archetypes, even as the pyramid was an archetype for the hierarchy systems and the zodiac shall be the archetype for the new world.

# 21

## The Law of Ascension

This law defines the high vibration frequency of the soul at which an incarnated being is resonating. To reach this stage a personality loses the illusion of separation from its God self and becomes one with the all. It signifies that one has gone through the process of purification. The vibration of such a person raises one to the point of ascension without going through the process of death.

This also means that this soul need no longer to reincarnate and leaves the earth plane to live a finer existence on a higher plane. Jesus ascended, as have many other Avatars before him and after him. We are meant to bring our loving energies to our every day existence, to set a good example and be a role model for others to emulate.

We can recognize this higher vibration frequency in others by the degree to which such a person is a magnet to others. All hierarchy and heavenly masters are ascended humans. Every one of them has had to go through the process of life as a human on this earth, the same as you and I. This law allows any one and every one to ascend provided one is willing to go through the required efforts and the disciplines of purification. This is not an easy task but it is possible.

See also the law of Vibration.

# 22

## The Law of Assembly

Through relinquishing one arrives to this law of Assembly. As the world makes progress through the law of Evolution there is a never-ending process of elimination going on, accompanied by a parallel process of substitution. The old and purposeless is constantly abandoned for the new and the more useful. Throughout history, that which is no longer useful is rejected and discarded, and is replaced by more useful elements.

We are presently, for example, experiencing a process of re-interpreting and re-arranging what is known as doctrinal structure underlying the relation between knowledge and wisdom. This involves the destruction of old outdated concepts and institutions, substituting them with new and more correct ideas. Whether it is economics, politics, education or religion this process of ending and replacement continues. Old concepts must be discarded and new concepts have to be found. A new world religion for example will eventually be founded upon a deeper spiritual perception of life. In other words a spiritual unfoldment must consciously give way to a much higher phase of perception.

This law also works on an individual level for each one of us. It requires us to continually re-evaluate our position in life and to discard the old and useless structures, ideas and beliefs that no longer serve us effectively and to replace these with the new and more useful.

## Cosmic and Universal Laws

On a lower physical level this would mean for us to review our immediate collection of material possessions and rather than hording things that accumulate dust and occupy space needlessly, serving no one, least of all ourselves, to clear things out, to throw away or give away what we have no need of, to make space for new things to enter our life. This is one of the basic teachings in the Chinese Feng Shui system. The same applies also for relationships, when we hang on to a dying relationship refusing to let go, we cannot possible have room for anything new to enter our life. The very same law applies to every aspect of our life. Most of all it applies to our mental state of mind. We are often stuck with ideas and habits that are old and redundant, holding us back from growing and expanding and moving on forward. It would behoove us to be constantly aware and when we find ourselves in a rut, to take whatever steps are necessary to get us out of the black hole we find ourselves in.

## 23

## The Law of Association

This law states that if two or more things have something in common, then the thing that they have in common can be used to influence or control the other thing. The degree of control depends upon the size of the thing in common. The more in common the things have, the more control can be used to influence the things.

# 24

## The Law of Attitude

This law states that it is our attitude that determines the quality of our life. Having the right attitude is one of the main keys to having a balanced and pleasant life. Having success and achieving our goals or failure to achieve our goals in life depend very much on the attitude we have towards life in general. Our thoughts and feelings determine our behavior patterns. Our innermost attitude that we do not necessarily reveal to others, dictates our outlook on life and our interaction with the world at large. When we are in harmony with our inner self this has a positive effect on our thoughts. If we are in conflict with our inner self, no matter how much we try to hide it, it will show itself in our attitude towards others. If we deal with our self with love and understanding, our attitude will project the same as we interact with our family, friends and strangers.

Attitude is the only weapon that can harm an individual. Nothing, absolutely nothing, can harm a human being but his or her own attitude. Each experience is put in its proper perspective and is hopefully resolved in a favorable manner. How you react toward those experiences, your attitude about them, determines how the experience affects you. Only you can control and change your perception and your attitude towards life and your experiences. The choice of your attitude is yours. An inner positive attitude towards life will bring you positive feedback from the world around you. A negative inner attitude will bring you only negative feedback. This is the law. Chronic complainers will always have something to complain about. Someone with a chronic ungrateful attitude will always be dissatisfied no matter how much they have. When you race through life without awareness you are bound to create many little scenarios that will boomerang on you, and cause you pain and it is usually no one's fault but your own.

As we all know all human faculties can be continually developed and improved. But even this depends on the attitude that we have. We have the freedom to choose our attitude to life and it is the attitude we choose to have, that determines whether we go through life happy enjoying many highs or, miserable suffering from many lows.

# 25

# The Law of Attraction

This is the basic law of all manifestation, the love aspect, and it governs the soul aspect. It is the paramount law for this solar system. The law of Economy is the basic law of one pole, that of the negative aspect, the negative electron; the law of Synthesis is the basic law of the positive pole, the positive central life; whilst the law of Attraction governs that which is produced by the relation of the two, it is the law for the fire which is produced by the merging during evolution of the two poles. This law of Attraction is itself controlled by a greater cosmic law, the law of Akasha, which is the principle of the intelligence of substance. It is the primary law of man.

The quality that emerges through the process of manifestation and under the impulse of divine life is love. Love functions through the medium of the law of Attraction. Love has one sole aim and that is to produce an ultimate synthesis in consciousness. The object of the present evolutionary process is the growth of conscious awareness and the entire process is directed towards that. Both love and sex express the meaning of the law of Attraction. Love is sex and sex is love, for in those two words the relation, the interplay and the union between God and the universe, between the human and God, between the human and the soul and between women and men are equally depicted. The sex referred to here is the act with higher emotions of love and respect for life and not, to the physical animal act that satisfies the lower physical senses.

*Cosmic and Universal Laws*

The law of Attraction determines the present and governs the immediate condition of the planetary types. It is concerned with the soul or the consciousness aspect.

On a practical level the law of Attraction is about 'like attracting like.' We attract to us what we are thinking about. We attract to us that which corresponds with our feelings. So if we have negative thoughts or negative feelings that is exactly what we attract to us, nothing more nothing less. No matter how much we wish to have it different, if it is the negative that we are focusing on, that is what we will attract to us. We attract situations, friends or lovers, in line with what we are thinking about, feeling and concentrating on in our private inner world.

See also the law of Attraction and Repulsion.

# 26

## The Law of Attraction and Repulsion

This is one of the three major cosmic laws. The law of Attraction is neutral because it is also called the law of Adjustment. This law is the fire that is produced by the merging during evolution of the two poles, the negative and the positive. It is the law of Akasha. Fundamentally, this law describes the compelling force of attraction that holds our solar system to the Sirian. It holds our planets revolving around our central unit, the sun. It holds the lesser systems of atomic and molecular matter circulating around a center in the planet, and that of the subtle bodies coordinated round their microcosmic center. This is the basic law of all manifestation, the love aspect and it governs the soul aspect.

The law of Attraction and Repulsion has eleven subsidiary laws—law of Chemical Affinity, law of Progress, law of Sex, law of Magnetism, law of Radiation, law of Lotus, law of Color, law of Gravitation, law of Planetary Affinity, law of Solar Unity and the law of the Schools. It is the primary law of man. The law of Synthesis is beginning to be felt. Like attracts like. We attract people of like energy. This means if you want to attract different friends, mates, circumstances, then you must change yourself within. If you are a negative thinking person, you will attract negative people. If you are co-dependent person, you will attract controlling people. You must first take control of your thoughts and that will change your life and your manifestations. If you change

## Cosmic and Universal Laws

yourself to being a positive thinker, or a non-co-dependent person you will become a healthier person in every way.

The law of attraction can be stated this way: As you seek, you attract and are attracted to that which will fulfill your search. This law applies only when you seek. You attract to yourself that which you put the energy of your thoughts into. If you desire something, you can attract it to you by positively anticipating its arrival into your life. Alternately, you can attract that which you do not want into your life by giving negative energy to your thoughts of receiving it. In practical words, as an example, if you constantly think while driving, I'm afraid I'll have an accident or I don't want to have an accident or I must watch out not to have an accident, then you are sure to attract an accident. If you are financially broke and you constantly talk about being broke and having no money then you will for sure continue to be broke. If you wish to attract more money to buy the things you want, then focus instead on what you want to have, how much money exactly you wish to have, imagine yourself having the thing you want to have. Be specific about what it is that you want. This will change the energy around you and will attract that what you want to you. Of course you need to help it happen on the physical level too. You can't sit back and expect it to drop into your lap, you will need to take the necessary steps towards your goal and the universe will do the rest for you. Do not doubt and do not become impatient. Expect it to happen, and when you do get it, acknowledge it and be genuinely grateful. The universe does not tolerate laziness nor ungratefulness.

The underlying law that regulates supply in the world of effects has two important phases one is desire and the other expectation. These mental attitudes represent lines of attractive forces, the former being the positive phase of the law and the latter the negative phase, while phases must be complied with to obtain the best and greatest results.

The first phase of desire embraces a positive process of attraction, that is, when an individual earnestly desires a thing, he sets up a line of force that connects him with the invisible side of the good that is desired. Should he weaken or change in his desire that particular line of force is disconnected or misses its goal. If, however, he remains constant in his desire or ambition the good remains constant in his desire and sooner or later it will be realized. The principle involved is that you cannot ask for anything unless it already exists, if not in form, then in substance and desire is the motive power for calling it forth to manifest into visible appearance or physical effect.

The first phase will not work unless you comply with the second phase of the law. It is of no use to desire a thing unless you expect to get it, either in part or in full. Desire without expectation is idle wishing or dreaming. You simply waste much valuable mental energy in doing this. Desire will put you in touch with the inner world of causes and connect you by invisible means with the substance of the thing desired; then, continuous expectation is necessary to bring it into a reality in your life. Much like the pull of gravitation in the physical realm, 'expectation' is a drawing force of the mind that acts in the invisible realm.

Often people desire good things they never expect nor make any real effort to grasp. They start out well and may get half way, but not any further. When they learn to comply with the other half of the process involved and learn to expect what they desire, most of their dreams or wishes will steadily materialize. We meet people who expect things they do not want but which often come. This proves that expectation is a powerful attractive force. Never expect a thing you do not want, and never desire a thing you do not expect. When you expect something you do not want, you attract the undesirable, and when you desire a thing that is not expected, you simply disintegrate valuable mental force. On the other hand, when you constantly expect that which you persistently desire, your ability to attract becomes irresistible. Desire connects you with the thing desired and expectation draws it into your life.

When we charge our thoughts so firmly with the idea that there are no failures, then we expect success. Our mind becomes strengthened with our conviction and, like a magnet, draws to us whatever desire is uppermost at the time. One attracts into one's life one's deepest desire. We do not get what we deserve, we get what we believe we deserve.

See also the law of Attraction and the law of Manifestation.

## 27

## The Law of Authority

This law states that whoever is liable has the authority, and to the degree of that liability the degree of authority should be given. The author of an action or work who is liable for that work has the authority over that work, to dispose of as he or she wishes, along with the liability. The creator has absolute authority over all creation.

# 28

## The Law of Averages

The law of Averages is the principle holding that probability will influence all occurrences in the long term. Eventually everything evens out.

# 29

## The Law of Avoidance

This law states that refusing to handle a highly emotional or unpleasant situation, to deny living up to one's full potential or neglecting to do something that should be done, will affect an individual's physical body and mental mind. It also affects the lifestyle affairs through each incarnation, until that person correctly balances with the situation. In other words avoiding difficult situations in life only prolongs the ordeal, it will repeat in the next incarnations until the lesson is learnt.

# 30

## The Law of Awareness

For most people, awareness depends on their five physical senses and each one is attached to different things. When the soul is aware of itself, however, and one is aware of one's soul, then the senses follow that which has awareness of the whole. All that one loves with the senses is temporary as one's body is perishable. Only the soul and God are infinite and eternal. The realization of this is a far greater gift than what one can possess here on earth. Material possessions cannot be taken when the soul has departed from the body. The soul, however, departs with the intangible refined qualities that may have been acquired during a lifetime.

This law is about observing our thoughts, feelings, behavior and actions, to be aware of the illusion and the separateness we experience and yet, not to be confused by this illusion and not to be caught in it. To be aware of the illusion of tragedy, free will or death and not to be caught in it and to realize it is nothing but illusion.

There are certain limitations placed upon this awareness, which the law cannot break. One of these is that it cannot break its own principles and laws. It cannot deny or reject those who would appear to separate themselves from this awareness. Having awareness is having the ability to distinguish and not to believe everything that one reads, sees or hears but always to question, to explore and to discover, to have soul awareness.

*Cosmic and Universal Laws*

The precepts of cosmic awareness are not to judge but to be humble and to always act in line with the law of Love and the law of Mercy. Each and every one of us has access to this cosmic awareness, wherein we move deep enough within ourselves, laying aside hostility, frustration and move into ourselves to find that pool of consciousness which emanates peace, tranquility and love for all living things.

# 31

## The Law of Balance

This is elaboration and continuation of the law of Equalities or Fair Exchange. The law of Balance is a universal law that supersedes all of man's laws, creating stability for all third dimension manifestation. Each thought must be balanced by whoever creates it. This is divine wisdom. For every action there is a reaction. The energy of the universe is continuously flowing from action to reaction in search of balance to achieve harmony. Where there is an imbalance we usually experience irritation, discomfort and pain.

Duality of perception leads to a perfect balance that governs the universal law of One. Negative and positive create a perfect balance and do not negate the law of One. Any message communicated in love validates equality. Low self-esteem is just as non-productive as a puffed up sense of self-esteem. They both deny equality. Another manifestation of the imbalance of this law is addiction.

The law of Cosmic Balance is considered to be the foundation of the universe wherein the forces of nature are in a state of constant equilibrium. However, the equilibrium of the universe is not absolute because there is a constant oscillation and it is this slight lack of equilibrium that keeps the universe in constant motion perpetually active. If there was a perfect balance and harmony the universe would be in a state of inertia, stagnant, absolutely immobile and manifestation would not be possible. The vital thing is that this imbalance should not be too great or else it would lead to total destruction. The key is to learn to work with the forces and not to sway too far from that golden middle line.

Interpreted to our daily lives, the law of Balance operates exactly the same. It is good to be perfectly and relaxed yet not so relaxed that one is unable to concentrate. A good example, imagine a bowman with a bow and arrow. The bowman should be relaxed yet totally focused. The bow and arrow should be taut, not too taut though nor too lax, to get that perfect balance to hit the mark. In other words we should avoid all extremes.

See also the law of Adjustment and the law of Attraction and Repulsion.

# 32

## The Law of Being

There is only One Being and only One Universal Soul—the many individual souls are all a part of the one Being. As in 'in Him we move and have our Being.' In the human the base of the spine is controlled and governed by the law of Being where spirit and matter meet.

According to eastern ancient scriptures the 'life principle' is seated in the heart, and the 'will to be' is seated in the base of the spine. From the angle of the esoteric sciences the base of the spine houses a threefold thread. This threefold thread within the spinal column is therefore, composed of three threads of energy which have channelled for themselves in the substance of the interior of the column a 'threefold way of approach and of withdrawal.' In Sanskrit terminology these are the 'ida', the 'pingala' and the 'sushumna' paths and they together form the path of life for the individual human. One of these paths is the one along which the energy which feeds matter is poured. Another is related to the path of consciousness and of sensitive psychic unfoldment. The third is the path of pure spirit.

At the base of the spine lies dormant the serpent of fire known as the 'kundalini fire.' Under normal circumstances this fire is aroused when the human has evolved to a certain degree of consciousness. It is popular in the west to have workshops specifically to arouse this kundalini fire permanently. This can be at times extremely dangerous mentally for the individual, because normally the kundalini fire when aroused naturally requires the person to have achieved a certain state of consciousness on the evolution ladder and for the body to have arrived to a certain vibratory level. When the kundalini is aroused or forced artificially before the person has through personal effort developed his physical instruments and spiritual faculties, the kundalini fire that rises through the nerves of the spine to the brain, can cause irreparable mental damage and mental disorientation.

## 33

# The Law of Believing and Knowing

This law states that we have the ability to create and it is through believing and knowing that we will manifest our desires. It is critical though that the believing comes from the emotional heart, i.e. that we believe with all our heart without any doubt, and most importantly, allowing this to happen. The knowing here does not refer to knowledge derived from books but the knowing beyond any doubt with every cell and fiber of our being.

See also the law of Attraction and the law of Creation.

# 34

## The Law of Catastrophe

This is also referred to in the human experience as the stage of drama or trauma. An absolute necessity for the volutionary process motivated by many laws of totality, when the seed cracks and growth is permitted to begin, this occurs in the human experience and in nature itself.

Think of the many national catastrophes of recent times, and how the material things of the world, which are forever changing and everlasting have been fought for. Man, it seems, is blinded by the material life disregarding the secret, the hidden very meaning of life.

In all worldwide upheavals there has not been one nation or race which was not involved, suffered, directly or indirectly, to a greater or a lesser degree. No corner of the globe, no race or religion has entirely escaped a catastrophe, in one form or another. This makes us think that the catastrophe of modern history is intended for humanity in general, as a cleansing purpose, inaugurating an ideal period of peace, which can only be possible when instead of the will of man the purpose of God is fulfilled.

We humans experience this law with our own personal life changes, traumas and personal catastrophes whether generated by us individually or imposed on us by circumstances beyond our control, to help us in our individual evolutionary process.

# 35

## The Law of Center

A basic principle in nature is that everything has a center from which it obtains its source energy, intelligence and pattern which is continually self renewing. Each center is connected to every other center and to the one center from which all life is vitalized.

Everything has a center the individual, the family, the enterprise, the country, the earth, the cosmos and so forth. In the Rig Veda, for example, it states, the universe is conceived as a spreading from a central point. The creation of man, which answers to the cosmogony, likewise took place at a central point, at the center of the world. According to Mesopotamian tradition, man was formed from the 'navel of the earth.' According to a Syrian tradition, paradise was the navel of the earth, established on a mountain higher than all others, The Sacred Mountain. According to Indian beliefs, Mount Meru rises at the center of the world and above it shines the polestar. The Iranians believe that the sacred mountain Haraberezaiiti is situated at the center of the earth and is linked with heaven. The Buddhists, north of Siam, know Mount Zinnalo to be the center of the world. Similar beliefs are found among the Japanese, The Finns and other peoples.

The center is the zone of the sacred, the zone of absolute reality. The road leading to the center is arduous and demanding. The seeker has a difficult road to the inner self, to the center of his being. The road is strenuous and gruelling, filled with perils and suffering, because it is a rite of the passage from the ungodly to the sacred, from the illusory to reality and eternity, from death to life and from the human to the divine.

## 36

## The Law of Challenge

This refers to communication with other levels of being. This law says that we have the right to ask another of his or her intent and whatever pertinent information we feel we require when encountering a disembodied being. Those who come to us in the role of information givers to channeling mediums, do not mind being challenged. Ask the entity your questions three times using the same words each time and you will be given the correct information.

## 37

## The Law of Chance

The law of Chance is that law that results when the law of Magic is initiated without being in harmony with the law of Unity. The law of Gratitue is that law which does bring justice and balance for the actions that occur under the law of Chance.

## 38

## The Law of Change

This law is one of the laws that we humans are very familiar with as it effects us every second of our lives. Whether we consciously activate this law or not, the law of Change is at work. In the ancient formulations of the Archives of the Hierarchy it is stated: 'Regard and recognize the changes in the hearts of men and change the rules as men in time and cyclic change approach the Ashram. The Ashram stands not still. New life pours in from either side.'

From this we learn that that the law of Change governs the hierarchy just as it governs humanity. The occult law holds good, 'as above so below.' What we also learn from this statement is that the disciple who functions under this law has to deal with (a) constant transformation in the personality and to adapt the self rapidly to developing and changing events which are taking place and (b) to contribute to the wise circulation and direction of the new energies which are pouring into and through the Ashram, this is done by realizing that one is the center of changing energies.

The new energies pouring through Shamballa into the hierarchy are of an extra planetary nature and have their source largely in the 'Aquarian' quality of the present cycle, the Acquarian age, and these energies are steadily eliminating the energies with the quality of the Piscean age.

On a more practical note for us humans, this law says that everything is constantly in a state of change and constantly growing and transforming to something better and higher. Changes occur in the physical structure, in the personality, in consciousness and in the changing events individually and collectively. This law does not tolerate stagnation on any level. Anything that stagnates is doomed to rot and die. We see this in plants around us all the time. What is not growing and transforming dies. We see this in our own bodies, from the day we are born until the day we die, we are in a constant mode of transformation every second of our lives. No two minutes are we the same, our body is constantly changing, first growing until we reach adulthood then at some stage as we begin to get into old age the body begins to deteriorate. This process depends on the health state of the individual physical body. When the body is neglected or abused during young age it deteriorates faster with old age. Emotional and mental stagnation violates this law of Change. But whether healthy or not the law of Change is always at work.

At present we humanity are witnessing a period in the history of mankind of extreme change and adjustment and of a far reaching cosmic organization. Evolutionary changes instinctively demand major reorganization and group recognition, great work and responsibility. The three lines of thought for us to urgently meditate on presently in our time are progressive change, re-ordering change and above all group responsibility on every level, social, economical, political and educational. As you read this if you observe the world around you, you will see these changes taking place.

In accordance with this law of Transmutation every condition can be transmuted and everything is always changing. The only consistent thing in the universe is the imperishability of energy and its changing form.

This law is also known as the law of Alchemy as it allows every condition in life to be transmuted into divine glory and made spiritually beautiful no matter what that condition is. If we can accept a situation, no matter how bad it is, bless it and are thankful to God, we can actually transmute even bitter heart breaking experiences into spiritual godliness. Through this law we can receive the power also to transmute our spiritual dreams to physical manifestation. This alchemy is the power of God in action and is eternal and immutable.

There is no escape from energies of this law of Change no matter how much we try to hold on to a situation. Like it or not everything inevitably is committed to change and transformation, all the more necessary for us to be aware of and to understand the importance of the power of Now.

See also the law of the Present Moment.

# 39

## The Law of Chaos and Order

Law provides order, structure, and justice to the world. Without that nothing material could exist. Law appears friendly to life, but a realm controlled by order alone becomes just as stagnant as one stifled by chaos. Chaos, disorder expresses the principle of possibility unfettered by rules. Magic and sorcery draw on the powers of chaos because they break the laws of nature. Where universal laws provide order, chaos provides balance. There are theories that chaos existed before order was established in the universe.

Under the law of Order you are born, you create your blue print of your incarnated life. You lay out the general path you want to take, the situations that need to occur to provide your opportunities for learning lessons, paying or receiving karmic debts, expanding your awareness and, hopefully, becoming more enlightened. This is the order of your life.

Under the law of Chaos, in each incarnated life, you have free will and choice. You walk on that path established in your spiritual blue print, but like all construction, once you're building the life, situations present themselves that require choices. This is the chaos that balances the order. Your free will and choice are the chaos in your life.

We only hope that we make the best choices and decisions for the evolution of our soul and spiritual growth. If life were totally preordained, then what's the purpose of learning? But the point is that life is not preordained. With your free will you create

*Cosmic and Universal Laws*

the chaos that by your decisions direct the outcome. You have the ability to continue your construction and spiritual evolution, or destroy it and face the same situation over and over until the lesson is learned.

# 40

# The Law of Chemical Affinity

In esoteric terms this law governs the soul aspect of the mineral kingdom. It concerns the marriage of the atoms and the romance of the elements. It serves to continue the life of the mineral kingdom and to preserve integrity.

In physical chemistry, chemical affinity, historically, refers to the force that causes chemical reactions. A broad definition, used generally throughout history, is that chemical affinity whereby substances enter into or resist decomposition. In current use, it can be defined as electronic properties by which dissimilar chemical species are capable of forming chemical compounds. Chemical affinity can also refer to the tendency of an atom or compound to combine by chemical reaction with atoms or compounds of unlike composition.

The term affinity has been used figuratively since c.1600 in discussions of structural relationships in chemistry, philology and natural attraction. According to chemistry historians, the influential text book of 1923 'Thermodynamics and the Free Energy of Chemical Reactions' by Gilbert Lewis and Merle Randall led to the replacement of the term 'affinity' by the term 'free energy.'

A chemical bond is the physical process responsible for the attractive interactions between atoms and molecules and that which confers stability to diatomic and polyatomic chemical compounds. The explanation of the attractive forces is a complex area that is described by the laws of quantum electrodynamics. In practice, however, chemists usually rely on quantum theory or qualitative descriptions that are less rigorous but more easily explained to describe chemical bonding. In general strong chemical bonding is associated with the sharing or transfer of electrons between the participating atoms. Molecules, crystals and diatomic gases, as most of the physical environment around us, are held together by chemical bonds, which dictate the structure of matter. Keeping in mind that opposite charges attract and electrons orbiting the nucleus are negatively charged while protons in the nucleus are positively charged, imagine two atoms near each other forming a covalent bond. In 1809 Johann Wolfgang von Goethe published a short novel 'Elective Affinities' which extended the chemical term 'elective affinities' through storyline to human relationships, both intimate and political.

To summarize the above in a few simple words on a practical level for our understanding it means, opposites attract. And now we understand also why we talk about the 'chemistry' being just right for two people. This chemistry is felt instantaneously on meeting one another, one could say, felt in every atom of the body, and this could be either right, and the two people will feel drawn to each other, or then the chemistry can be all wrong and the two people for no apparent reason at all can't stand each other.

# 41

## The Law of Choice

This law states that we are free beings and have the power to make choices. We humans are given the freedom to choose whatever it is we desire to do or not do, for better or for worse, and no one should influence us or rob us of that choice.

Throughout history individuals have exercised power over others, and continue to do so today, thereby, consistently violating this law.

On a personal level each one of us has the freedom to choose the way we want to go. There are two ways to go, the positive or the negative; the possible or the impossible attitude; the 'I can' or the 'I cannot' road. With the positive approach we expand our possibilities and opportunities with the negative approach loaded with fear or doubts we limit our existence and miss out on much of the abundance of life.

For every situation, in every circumstance, on every level, we are able to make a choice. We can choose to be happy or unhappy, we can choose to be active or passive, we can choose change or remain stagnant, we can choose to love or not to love. So we have no one but ourselves to blame. We create our life with our every choice that we make.

See also the law of Free Will.

# 42

## The Law of Circle/Circulation

Experiences in life both the positive and the negative are nothing but lessons presented to us individually and collectively on the stage of life. Each time a lesson is presented to you, and you do not learn from this particular experience, or you avoid the lesson, it will be repeated with more energy, presenting you with another opportunity to learn. This is repeated again and again until you have learned the lesson from the experience so you can evolve on to a higher level of being, a higher consciousness level. If you think that by ignoring or postponing an unpleasant situation that it will disappear forever or at best take care of itself eventually, you are mistaken. The problem will confront you again challenging you to remember and to act, and this will repeat itself, until you face the challenge and successfully deal with it to your soul's satisfaction.

Everything in life goes round in a circle. This also means that whatever energy you send out, whatever the quality will ultimately go round the circle and in time find its way back to you. This law also states that which is in circulation increases and that which is hoarded decreases. A classical example of this is the circulation of money and economics.

In the eastern tradition of feng shui, the studies of energy, we speak of stagnating energy which blocks the general flow of energy. For example, if we wish to have something new in our life, we have to first move, re-arrange and clear out old things in order to allow space for the new. If we wish to have a new relationship we should first have closure with all old relationships in order to welcome a new relationship into our life. The closing of a circle also means the completion of something. This law of Circulation does not allow loose ends. We all know from our life experiences, that loose ends have a way of coming back to haunt you.

In summary, be careful of what energies you send out because these will eventually return to you. Also make sure to have closure with projects, relationships, and other issues so that you are able to move forward with your life unburdened.

# 43

## The Law of Coalescence

On the path of involution this law controls the primal gathering together of molecular matter, beneath the atomic sub plane. It is the basis of the attractive quality that sets in motion the molecules and draws them into the needed aggregations. It is the measure of the sub planes. The atomic sub plane sets the rate of vibration. The law of Cohesion fixes the coloring of each plane.

See also the law of Cohesion.

# 44

## The Law of Co-creation

The law of Co-creation states that two people working in co-creative action have the power of four people working individually, and three working in co-creative activity have the power of nine people working individually. Four working in co-creative activity have the power of sixteen and one hundred and forty-four persons working in harmony can change the world.

When large groups of beings believe and agree on certain images as real and being stable, this agreement holds the power of many times that number of energies than if such energies were held by individuals working separately. Wherein groups agree upon certain images, these images do tend to manifest and hold their being in a magnified manner.

Jesus said: 'All these things ye shall do also.' Meaning exactly that. It is within our power to do miracles like he did. We humans are co-creators with the higher powers but a human being must reach a certain height in the evolution ladder in order to have the power to be able to create. To get to that stage, we have to go through a process of purification and self-transformation.

See also the law of the Earth.

# 45

## The Law of Cohesion

This law is one of the seven laws of the solar system under the three major laws and is also referred to as the law of Birth. It is a branch of the cosmic law of Attraction. This law demonstrates itself in this love system in a threefold manner.

On the plane of the Monad, as the law of Cohesion, the law of Birth, resulting in the appearance of the Monads in their seven groups, Love the source, and the result, the Monad of love.

On the plane of the buddhi, it shows as the law of Magnetic Control. It shows itself as the love-wisdom aspect, irradiating the soul, and eventually gathering to itself the essence of all experiences, via the soul, via the personality lives, and controlled throughout from the plane of Buddhi.

On the astral plane, as love demonstrating through the personality. All branches of the law of Attraction, in this system, show themselves as a force that tends to coherence which leads to absorption.

This law states that it is the aim of all things to unite. Unification, is a simultaneous attraction between two or more, as in sex, business partners and organization, political groups and so on.

See also the law of Coalescence.

# 46

## The Law of Color

All colors emanate from one primary color, one source, the cosmic ray of indigo, veiling cosmic love and wisdom. This indigo color splits into three major colors and then into the four minor, making the seven colors of the spectrum. It is written in ancient scriptures that colors as they manifest on the physical level as seen by the physical eye are at their crudest and hardest in comparison as they appear on the emotional plane of existence. Many have through meditation and receptiveness to higher teaching gone through the Hall of Learning to the Hall of Wisdom that is where the true esoteric interpretation of the colors can be known. Meditation prepares one for the initiation that opens the door to the Hall of Wisdom.

This law states that color serves a twofold purpose. It acts as a veil for something that lies behind and is therefore attracted to the central spark. All colors are centers of attraction and are complimentary or are antipathetic to each other. Color like music can be healing and impacts the physical, emotional, mental and human body profoundly. Man is also partially composed of color in the aura. We are color, tone symbols and speed of vibration and light. When intense rays of one or more colors are sent to a specific area of the body, the result is change in our psyche and structure.

We in the west are beginning to rediscover the importance that color plays in our environment and the effects that colors have on our health. With color therapy we are able to heal illness, of a psychic nature, since the physical is dependent on the psyche. We can direct our emotional and mental health by surrounding ourselves with harmonic rainbow and bright colors. This we can, just the same as we can do with essence and smell of various natural herbs and flowers. Crystals most of which also come in colors are another source of healing. In nature which itself gives us a magnificent combination and variety of colors there exists all that we need to heal ourselves. Different people have different color affinity and reactions to different colors. Colors are frequencies and, therefore, affect our moods, so we need to choose colors that suit us, colors that appeal to us at any certain time, for our choice of colors also changes in accordance to our consciousness level.

# 47

## The Law of Common Ground

This law is viewed as a problem solving approach and is an area where two or more people can gather to blend their differences.

The law requires that the area be cleansed of previous energy left by others who historically have passed through, or have lived on the spot. Two or more people sending loving energy to the area for a specified period of time do this. After the cleansing process one surrounds the area with a gold net to keep it cleansed and protected from other negative energies. The energy left after using the space for the blending of differences can be cleansed in the same manner. All this is done on a psychic level through the power of the higher mind and imagination.

Through the power of meditation, concentration and imagination you can do this exactly as is stated here. It is as simple as that. Write out your decree in clear simple words and when you are ready say it out loudly with a firm voice combined with your imagination and faith that it is done exactly as you say it.

In many civilizations there are customs of space cleansing using incense. The middle eastern people use incense sticks used commonly by many religions. Some people resist this practice, but there shouldn't be separation between religions and customs, everything we see is the manifestation of God. We see God through his creations. More separation means less Godliness. When we see everything as a manifestation of good, we become more loving to everything. With the practice of love, praise and gratitude we don't need religious scriptures. Gratitude opens a door in our heart, so that abundance can flow in. Mindless gratitude however will not work. Gratitude must come from the heart. If you practice love, praise and gratitude, you will see your life changing for the better immediately.

# 48

## The Law of Communication

Every unit from the single atom to the galaxy system is plugged into a giant switchboard. Each unit has the ability to communicate with all other units through its own vibrational frequency. This communication system makes it possible for all beings to have psychic possibilities, and to communicate or share information with each other on a psychic level.

Spirit communicates with itself. Language does not exist except as a physical manifestation. Therefore, communication is a divine aspect of God, and excludes no soul. All that may be known truly is known depending on the level of growth of each soul. The higher evolved the soul is, the more clear is the communication with the spirit. Evolved souls are able to communicate with each other without words and through telepathy over great distances.

On a practical level no harmonious inter relationship between people can exist without clear communication. It is the duty of the more educated, the more evolved, the older or the wiser to be patient and to make that extra effort to establish better communication with fellow humans.

# 49

## The Law of Compassion

The deepest human value is compassion, a sense of caring and commitment to life, not limited to any specific time, place, society or culture. It is the ultimate source of success in life.

Having compassion for another soul is having compassion for the spirit. Judgement, which excludes compassion, is without merit. Failure to show compassion is a violation of the universal law of Love and sets into motion the universal law of Karma. One has to feel compassion first before one can feel the energy of love.

Having compassion does not mean feeling pity for someone. It is rather the feeling with someone of pain and suffering as if it were our own pain. It is having empathy with someone rather than feeling sympathy. The feeling of compassion is free of any judgement and criticism. Compassion is the wish for another being to be free of suffering, as love is wanting them to have happiness. It is a genuine wish for the wellbeing of others and is the ultimate and most meaningful embodiment of emotional maturity. It is through feeling compassion that a human achieves the highest peak and the deepest in her or his search for self-fulfillment.

A compassionate human being has a keen awareness of the inter-dependence of all things on earth. The virtue of compassion and a good heart can be developed through constant and conscious effort.

# 50

## The Law of Compensation

The law of Compensation is closely related to the law of Sacrifice. For this law to become active in your life and to become a recognized factor in daily living sacrifice is required. Sacrifice has nothing to do with animal or blood offerings. The compensation comes later into recognition. The rewards for a happy and fruitful life are attainable if you understand the terms of this law.

The abundant supply of all we need is ever attainable and at hand, if we take responsibility to change our application of natural law in order to bring about the conditions that we aspire for. If you think you do not deserve compensation you will not get it. The law follows your belief. If you think you are unjustly treated by life and others are getting more than you are, then perhaps you should look at yourself again and ask yourself whether you have really paid your dues. Paying your dues is a popular term. In other words you must have done some work, sacrificed something, given of yourself in some way in order to get the compensation in return. This law sees to it that we all get what we are owed. What you invest in life is the return you receive. What effort and energy you place in your actions of giving plays a big role in what your return will be, the main aspect of this law of balance, which regulates that what is returned to us for our efforts. When we apply honor, integrity and purity in our efforts, thoughts and actions we initiate a purity of compensative response. You know this saying for sure 'what goes around comes around,' this gesture holds true, for if

*Cosmic and Universal Laws*

we cheat, deceive and lie through our efforts we receive nothing in compensation but grief. We must work within the parameters of natural law, and when we work diligently and consistently we find our efforts are rewarded, the foundation and walls of our house of success are strong and coinciding with the workings of natural forces. Compensation is an equal return for that which is given. It is a balance of that quality or service that is extended to another.

In order to receive anything worthwhile in life we must first give. Often we think we are working hard or contributing and doing our share, but in reality we are being short sighted and selfish concentrating on our own self-centered needs and satisfactions. Our striving and our achievements should be in accordance with our gifts, abilities and talents, which we should endeavor to put to work for the good of the whole. The more we give, the more we do, the more we contribute with unselfish genuine motives, the more we will be compensated and the compensation might not always be that what we imagined it to be.

# 51

## The Law of Completion

On a cosmic level, at the point of Omega all souls transmute to become the energy vibration of God at which point the group soul begins as Alpha.

In practical terms, we could interpret this law for us on the physical level, as one that requires us to bring everything to a close, be that a project or a relationship. Unfinished business, open loose ends are not tolerated by nature. If we really give this a further thought, we ourselves are very aware of this, as we feel uncomfortable when any issue in our life remains unfinished. We have this inner gnawing feeling that haunts us, and will not let loose until we attend to the matter in one way or another. This tells us to always listen to our feelings and to always seek closure to any given situation.

# 52

# The Law of Concentration

Concentration is a quality of the soul. The focus of the soul strengthens thought and brings thought into physical manifestation. It is through this law that we are able to create all that we wish for in our life. Closely associated with concentration is will power. The relationship between the two is totally dependent, without one you cannot have the other. You need both the will power and the concentration power to achieve any goal you want to attain in your life. Distraction, which is a function of the lower mind, is a tool of the soul created in order to develop concentration and thus aids in manifestation. One needs to cultivate both will power and concentration power in order to create and manifest into the material world. Without total focus and concentration nothing can be properly achieved. We are meant to have plenty of everything and not merely the basics as so many have or nothing at all to live on. All our natural desires can be realized. The Infinite has arranged it so that anything that we want can be supplied.

It is in your soul power to think, as thought is the essence of all created things. Every instinct of man leads to thought and in every thought there is that great possibility. Thought development when allied with the mysterious powers of the universe has been the cause of all the world's true progress. Silent concentrated thought is more potent than words, for speech distract from the focusing power of the mind. By the law of concentration you can achieve

*Cosmic and Universal Laws*

your heart's desire. This law is so powerful that that which at first seems impossible becomes attainable.

See also the law of Will Power, the law of Balance, and the law of Meditation.

# 53

## The Law of Condensing Light

This law is for those who are ready to create profound changes in their consciousness, in their spiritual path and in their daily life. Working with the solar light, is one of the most powerful forces in the universe. It is a light of higher will and universal love. It is the light of the soul plane.

The essence of your purpose on earth is to work with the solar light to fulfil the essence of your soul's higher purpose that is to become a more perfect light, to find light, to draw light into yourself, and to become the light as your radiance lights the way for others. In the process of working with solar light, you are guided to meet the solar light and draw it into your mind, emotions, body, aura, atoms, and every part of your life. You will learn how to bring solar light and its qualities of radiance into your circumstances, projects, relationships, and activities to enhance all the light that is there and to release anything that is not of the light.

You discover how to recognize who and what increases your light, and how to work with those things that decrease your light. Your vision of what is possible in your life can expand and you will know what steps to take to create what you want. You learn how to manifest those forms that hold the most light for you. You learn how to create matter and form out of light. You learn to manifest those things that increase your light and that are in harmony with your higher purpose.

*Cosmic and Universal Laws*

You link your mind with the universal mind to know what actions to take to bring about what you want. You work with and become aware of the solar light from moment to moment. As you become aware of both the higher dimensions of light and your ordinary reality simultaneously, you can consistently see and choose your path of most light in everything you do, making those choices in every moment that assist you in becoming a more perfect light. All this is possible for you to do through focus, vision, concentration, meditation and prayer. Just focus on the solar light and with your thought power, flood it through any form or situation to cleanse, to purify and to protect.

# 54

## The Law of Consciousness

Totality is all Consciousness, all there is—is. This is the conscious of being or awareness of its existence. In other words, what we know at a given moment is reality for us as a conscious individual. What one perceives in consciousness from moment to moment is our individual reality and therefore real for us.

The development of the human being is but the passing from one state of consciousness to another in a succession of expansions and a growth of awareness. Consciousness is dependent upon life and energy for existence. It is the expansion of consciousness and increase in sensitivity and awareness that is the goal of all divine and hierarchical effort.

This consciousness is the soul of all things. It underlies all forms, it is objective energy, whether it be the form of that unit of energy which we call an atom or the form of a man, a planet or a solar system. The more we are in contact and in union with the individual soul the more the soul can manifest itself through the personality on this earth. As consciousness expands, the space for events increases and therefore, the dimension which one recognizes good and evil, opportunities and possibilities, past, present, future, enlarge to reveal the outstanding needs in this present world cycle.

There is individual consciousness, group consciousness, nation consciousness, global consciousness and universal consciousness, consciousness of God. Spirit is pure consciousness and pure

## Cosmic and Universal Laws

thought. Nothing exists outside of thought. Everything in the universe has its origin in idea, in thought and it has its completion in the manifestation of thought through form. Soul is the thinker of thoughts.

The consciousness responds when directed by soul, which is beyond all thought, beyond all matter, beyond all energy, space and time. As we change in our state of consciousness our physical body responds to this change, and everything around us begins to change for us, including our likes and dislikes. Even our nutritional diet changes according to our state of consciousness. We each are born with a certain amount of consciousness but from then until our death, we are responsible to make the effort to reach higher and beyond, to reach greater states of consciousness.

When you hold your consciousness firmly upon something, you bring exactly that into existence in yourself. It is impossible for your life to contain anything other than what is in your present or past accumulation of consciousness. Whatever it is that you are conscious of, in thought and feeling, stamps itself upon the universal substance in and around you and brings it ultimately forth into your life.

The goal is to be constantly aware of what you are thinking about, to be aware of your surroundings, the environment, to be aware of the company you keep, of your every activity, which you read and what you expose yourself to. All of these things leave a stamp on your consciousness and on the universal consciousness that in turn manifests this again in your life.

When a human is group conscious, he or she is aware of his or her soul group, of the soul in all forms and has attained a stage of Christ-like perfection as the 'measure of the stature of the fullness of the Christ' (Eph.IV:13).

See also the law of Thought, the law of Rebirth and the law of the Soul.

## 55

## The Law of Contact

This law states that things, animate or inanimate, once in contact with each other will continue to act upon each other even at a distance, long after the physical contact has been made.

# 56

## The Law of Continuity of Consciousness

Nothing in the universe ever dies, is lost or destroyed. It just changes form. Everything becomes a part of everything forever. Matter and energy are never destroyed only transformed and changed.

The universe is in a continuous and endless process of creation. Cosmic consciousness is a reality and everything in creation is connected to everything else. The medium for the 'implicate order' of this relationship is consciousness. The fusion of individual consciousness and the universal consciousness which is known in occult language as the building of the 'antahkarana bridge' results in the development of universal knowledge, of omniscience, all science and all knowledge. Continuity of consciousness is achieved after the soul has been acknowledged, awakened, liberated and identified with the whole. This is known as 'enlightenment.' A step nearer to achieving enlightenment is to be aware of our thoughts, emotions and actions, a faculty that enables us to be vigilant, observant and knowing. Destruction of God's creation is not possible. Continuity is absolute.

See the law of the Soul.

# 57

## The Law of Correlation

For every manifestation of spirit in the physical reality the corresponding thought first appears in spirit, 'as above so below.'

Nothing can manifest on earth if it does not exist in the spiritual world.

# 58

## The Law of Correspondence

In ancient times this law of Correspondence was clearly understood by human beings as they were not bombarded with thoughts, words, ideas and noise to the extent that they are today. The ancient Hermetic axiom that states 'as above so below' was a clear and meaningful experience. For prior to the multiplication of words and language, where few words were used and words were simple, like the times, human beings knew how to look beyond the words at the inner meanings, whereby the words stood halfway between the seeker and the sought, and the words themselves were like sign posts pointing toward a city, rather than the final destination for the questioner, as in present time, whereby the question is asked and the words are answered, and the answer is the final movement of the mind which perceives no further than the word which was given as an answer.

The true meaning of this law of Correspondence, 'as above so below' teaches you, as it is above, so likewise there is a corresponding action below. As it is within, so likewise there is a corresponding action without. As it is in the past, so likewise, there shall be a corresponding action in the future and in the present. Yet these correspondences may not be exact, they may be distorted, likened unto a reflective mirror that does not have a perfectly flat surface. As the cycle of one level in correspondence to the cycle of another level, so likewise, the souls of one entity have a correspondence to the souls of humanity.

## Cosmic and Universal Laws

This law of Correspondence states that our outer world is a mirror of our inner world. The thoughts and the images that we hold in our conscious and subconscious minds will manifest their mirror likeness in our daily external circumstances. Earth is a school for practicing these laws of mind control. There is a correspondence between the laws of Phenomena on the various planes of *being* and *life*, such as intuition, hunches, remote viewing and out of body experiences. The law of Correspondence enables that which is normally unknowable, to become known to the individual who learns and knows how to use this principle. Some use it in a conscious manner while others are not even aware that they are using it. When, however, it is used knowingly, it will enhance the clarity of vision and enables the mind to penetrate the most secret of secrets, and can shed light on many a dark paradox.

Correspondence establishes the interconnectedness between all things in the universe and keeps all things relative to each other. Known to the adepts and masters of ancient Egypt as the substance of the ethereal, the spirit substance or web that pervades and interpenetrates the universe. This substance acts as a medium for the transmission of light, heat and electricity. It is non-material in nature. Also known as the uncreated substance, or universal substance, the substance in which all suns, worlds, and galaxies are suspended in space and time. All of us are intimately connected to all of the above mentioned events, and to each other, whether or not it is realized. The ethers are where spirit substance is manifesting the beginning of matter. Science refers to this substance as dark matter that cannot be seen, touched, smelled, or weighed. Dark matter does not absorb or reflect light and is therefore invisible. It is considered to be a non material substance. It was first discovered on earth while doing research with the Hubble space telescope. The planes of Correspondence in the order of manifestation are, the spiritual plane, the mental plane, the physical plane, or the Trinity.

See also the law of Analogy.

## 59

# The Law of Cosmic Equation

The tables of law hidden in the Arc of the Covenant are the Logos, the word of reason, measure, relationship and number. In Genesis the Lord God said: 'I have made everything with number, measure and weight.' To possess the tables, is to have the possibility of access to the great 'law of Unity' that rules the worlds, of relating effects with their causes and consequently of acting on the phenomena that the causes produce as they diversify into plurality. However, man is still unable to make use of this information unless he has been initiated into the secret of reading them. The secret was sealed in a cryptic writing in a numerical system, which was given in the Semitic language by Moses, now known as the Kabbala.

All numbers, measure and geometric forms have a meaning and only those who are initiated are able to understand this. The one who understands this understands the universe.

See also the law of Number, Measure and Weight.

# 60

## The Law of Cosmic Manifestation

Every human desire defies the cosmic law of the constructive use of energy. It is said that under every human desire lies a serpent coiled that will demand payment as sure as you are born. Just as sure as you exist in this universe will you find every human desire coming back to you one day, demanding a price in pain, limitation and unhappiness for no other reason in the universe except that those desires defy the law of cosmic manifestation. This reminds us of the Buddhist teaching namely, to be free of all desire. Some contemplation is required here to understand this correctly.

See also the law of Desire.

# 61

## The Law of Cosmic Web

Every point in space regardless of vibrational frequency connects with every other point in space and interconnects with every point of time: past, present and future.

# 62

## The Law of Courage

The law of Courage states that courage is the ability to not only face a danger but to risk an action to defuse that danger. When action is taken fear departs. The degree of courage is in proportion to the degree of danger, risk and fear a courageous action must defuse. Courage is a quality of an evolved soul in manifestation. The more evolved the soul is the more courage the person has and the less fear one feels.

Courage is a soul quality, its vice of deficiency being cowardice and it its vice of excess recklessness. Courage is one of the four cardinal virtues, along with prudence, justice and temperance in Roman Catholicism. In both Catholicism and Anglicanism, courage is also one of the seven gifts of the Holy Spirit. There are also more subtle distinctions in the definition of courage. Some distinguish between courage and foolhardiness for example. If a courageous person overcomes a justifiable fear for an even more noble purpose, or if the fear is not justifiable, then the courage is either false or foolhardy. There is physical courage, moral courage as in the case of facing prejudice or discouragement, or civil or social courage defining many standards.

## 63

## The Law of Creativity

There are physical laws like gravity and relativity that govern our physical world and there are laws that govern our mental world, just as there is law and order in the realm of creativity as well. People who accomplish their ideals are cooperating with the universal laws of nature. When we know and understand universal laws and cooperate with them we will be able to expend less energy and direct it more efficiently enabling us to create always higher and greater achievements. Through the practice of daily mental and spiritual discipline we are able to develop greater awareness of the universal laws. The Creator is absolutely creative and as extensions of the Creator we are creative and we are co-creators with God. Nothing exists for us in our individual and collective world, which we did not create ourselves. As soon as we formulate a desire in our heart it becomes a reality on a subtler level. We are responsible for all of our creations. Every human being has this deep instinct within him to seek and to create something better.

The power of imagination is essential for creativity. Everybody dreams, wishes and imagines but one needs to understand how this works in order to be creative. The imagination can be described as a screen that lies between the visible and the invisible worlds, and images and entities are projected on this screen that we are normally unaware of in our field of consciousness. Those who have a developed imagination are able to use this faculty of imagination, to receive and to record these impressions, which they then try to express or describe or realize on the physical plane.

When one knows how to model and govern his own thoughts and feelings, he is capable of purifying his psyche to such an extent that his imagination becomes transparent and crystal clear and he begins to 'see' with his third eye, the things on the subtler plane. At this level imagination and vision are one. The power of imagination is formative but it is the thought combined with emotion that creates. If the imagination is allowed to roam randomly, if it is not guided to some useful task by an intelligent will, it remains fruitless. Thousands all over the globe might have the same great idea all at the same time, but it is only the one who knows how to control and discipline the imagination who is able to manifest the idea on the material plane. Ideas are constantly received from the universal mind where all knowledge is, when one is relaxed and in tune with the universe. Only the very few are capable to follow up by taking the necessary actions to manifest the idea received.

See also the law of Abstraction and the law of Attraction.

# 64

## The Law of Credibility

This law states that credibility is the ability of entities to earn, receive and accept credit for what they do, and to refuse credit for anything they have not done. Your credibility is the standard by which others may evaluate you to determine how they will relate to you. A credible person is skilled, qualified, experienced, intelligent, honest, caring, fair and trustworthy. It takes time to establish credibility but it can be lost very quickly, by one dishonest act. Once lost it is very hard to establish credibility.

# 65

## The Law of Currency Exchange

This law states that energy flows like water or electricity. Energy flows in currents that may be tapped for use elsewhere, and may be exchanged for other energies, or may be stored in containers such as containers, foods, bottles, cups, batteries, valuables, ideas, properties, bodies, words, monies, contracts, banks, friendships, gardens, music, titles, talents, and all other areas of consciousness to be used or exchanged at another time or place.

An excess of energy in a container unable to handle it, creates friction, heat, fever, rashes, combustion, temper, rash behaviour, an over load on the circuit or circulation system, or an inflamed, short circuited or an explosive situation. Containers vary in nature, purpose, dependability, durability, utility and adaptability as they may diffuse, leak, lose, transform, absorb or deplete energies. Containers may give, take, store or deny energies from others, but it is energy in movement that serves to move other energies. Energy currents are alive, while stored energy is stagnant, dead until it is released. A few small energies, carefully placed, can tap into greater energies in such a way that multitudes are fed, clothed and sheltered and entire civilizations are raised to higher energy levels.

# 66

## The Law of Cycles

The world of nature exists within a larger pattern of cycles, such as day and night and the passing of the seasons. The seasons do not push one another neither do clouds race the wind across the sky or vice versa. All things happen in good time and in their own time. Everything has a time to rise and a time to fall. Whatever rises falls and whatever falls eventually rises. That is the principle of cycles.

This law is active everywhere, in everything and in all of us, in circumstances and events. History proves this. There are smaller cycles and there are larger cycles. With observation we can see and understand this law of cycles working in our own lives. All of life exists in cycles. For everything there is a beginning, an existence and an end. To everything there is a season, and a time to every purpose under the heaven. Through observing our own life closely and understanding the cycles of the highs and the lows, which can be three, seven or nine years cycles, we can figure out the rhythm of the cycles in our own lives for outer activity, for intake and re-energizing and for rest and contemplation. This would help us to do the right thing at the right time, as we go with the energy flow and have it work for us so we can meet with success in our endeavors.

There is a cycle of the life of the world, and the cycle of the creation of man and his destruction, the cycles of the reign of races and nations and cycles of time, such as a year, a month, a week, day and hour. The nature of each of these cycles has three aspects: the beginning, the culmination and the end. For example, new moon, full moon and waning moon, or sunrise, zenith and sunset. These cycles, sub-cycles and under-cycles, and the three aspects of their nature, are divided and distinguished by the nature and course of light. As the light of the sun and moon and of the planets plays the most important part in the life of the world, individually and collectively, so the light of the Spirit of Guidance also divides time into cycles. And each cycle has been under the influence of a certain Master with many controllers under him, working in the spiritual hierarchy that controls the affairs of the whole world, mainly those concerning the inward spiritual condition of the world.

# 67

## The Law of Cyclic Returns

Also known as the wheel of reincarnation. Reincarnation is that process by which the 'consciousness of the permanent atom' manifests in another body through the human birthing process. This accounts for genius in the very young. Once a soul qualifies for an incarnation to the third dimension, there is an understanding that it must be completed. All karma must be cleared or forgiven and certain aspects of soul growth accomplished before the entire cycle of reincarnation growth is considered completed.

Disintegration and death for all periods of transition are periods of the destruction and building of forms and the shattering of the old so that the newer and better chalices of life may be constructed. This law governs the gradual disintegration of the concrete forms and their sacrifice to the evolving life.

In a way this is the reverse side of the law of Vibration, it is the law that governs the end of a system. The law of Sacrifice and Death is the controlling factor of this aspect of the physical plane. The destruction of the form in order that the evolving life may progress is one of the fundamental methods in evolution. True death, under the law, is brought about by the attainment of the objective and hence by the cessation of aspiration. The etheric body of a human, a planetary Logos and a Solar Logos, being shattered, becomes non-polarized as regards its in-dweller and permits therefore an escape. It is no longer a source of attraction, nor a focal magnetic point. It becomes non-magnetic and the great law of Attraction ceases to control it, and so the form disintegrates.

The result is freedom from the handicaps of the physical vehicle allowing entrance into a fuller life.

See also the law of Sacrifice and Death, the Law of the Soul and the law Reincarnation.

# 68

## The Law of Description

The law of Description is a law that serves as a tool for creative purposes. This is likened unto the paintbrush of the artist and the chisel of the sculptor. Description as that which carves out images, creates boundaries, creates shapes and forms, creates limitations, creates confinements, and creates also those concepts that expand those boundaries to release from confinement.

The law of Description is capable of creating anything for anyone. This relates unto the law of Magic in that anything described is on its course toward creating a manifestation to the decree of impact on its description. The nature of manifestation depends upon the intensity of the collective or disruptive energies involved.

In practice this means when we desire to manifest anything we need to visualize and imagine the picture in its totality with every minute detail, including shape, color, size, texture, etc. and focus our concentration on this fixed image unchanged for it to materialize on the physical plane. The more we can focus on the image the more energy we can feed it and the more likely it is to materialize.

See also the law of Manifestation.

# 69

## The Law of Desire

What one desires, one wills to be. What one wills to oneself, one first desired. To achieve one's goals in life, one must first desire them.

*'Ask and it shall be given unto you.' 'Seek and ye shall find.' 'Knock and it shall opened unto you.'* We have been told again and again that it is we who should take the initiative first. We need to take the first step, to ask, to seek and to knock. We are not meant to sit back, to fantasize and to expect our wishes to come true without any effort or action on our part.

Buddhism teaches us that in order to be happy, we have to be free of all desire. This is true, of course, but impractical if taken literally, as we would float through life aimlessly, without a purpose or goal. I like to think of desire as aspiration. When we watch life in action, we see that everything around us is in the process of moving, growing and changing. Nothing in life remains stagnant. A child aspires to crawl, to walk upright, a plant aspires for the sun, it breaks through the darkness of the earth to reach out for sun and light that help it grow. Likewise, we humans aspire for growth, for knowledge and progress. Perhaps a good description is that desire is ego based i.e. to satisfy the ego, while aspiration is soul based i.e. to follow our soul path.

One very important point we should keep in mind. What ever it is that we desire or aspire for should always be for the good of all concerned, free of all selfish motives.

Refer also to the law of Cosmic Manifestation.

# 70

## The Law of Destiny

This law does not really apply to us, not at the present time anyway. This law affects the ashram and the hierarchy as a whole. This law of Destiny has been brought into being since the foundation of the hierarchy on earth. It is the result of the pledged and united dedication to service that is the outstanding note of the united ashrams. It is a sevenfold law, for it takes on the seven colors of the seven rays, the seven qualifications, modes, methods and energy expressions of all the seven rays. As far as humanity is concerned it is free from all evil because it is selflessly motivated. This law will become effective when humanity achieves increased purity in the three worlds.

Through the universal law of Planning, the blueprint for each soul, once created by the higher intelligence, cannot be subverted. Contrary to all beliefs we do not create our future but we do choose which direction our life should take. It is we who set our course but our destination is already there waiting for us. There are thousands of different regions and spheres in space and our path can lead us upwards or downwards all we have to do is make our choice.

# 71

## The Law of Dharma

This law represents the purpose of life. The law of Dharma is that which may be described as the principle of 'right action.' This refers to that which universally right, right for all who are affected by the action. An action by an individual, a group, a nation or culture is right only when everyone is rightly served by the action according to their needs and earnings. Dharma brings about that which may be called 'good karma' or 'right results.' Each living thing has a purpose for existence and a special experience to provide to this world. Utilizing our unique talents in service of others exalts our spirits to attain our ultimate goals.

To live a life without creating further karma is to do everything in the name of God or in the name of that Inner Master within you, to live in flow with the universal laws.

# 72

## The Law of Differentiation

Also known as the law of Discernment. This law allows us to tap into our own unique piece of the divine blueprint. It is about being totally in tune with the next step in our personal evolution path and we are connected without judgement of other realities. It is about the recognition that there are many instruments in the 'divine orchestra' and knowing your place within this orchestra, what instrument you are to play and learning how to play harmoniously together with all the other instruments. We have learned through our many embodiments that the more finely we tune the physical vehicle, the stronger it is and the higher the voltage, frequency or light quota, we can attract and emit.

The sound, which was the first indication of the activity of the planetary Logos, is not a word, but a full reverberating sound holding within itself all other sounds, all chord and certain musical tones, which collectively, have been given the name 'music of the spheres.' It is this sound that the rising one must recognize and respond to. The student can achieve this at the fourth initiation, once she or he has let go of the ego. From the silence, which is the sound, the reverberating note of shamballa, the sound focuses itself depending on the status of the initiate. At this stage the initiate is confronted with the seven paths, because each path constitutes a mode of penetrating into a realm of realization beyond our planet. The initiate must demonstrate his mastery of the law of Differentiation and arrive at knowledge of the seven paths through differentiating the seven sounds, which make up the one sound, but which are not related to the seven sounds which compose the threefold AUM.

Being a 'refined human being' tuned to the beat of oneness brings rewards of joy, magic, bliss, fulfilment, great 'soul to soul' relationships, health, vitality and much more. We move from surviving to thriving, we activate four fifths of the brain housing higher consciousness, and we are conscious to the divine plan as we witness it unfold with great joy.

# 73

## The Law of Discipline

Many problems can be avoided through exercising self-discipline, a quality one can cultivate. Discipline on an inner level has to do with self-knowledge, knowing yourself, your strengths and limitations. It is recognizing your potential and how you can go beyond your limits. Discipline is the surest means to greatest freedom and independence. By practicing discipline, one expands to a greater degree than almost any other action. It provides the focus to achieve the skill level and depth of knowledge that translates into more options in life. Commitment involves discipline over a specific period of time. Discipline and commitment provide the bridge between here and our goals. Nothing can be achieved without practicing discipline.

Discipline is practiced in all areas of life, without discipline our world cannot function. With self-discipline we can learn to control our emotions. Without us having our emotions under control, we cannot cultivate our mental faculties. Without developing our will power we cannot develop self-discipline. If we gave in to every emotion we had, without restrictions or understanding, our life would be chaotic.

We have to take care though that we do not cross the middle line and become too rigid and inflexible, that would not be self-discipline. As a matter of fact the more discipline we exercise the more comfortable and flexible we can be. Spiritual teachings advise us to practice self-discipline, to conquer the self in order to get rid of our suffering. They teach us that the path of freedom from sorrow is to overcome our passions and desires. They teach us that no living creature seeks pain; that we should perceive unity in diversity; that all beings are equal and not to resort to the use of arms. He, who rises above the use of armament, has a tranquil mind, they say. A person who has a calm mind is not tormented by the physical five senses. The passions of a man who has conquered the senses, such as anger, pride, attachment and greed are not activated of themselves. The factor behind the insecurity of the soul is nothing else than the fickleness of the senses and the untrained mind that grows restless because of non-awareness. The person, who understands the role of the senses and has them under control, becomes his own master and is able to overcome all obstacles to achieve his goal. Without overcoming illusion, mental instability or personal insecurities, it is not possible to succeed. The qualities required are faith in oneself and one's aim, total dedication, constant effort and practice in discipline over the mind, speech and body.

# 74

## The Law of Disintegration

This is one of the seven laws of the solar system. On the third plane comes the final casting off, the ultimate shedding of the sheaths, of the fivefold superman. A Chohan of the sixth initiation discards all the sheaths beneath the monadic vehicle, from the atmic to the physical. It is the reverse aspect of the law of Cohesion. The law of Economy holds the key to this law.

When the Monad has circled through all disintegrating forms and has achieved the sixth initiation, the five lesser sheaths are destroyed. This law governs the physical plane catastrophes and disruptions, the astral and the lower mental thoughts plane disintegration. This law breaks up the forms and the law of Attraction builds up the forms again.

We experience the break up of the forms of political control, great religious thought forms, art and science etc. All eventually break under the working of this law. The process is slow. A form comes into being and grows into a perfect form and at the moment it has reached perfection loses its usefulness, it crystallizes and breaks and the evolving life escapes to find itself new forms of greater adequacy. This is the case for all life as we know it and through all cosmic processes. The same law applies to us humans.

We go through the process of life, birth, growing, changing and expanding in consciousness, getting old and disintegrating and dying so that the soul can move on to another more adequate form, to continue with the growth of consciousness and going through initiations. Nothing is static in the universe everything must move on constantly growing, changing reaching its full potential and finally disintegrating releasing the spirit within. There is no escape from this law.

## 75

## The Law of Dissolution

Disease and death are essentially conditions inherent in substance. Just as long as a woman or man identifies her or himself with the form aspect, so will she or he, be conditioned by the law of Dissolution. This law is a fundamental and natural law governing the life of the form in all the kingdoms of nature.

When the disciple or the initiate is identifying her or himself with the soul and when the antahkarana, also known as the rainbow bridge, is built by means of the life principle at the demand of the spiritual will or through recognition of the necessities of the hierarchy or the purposes of shamballa, natural law uses or discards the body at will.

# 76

## The Law of Divine Flow

We live in the law of divine flow by living in the moment, by being centered and by being in service to others, as opposed to service to the self. We stay in the 'moment by moment' flowing of our higher self, creating actions that reflect love, generosity and allowing of others to be.

When we are able to do this, we notice how we say just the right things, do what is best for all, and refrain from doing that which we previously disliked in ourselves or in others.

Through the energies of this law we maintain a stronger connection to our 'Godself.' The more we do this, the more we are able to go on doing this. To a degree, the deliberate letting go of this flow is the allowing of our spiritual integrity to be compromised.

See also the law of Divine Union.

# The Law of Divine Union

Divine union does not require two or more people in order to occur. One can experience divine union alone, while watching a sunset at the beach or from sitting on the terrace, taking a walk in the mountains or red wood forest, or just meditating or praying quietly at home alone. Divine union requires only the ability of the initiate to honor, his or herself and whomever or whatever is around them. In a state of honor, magic is generated through the love of one's own I AM Presence, the Higher Self to the human being.

The experience of divine union is created when love from the higher self pours through every cell of one's physical body, emotional, mental, etheric body and all the energy bodies. As the love of 'All that is' pours through one's energy field, this love blesses not only the person but all who are present and offers others an opportunity to begin to wake up from the third dimensional mass conscious dream.

As initiates transcend the kumara of fear, they begin to embody a state of divine union. Fear can be equated to the emotion that is experienced when one feels separated from God and the Higher Self. Once the experience of separation is transcended, the feeling of fear departs as one experiences divine union.

A state of divine union also requires that the masculine and feminine sides of an initiate come to a working balance within. It is the competition between the masculine and the feminine or between the masculine and God, that is the root of lack of balance required to sustain the state of divine union. Total relaxation as well as awareness is required to achieve the state of divine union. One knows without a doubt when one has experienced this divine union, it is a feeling of total bliss.

# 78

## The Law of Drama

The law of Drama is closely linked to the law of Karma, also known as the law of Cause and Effect and the law of Dharma. Right action, is the law of Drama.

The law of Drama expresses itself as the struggle that comes from the action right or wrong, on the way to the result. The law of Drama demonstrates that it is not the external result of an action that is of greatest significance, but the inner character growth, or decay that develops during the struggle.

# 79

## The Law of Duality

Life in manifestation produces existence and being its root cause is duality. As in spirit and matter, life and form, father and mother, positive and negative, darkness and light, etc. This duality is everywhere and produces a third factor, consciousness. This consciousness is the soul of all things.

Life in the physical body is preserved, physically and spiritually, under the impulse of the powerful will-to-be of the incarnated soul. This upon the magnetic power of the planetary life inherent in every atom of the form nature, by means of these atoms isolated and held by the law of attraction in form. It is a projection of consciousness into an isolated form, created, occupied and in dwelt by a soul, by a living being. It is a peculiar aspect of isolation which conditions the physical body of the human or any living form, rendering it detached, coherent and temporarily living its own life in response to the imposition of the livingness of the incarnating soul.

Two aspects of life and two forms of will or purpose are brought together. The higher type of energy is evolutionary the lower type of energy is involutionary in nature. This creates two aspects of livingness that of the spirit of the earth and that of the spiritual man. It is these conflicting forces that present the problem of dualism. The swing of the pairs of opposites is felt strongly when the soul is one the probationary path, joy and bliss then gloom and depression as the disciple swings back and forth between the dualities, astral in nature and sensuous in quality. This is not a quality of the soul and causes separateness.

Duality is opposing forces of energy that play against one another through judgement and competition, creating the ego as part of the personality. Looking at duality from occupying the middle golden line, we can deal with the complexities. It is accepting and embracing duality in life that makes it possible for us to find this golden middle line in all our endeavors. As we live on this plane of duality we need to exercise the law of Balance to create a polarity of female/male, negative/positive energies to achieve harmony and integration. This is the first step towards enlightenment. The state of harmony, however, is not meant to be stagnant but is a constant slight motion in one way or the other though avoiding any extremes.

See also the law of Balance and the law of Polarity.

# 80

## The Law of Duplication

This law states that if one person can do something, then this very thing can be done by others too, to a lesser, a higher degree or equally to equalize with the activity.

# 81

## The Law of Duration and Density

The closest contact to death is that which is a shift in the psyche on several levels simultaneously, wherein many changes on different levels occur. There is a giving up of certain descriptions of the self on one level while being forced to re-identify and re-describe oneself on another level.

One is capable of visualizing one's health to what would be more to one's own liking, for as you visualize yourself so you are. It all depends on how long and how intense you see yourself and in what vision. The longer and the more intense you are in your vision, this being in line with the law of Duration and Density, then the more substance you have in that vision and the more you can change yourself.

It is necessary for one to see oneself as one is, otherwise one does not know what they change from and toward, the images or visions can be scattered and fleeting. When you are one who sees yourself as you are and, therefore, are capable of holding an image of yourself changing slightly toward that which you want to be, you may think not in terms of becoming so much as in terms of being, for when you visualize something, you image it best by being it.

# 82

## The Law of Dying

When an entity has completed one stage or area of growth, it gathers all the knowledge from this area of growth and all the knowledge from the Group Soul of its element and withdraws this knowledge into itself, ready to expand into enlightenment. Physical death is not the end of soul life but a transformation.

# 83

## The Law of the Earth

No condition can be corrected or changed in the physical world without having the understanding, the use and the recognition of the love of the Ascended Hosts and Masters, the Great Seven Mighty Elohim. The more you remember to qualify your every thought, feeling and action with love, the more love will teach you about itself and the more understanding you will have of the many powers of love.

With the power of love present, in your electronic belt that surrounds you, of the Ascended Beings protecting you, you will not be at the mercy of the negative or destructive forces. This is the law of the Earth.

The cosmic law does not allow the Ascended Beings to help you unless you recognize, accept and make conscious use of the power of their love, into all your affairs. This must be done of your own free will. As you keep charging the hearts flame of love into the electronic circle around you, you increase the power into the reservoir by which you produce instant manifestation in your physical world. The more you do this the more the memory will come back to you of having had the use of this before.

The people of certain nations in the east have always been aware of and have accepted the Presence of the Ascended Beings, recognizing them to be the elder brothers of mankind constantly assisting life to be free. It is the confusion and the doubt and the incessant loud fast activities and demands in the western way of

*Cosmic and Universal Laws*

life, that have created a veil making it difficult for most people to accept the existence of higher beings.

The Ascended Masters are higher beings who have all gone through the incarnation process of life on this earth, who have evolved through the same experiences, trials and errors on the physical plane, to enlightenment and to existence on higher planes of being. Krishna, Moses, Jesus, Buddha are examples of the more widely known Masters, also known as Avatars. There are many others Avatars who are less widely known, some perhaps even long forgotten.

See also the law of Creation.

# 84

## The Law of Economy

This law of Economy causes matter always to follow the line of least resistance, and is the basis of the separate action of atomic matter. It governs matter, the opposite pole of spirit. Initiates must master this law before they can achieve liberation, or enlightenment.

The universe is economical with its energy to give the greatest amount of creation. That is why we don't have affinity for people who take too much of our energy. We avoid troublesome people because they suck our energy away. We normally intuitively avoid such people i.e. negative people, chronic complainers, chronic sick people, people who talk endlessly without meaning, etc. as they literally drain us of our energy.

Conversely the more we can save the energy of other people the more they will love us. Remember nobody has to live their life, for us.

# 85

# The Law of Economy of Force

This is one of the three major cosmic laws. The law of Economy of Force is the basic law of one pole, the negative aspect. This third cosmic law governs matter, the opposite of spirit, and causes matter to follow the line of least resistance. This law adjusts all that concerns the material and spiritual evolution of the cosmos with a rhythmic expenditure of force. This is done to the best possible advantage with the proper adjustment of equilibrium and with the necessary rate of rhythm. Unevenness of rhythm does not exist on the cosmic level. The person who aims at providing point of contact between conditions of chaos and those who work for constructive ends and order, should likewise use that most necessary factor of common sense in all activities.

For example, in a dual you do not just hit your opponent instead you use your opponent's force in order to strike back. Where this is done time is wisely distributed and energy is economized, something that one cannot do with zealousness. Zealousness does not rationalize nor does it know how to differentiate. This involves obedience to the law of Economy of Force, due to discrimination and a true sense of values. The Ascended Beings find a helper in an aspirant with such common sense, a dynamic way of thinking, seeing, relating and acting, with intuitive and rhythmic logic and inner knowing.

*Cosmic and Universal Laws*

The law of Economy of Force starts on the physical plane to the lower mental plane. On the higher spiritual planes it becomes the law of Love.

See also the law of Love.

# 86

## The Law of Education

We are all students and all teachers from the day we are born to the day we die. Knowledge is a divine aspect of the Creator and is gained through education. Life offers us limitless educational opportunities both academic and practical. All souls are in the process of education. This does not necessarily refer to the traditional book education only but more to the practical, emotional and spiritual education a soul goes through the school of life and experiences gained during each lifetime by its personal endeavors and relationships. This explains maturity found in younger children and immaturity in many adults, as it is the soul position on the evolution ladder, that is meant here and which mostly reveals itself through the personality.

On the physical level, a fundamental change in the methods of teaching in the future is inevitable, where the emphasis will be laid upon the fact of soul existence on its own plane, its alignment with the lower self and for direct communication with the physical brain. The faculty of intuition will be developed and men and women will be taught to think, to control their mental body and to discover their full potential. Education will focus on the true science of linking up the integral parts of man and to link him in turn with his immediate environment and with the greater whole in which he has to play his part. One of the main immediate objectives must be the elimination of the competitive spirit and the substitution of the cooperative consciousness. The world itself is a great blending pot out of which the 'one humanity' is emerging.

Through new methods of education, barriers will be removed. The fact that great art and literature have always belonged to the world is emphasized, confirming our similarities rather than differences, spiritual idealism and creative achievements. Two major ideas that should be taught are the value of the individual and the fact of the 'one humanity.' The effort of education to civilize the child will be to train and rightly direct its instincts, to develop and use its intellect correctly and elicit and develop the intuition. when these faculties are developed and are functioning correctly we will have a civilized, cultured and spiritual awakened human being. The adult will be instinctively correct, intellectually sound, and intuitively aware. The soul, the mind and the brain will function in the right relation to each other and as they should.

It is the responsibility of parents and educators to provide the child with an atmosphere of love and understanding, patience and courtesy plus to have regular ordered activities. This will encourage the child to grow without fear, shyness or timidity, accepting small duties and sharing of responsibility and likewise to be patient and courteous to all alike. An atmosphere of understanding is important so that the child is sure that the reasons and motives of his actions are recognized and the nature of his motivation is comprehended, even though parents or educators might not agree or approve of his actions.

An educational system must be worked out that makes it possible for all barriers to be removed and prejudices of every kind eliminated, and a training given to the developing child to enable him or her to grow and live with harmony and goodwill.

## 87

## The Law of Elements

Each unit has its own frequency and each element in that unit has its frequency of emanations connecting it to and compatible with the parent unit. When these elements separate from the parent unit, they will still have the same emanations that connect them to the parent unit.

## 88

### The Law of Elevation

The law of Elevation is for individuals who have been elevated to be governed by soul laws who are welded together as a group by a united aspiration and objective. In the past successful groups were composed of kindred souls who are all thinking alike, none of whom think with intuition, who are governed by some school of thought, or because some central figure dominates all the rest, hypnotizing them into an instinctual static condition. This served the purpose perhaps for the teacher and the group but not that of the Divine.

The new groups consist of free souls, individual and developed souls, who recognize no authority but that of their own individual souls, and submerge their interests to the soul purpose of the group as a whole. Just as the achievement of an individual has down the ages, served to raise the race of mankind, so a paralleling achievement in group formation will tend to raise humanity, still more rapidly.

See also the law of Group Endeavor.

# 89

## The Law of Energy

God is pure thought and energy is also pure thought. Spirit is *energy-in-motion*, and energy is the physical world manifests as e-motion. *Energy > thought > action > manifestation*. The universe is made up of energy, it is, therefore, not possible to dissipate energy. The language of energy is waves and frequencies and scientists have detected that at every dimension of life, including the human body, subtle energy layers are vibrating beneath the visible world of matter.

Emotions arise from thoughts so if you do not like the way you feel, just change your thoughts. Each emotion we have vibrates at a different frequency. The energy of love has the highest frequency of vibration, whereas, the energies of emotions of guilt, jealousy or shame vibrate at a very slow rate. Happy people vibrate at a very high level with emotions of joy, love, compassion, acceptance and forgiveness.

Energy is neutral and it is the use of energy that causes constructive or destructive movement. In other words, the same neutral energy is available to the good-doers and to the evil-doers. Energy does not discriminate. The energy that is used by any living being is colored with the quality of the thoughts of the entity that it manifests through. That is why it makes no sense to say 'how can God allow this evil to happen' or 'there is no God or this evil would not happen' etc. It is we, humans, who make things happen for good or for evil by activating the law of Energy.

Particle physicists like *Albert Einstein* and *Neils Bohr* proved that their perception and thoughts repeatedly influenced the dance of the electron and the outcome of their experiments. This means our predominant thoughts not only program our subconscious behavior, but that our repeated and focused thoughts manifest into physical reality by influencing the fundamental building block of all creation—*the atom*. In other words, we are all co-Creators with God but this we can only do when we vibrate at the highest levels so that we influence the dance of the atom. *It is our subtle thoughts that influence the forces of creation.*

Although traditional science can to date detect the vibrations of four layers of energy, Indian teachings tell us there are actually six layers of energy. Let me explain the six layers of energy—the physical, the electrical, the mental, the emotional, the intuitive and the soul layer. It is the sixth layer of the soul that is the same as the creative God force within.

The mind is where thoughts originate as an energy field and the brain is the physical medium in which thought waves vibrate. On the mind plane we have three levels, the intuitive mind that can tap into all universal information, the rational mind that analyses and categorizes and the subconscious mind. Our behavior is controlled mostly by the subconscious mind, the storehouse of our memories, emotions and core beliefs. Our success on the physical plane is controlled by our subconscious mind. In other words, if you believe you can't succeed then you will never succeed. You can, however, change your negative or limiting subconscious belief system by repeating affirmations and auto-suggestion to the contrary. Through regular meditation you can learn to tune in to the higher frequencies. To compare, if non meditators vibrate at 350 cycles per second, regular meditators can vibrate as high as 200'000 cycles per second, at which frequency it is possible to tap into the universal energy Force, the universal Mind that has all the information.

It is your free choice, to raise your energy vibrational level at any time. As mentioned above, energy does not discriminate. You do that by changing your every negative thought with an uplifting positive thought, by accepting things as they are, by not feeling constantly irritated with people or with circumstances that don't go your way and last but not least, by cultivating the feeling of love and compassion rather than fear or anger. Daily short prayers and regular meditation will definitely help to raise your vibrational frequency.

Energy does not change forms, but is as spirit energy eternal. Lack of energy does not exist. We have an inexhaustible reservoir of energy to draw upon, something that we should always remember. Tune in to the right frequency and join the new world of enlightened people.

See also the law of Vibration, the law of Meditation and the law of Manifestation.

# 90

# The Law of Enthusiasm

An enthusiast is one who is one possessed by God and celestial inspiration, full of rapturous intensity of feeling, in pursuit of a goal with passionate eagerness, proceeding from an intense conviction of the worthiness of an object. Enthusiasm is a soul quality. This law of Enthusiasm indicates that which allows one to be filled with spirit that, in turn may be used for purposes that can create greater expressions of spirit. Awareness indicates when one moves along in actions wherein new discoveries relating to self, new self-discoveries are made, one then purges oneself of the old and brings in the new energies of the discovery.

Action increases enthusiasm. This awareness indicates that the word 'enthusiasm' relates unto spirit within, and the spirit within is that which enhances the life-force factor. This awareness also indicates that those who use the law of Enthusiasm for destructive purposes, are those who shall reap the whirlwind of devastation on many planes and many levels, thereafter activating the law of Karma.

Awareness of this law indicates that essentially, when one begins to stagnate and move through life in a robot type of behavior pattern, one loses enthusiasm for life. Life then becomes mechanical in nature because even if one indulges in the thrills and desires nothing seems to change any more. One is bored and does not progress. When one stagnates one loses more and more of the protective aura around the body and around the psyche. One loses vitality of the physical and spiritual body. When the vitality is depleted the aura tends to draw in the forces, which result in illness or accident or further weakening of the bodies. This becomes likened unto an invitation to the higher forces, the so-called Lords of Karma, to take action to remove the entity from this plane. This law makes it clear to us that it is desirable for us to strive always for higher achievements and to do that with great enthusiasm.

# 91

## The Law of Essence

The Law of Essence states that, what 'is'—is, and what is not changed by any opinions or beliefs about it, but is what it is, while it is. This law states that actions and motives which are of the highest and the best quality, the most inclusive and encompassing, the most appropriate and essential, create those movements that lead to the Gate of Essence, behind which all things are exactly as they are, while they are. Essence is the ever-changing truth that was, is and forever shall be. The essence is the is-ness of what is happening at any moment regardless of the length of time included in that moment. This *awareness* indicates that awareness of what 'is' is total bliss and total union with the Godhead. The Sufis refer to the essence in the human. We talk about the essence of a person. When we are in touch with our own essence there is no limit to what we can do.

# 92

## The Law of Essential Integrity

This law concerns the integrity and activity of the soul in form. This law has ten subsidiary laws with which the true healer must work and is important for healers as well as for those souls who are ill and might be seeking help from therapists and healers.

The healer must be trained to know the source of the problem of the one who seeks help, the innermost stage of thought and of desires, to know of the cause and the effect of the disease. The healer must achieve magnetic purity for the self through purity of life and must attain that dispelling radiance that shows itself when the centers in the head are linked. It is through this magnetic field when established that the radiation for healing goes forth. The healer must seek to link soul, heart, brain and hands and only then can the healer pour vital healing force upon the patient. This is known as magnetic work. It can cure the disease but it can also increase the evil state according to the knowledge and purity of the healer. When the healer has linked soul, brain, heart and auric emanation of the self, then the mere presence of the healer can feed the soul life of the patient. This is known as the work of radiation. For this the hands are not needed for the soul displays its power. The soul of patient responds likewise through the aura. The healer heals through love and not through the will.

See also the law of Healing.

## 93

## The Law of Evolution

An aspect of the law of Evolution is that achievement, is ever followed by sacrifice and the giving, of the greater for the lesser. This is the theme of the entire creative process and is the basic meaning of the phrase 'God is love,' for love, in this solar system, signifies giving and sacrifice. Therefore, forgiveness sacrifice in order to save others is the keynote at this time. What is meant here is that the 'giving for' and 'sacrifice' involves right living upon the physical plane and not as often misinterpreted, the dying of the physical body as a sacrifice. It is the sacrifice day by day, in the process of our daily living that can save the world. It involves the sacrifice of our selfish personal interests, for the good of the whole and the giving up of our practical life to the salvage of the world. It is living in order that others may live. When all this is understood correctly and practiced by humanity, the new age will be realized and teachings of the true meanings of esotericism will be known.

In the total evolution of the spiritual man through physical incarnation during untold hundreds of lives, the entire process is simply one of expanding consciousness and of attaining sequentially and stage by stage an ever, more inclusive awareness. The entire story of evolution is covered in a few words that Jesus Christ said: 'If any man shall do His will, he shall know.' In other words, doing precedes knowing because knowledge is gained through experimenting and experiencing.

We must keep in mind that space is an entity and the aphorism explains this, 'in Him we live and move and have our being' and we must see ourselves in relation to this 'all-enveloping entity.' We are always moving in a world of energies that make an impact upon us from varying directions. Because completion is guaranteed so also is evolution. Evolution may be temporarily subverted but will always prevail. Evolution is a by-product of knowledge that is itself a by-product of divine intelligence and is a constant rising towards the higher spheres, spiralling towards God, and when someone is drab, hard and resistant it means that one is going in the opposite direction, the way of regress rather than progress.

# 94

## The Law of Example

The law of Example states that any person, concept or thing which is placed in a position of significance, may serve as an example for others to follow.

Those who have served as examples of power, lust and greed, have helped to create the tragedies that they and their followers have spawned. Those who have served as examples of love, service and the sharing of their better parts have helped to bring about freedom, beauty, joy and peace that has been allowed upon this plane. If we wish ourselves a better world and inner peace then all we need to do is to exemplify and portray the qualities of love, joy, peace and render service to others, particularly to the children who are searching for examples in their world.

# 95

## The Law of Exclusion

This law of Exclusion or contraction is the opposite of the law of Expansion. One becomes reductive in describing oneself as less than what all that is. One is either this or that, not this and not that, reducing oneself and one's world into oblivion.

Reductiveness does not allow intrinsic aspects of our being to come forth and inhibits the material imagination that is a magical participation in life. This law denies the depth, the warmth, action, poetry, ambivalence, dreams of our secret being and longings. When this law of energies is activated all is denied, dreams, desires, imagination and growth.

In some practical areas the law of Exclusion has its merits. We see many examples in our daily lives. Example, one way streets, which exclude traffic going the opposite way. This is good because it allows order in traffic and reduces accidents. Another example, you order chicken in a restaurant, which automatically excludes meat or fish, because this is what you want. Or you choose to buy a book in English, which excludes Russian or any other language, because you wish to read the book in English.

In other areas such as religion, tradition set by old clergy says that the Jewish holy day is the Sabbath excluding all other days, for the Christians its Sunday and so forth. However, in matters of the spirit, if this law is exercised then one goes against nature itself, for the spirit is forever free, forever in need for growth and expansion.

See the Law of Expansion.

# 96

## The Law of Expansion

This law of a gradual evolutionary expansion of the consciousness indwelling every form, is the cause of the spheroidal form of every life in the entire solar system. This awareness indicates that the law of Expansion is that inclusion which results when the definition and description of a part or a situation is expanded to include something else. The law of Expansion is that which is never-ending as long as there is more, which may be included by re-describing.

Those who understand the law of Expansion will understand that they are more than a physical body, more than a name, more than a social being, more than a life of action, more than a center of a society, more than an observer and an observed, more than a symbol for humanity, more than the awareness of the earth and solar system, more than the confines of form: that they are all that is and all that can possibly be.

Those who move from the law of Expansion into the law of Exclusion or Contraction would describe themselves as being something less than all that is, this being an exclusive law which describes them as being is, but not that; and this but not that until they are almost nothing at all in a universe of overwhelming forces.

Beware of the law of Exclusion, lest you exclude yourself from all else into the oblivion of the bottomless pit. Any values must remain vulnerable and those that do not are dead. In other words this

*Cosmic and Universal Laws*

law demands that we are not singular about any of one thought. Imagination and dreaming are part of this law of Expansion. The opposite of this law is when one becomes reductive and denies multiplicity of perspectiveness.

See also the law of Exclusion, which is the opposite of the law of Expansion.

# 97

## The Law of Expectation

According to this law, energy follows thought. We move toward but not beyond that what we can imagine. What we assume, expect or believe influences and creates our experiences and our world. By changing our thoughts and expectations, we can change without fault our experiences of every aspect of our lives.

It is all in our mind, our largeness and our smallness. The power of Expectancy is a state of mind and of spirit that gives life to our creative powers. If you expect much, you will obtain much! If you expect little, you will get little! If you expect nothing, then you will receive nothing.

Even if you are in a world of turmoil and confusion, practice abstract thought and activate your understanding of the laws to your own life so that your world can be one of peace, order and joy. Your world depends on how you choose to create it through your beliefs, your application of the universal laws and your expectancy.

# 98

## The Law of Faith

The law of Faith is founded upon the recognition that we all know more than what we have read, heard or studied. We know more because WE are a part of the ALL.

We have a direct link to the universal wisdom. We just need to learn and to remember how to access this link and this we can do, if we quiet our mind and look within, listen, discern, and most of all if we trust. We need to learn to develop more trust in our own deepest intuition and wisdom as the final arbiter and source of our decisions.

Faith being a vibration of the highest frequency will always prevail. Doubt never succeeds but faith always does. Faith is the feeling of light. It does not take faith it takes application. If you have faith, which is the feeling of light, it will act more rapidly but if you make your application, the law is compelled to act for you. Faith is the presentiment of knowledge. Like a motive force, faith intensifies the energy. Despair is the death of faith. When faith is knowledge then despair is the death of knowledge.

# 99

## The Law of Fixation

This is one of the seven laws of the solar system. By means of the law of Fixation the mind controls and stabilizes. This is the governing law on the mental plane. 'As a man thinks so is he.' According to his thoughts are his desires and acts and so results his future. He fixes for himself the resultant karma.

This law governs the crystallization of all forms prior to their shattering in the process of evolution. The word fixation implies the capacity of the thinker to shape his own destiny. His desires and acts are in accordance with his thoughts and so is his future. He fixes for himself the resultant karma. He fixes his future through his thoughts. It is the concentration and the focus on the goal. Wherever we have our focus and whatever we concentrate on we energize and bring into form. This law also governs the time of rebirth.

See also the law of Rebirth.

# 100

## The Law of Flexibility

This law involves a pragmatic acceptance of the present moment. It demands that we accept ourselves, others and current circumstances. That we do not exercise a rigid resistance of what is occurring at the moment. It requires an alert and extensive state of awareness and embracing and making constructive use of the moment. Stumbling blocks become stepping-stones and problems become opportunities. Everything serves our highest good and that of others related to us, if we can learn to make good use of it.

The serenity prayer used by Alcoholics Anonymous and other twelve step programs reflect this law. 'God grant me the serenity to accept the things I cannot change, the courage to change the things I can, and the wisdom to know the difference.' This prayer is drawn from the Vedas, also from Buddha's writings.

Another Chinese proverb says that we should learn to bend and sway like a tree in a storm. If a tree is too rigid in harsh winds it would snap and break, and so would we, unless we too learn to be flexible, without moaning and groaning, with the circumstances that life challenges us with. We activate this law in a positive way when we go with the flow and do the best we can out of every situation.

# 101

## The Law of Forgiveness

This law works with the energy of openness, and the ability to see all as love, so one may dispense with the unnatural feeling of getting even or of taking revenge. The old energy of eye for an eye keeps the vibrations of a person very low. To forgive, to release old stored anger allows the law of grace to intercede and dispense with amounts of karma an individual has stored on the astral level.

Non-violence is the natural outgrowth of the law of forgiveness and love. All good comes from forgiveness. It is a truth that the continuation of the human species is due to human's being forgiving. Forgiveness is holiness and it is by forgiveness that the universe is held together. Forgiveness is the might of the mighty. Forgiveness gives peace of mind. Forgiveness and gentleness are the soul qualities of the self-possessed and represent eternal virtue. One is only forgiven when one forgives. Failure to forgive one's self or others is a violation of this law.

Forgiveness is healing and fills one with light and perfection. When forgiveness is sincere, the individual will find his world re-ordered and filled with all good things as if by magic. But it must be remembered that unless a discord is forgotten it is not forgiven because you cannot release yourself from it until it is out of your consciousness. As long as you remember an injustice and harbor an inner disturbed feeling you have not really forgiven either the person or the condition. When forgiveness is complete, the emotional body experiences peace, freedom, health and vitality.

*Cosmic and Universal Laws*

Forgiving someone does not necessarily mean that you have to like the person or that you have to be eternal friends, but it does mean that you have to wish them well and let them go on their way with no anger or resentments. Should they happen to cross your path and you can't avoid them, be friendly, be polite and go on your way. Just don't hold any grudges or resentments against them but be genuine about wishing them well.

# 102

## The Law of Freedom

The law of Freedom allows that movement which gives all living beings the space to expand and grow in their ability to function in a manner that will allow others their freedom and space to grow, in order to free still others. Freedom is not a final state of being. It is an ever-expanding action of giving each other the space to create spaces for others, to create more spaces for still others yet to come. Freedom may be helped or hindered by laws, definitions, principles, descriptions, disciplines and boundaries. Universal laws free each and every one. Any law that fails to do that is subject to the rule of a still greater law. No one is free until each is free and all are freeing each other.

The Violet Consuming Flame is the law of Freedom to the earth and is the law and the authority that governs the action of mankind in the centuries yet to come. It is said that the Violet Consuming Flame must be intensified upon this planet for the next ten thousand years in order to keep mankind purified long enough to let the divine plan manifest its reality and blessings for the future. One can purify oneself with the Violet Flame through one's own mind, thoughts and imagination.

One imagines oneself standing and being completely enveloped, surrounded and purified by the Violet Flame, cleansing negative emotions such as fear, anger, greed, selfishness or any other vice that one might have. Do this for a few minutes as often as you can remember. Know that as soon as you consciously make your decree it manifests on the psychic level. The fact that it is invisible does not make it less effective. When you have faith and you repeatedly consciously make your decrees you will soon experience definite positive changes in your life on the physical plane.

# 103

## The Law of Free Will

We are a privileged species to have been given intelligence and the free will for freedom of choice. We are free to choose our direction. Predestination determines what our destiny in life would be, if we choose to fulfil that destiny. This law works the same for every one of us regardless who we are and no one has the right to infringe on this freedom of will. Anyone who robs any individual the freedom of choice is violating this universal law.

The law of Free Will states that divine will grants each individual the right to direct and pursue his or her life and the quality of that life, so long as he or she does not violate this same right of others. A right that excludes the rights of others is other than divine. Although through God's grace we have been given free will, the only purpose of free will is to surrender it back to the Creator. Free will is a learning tool of the lower mind, the ego. We are absolutely free to choose opposition to God during the process of spiritual growth, however, opposition to God is a violation of the universal law of One.

Free will when properly exercised simply allows each soul to grow at its own pace and in its own way, choosing its own path, reflecting the basic personality of the soul as assigned by God.

This is also a good reason why no one has the right to exercise any force on another individual in spiritual development or change in their belief system. Everything must be achieved through the individual free will.

See also the law of Choice.

# 104

# The Law of Friction

This law is a subsidiary law under the law of Economy along with three others, namely, the law of Vibration, the law of Adaptation and the law of Repulsion. The law of Friction governs the heat aspect of any atom, the radiation of an atom, and the effect of that radiation on any other atom. Every atom of matter can be studied in four aspects and is governed by one or other, or all of the four above mentioned laws.

Modern science is still at a loss here. Leonardo da Vinci stated the two basic laws of friction 200 years before Newton even defined what force is. David Kessler of Barllan University, has mentioned in *Nature* magazine, 'that while we physicists can tell you a lot about quarks, quasars, and other exotica, there is still no universally accepted explanation of the basic laws of friction.'

# 105

## The Law of Fulfilment

This law has to do more with the work of the Ashrams rather than with us. Part of the service rendered by members of an Ashram is to make way for new aspirants. They do this by hastening their own progress and moving forward so that they are admitted to a higher Ashram, leaving a vacancy for new disciples, which are promptly filled. By fulfilment is meant the full compliance of a disciple with the service demands upon the outer plane. When these demands are met and the service is effective then the outer effectiveness produces inner effectiveness.

## 106

## The Law of Garment of Light

Youth is a garment of light. Light is a garment of knowledge. Water is a garment of health. Life without virtues is like a garden without flowers or trees without fruit. The beginning of all things is spirit. The beginning of spirit is love. The zenith of the spirit is wisdom. The end of all things is truth that brings freedom. There is only an end where all contradictions cease. There is only a beginning where all is in accord. If the heart does not feel, the beautiful cannot come. If the mind does not think, the great will remain unknown. One can, through regular meditation, concentration and decree, establish a garment of light in one's aura as a protective device against all negative and adversary vibrations.

See also the law of Freedom.

# 107

## The Law of Gender

This law embodies the truth that gender is manifested in everything. The masculine and the feminine is ever at work on all planes of causation. Gender manifests on all three planes of causation the physical plane, the mental plane and the spiritual plane. The law is the same on all planes but on the higher planes, it takes higher forms of manifestation. This law works in the direction of generation, regeneration, and creation.

All life forms contain within them the two elements of gender the masculine and the feminine. On the great physical plane, the sexes of all species are manifested as male and female and the role they play in sexual reproduction. On the great mental plane, gender manifests as masculine and feminine energies that exist within each and every person. Every male has its female element, and every female has its male element within.

On the great spiritual plane, gender manifests as the Father Mother principle of the Infinite Omnipresent God in whose mind the universe is conceived and firmly held. It is written 'In him we live, move and have our being.' When balance and learning reach a critical mass, the personality achieves the merger of God, and will see self as neither male nor female but as the one blended Self.

# 108

## The Law of Giving

Giving and receiving are part of the exchange that perpetuates the energy flow of the universe. As we are receptive to the premise of giving that which we desire to receive, the abundance of the universe is perpetuated in our lives. We must give in order to receive, and we must receive in order to give. The energy of each is equal, and the universe will respond to either, with a pull of the energy of the other.

Some people say, 'well, I do give but I seldom see any sign of return.' There is a right way and wrong way to give. There is careless impulsive giving, and there is careful, scientific giving. When we give impulsively we are retarding progress, we are wasting our substance. Where we give to one who doesn't put forth the effort to help himself we need not expect a good return. Nature does not support a parasite or a loafer, but she gives her energy to the ones who are struggling forward. She lets the parasite and the loafer see that she will help if they put forth the effort to help themselves. But with us, if we support a loafer in what he is in, how can we expect any good returns? Rather the loafer becomes arrogant and demanding for more and more relief, until we wonder where and when it will end.

After giving, our next step is to prepare to receive the response or results of our giving and to receive, as the law states, 'good measure, pressed down, shaken together, and running over.' This is the exciting part, because our preparation shows our active faith.

*Cosmic and Universal Laws*

Instead of rocking and waiting, we are prepared and working. This in turn enlarges our view. It stimulates our interest, it disperses our doubt, our fear, and energizes our power of reception. The key to this law is that we are continually drawing into our life what we give and expect.

Therefore, what we receive will be in accordance with our actions and intentions. If you want smiles and kindness from others then give smiles and kindness to others. If you want help from angels then find someone who is less privileged than you are and share your light with this person, your actions will be reflected in the invisible world and it will be a call for entities to come and do likewise for you.

## 109

## The Law of Goodness

Although the universal law of Balance applies in true reality, there is nothing outside of goodness or of Godliness. Therefore all there is, is good and all there is, is God.

## 110

### The Law of Goodwill

Knowledge of this law will help those who have feelings of hopelessness when thinking about the course of world events. By viewing life in terms of energy, we understand that our higher self, coupled with our thought-mind creates energy and action-energy solidifies this thought into matter or results.

In an energy relationship, there is always a positive, creating side and a negative receiving side of that creative relation. This is simply how the world works. The will-to-good is the positive, creative impetus, which when received, makes the manifestation of goodwill possible. We are either mentally polarized or emotionally polarized and only those who are mentally polarized can begin to appropriate this energy through will on the mental plane. When this is fully comprehended, we begin to realize why the manifestation of goodwill is not more widespread.

An initiate states that it is absolutely essential that the will-to-good be unfolded by the disciples of the world, so that goodwill can be expressed by the 'rank and the file' of mankind. The will-to-good of the world *knowers* is the magnetic seed of the future. Our mental capacity today readily contacts those ideas that constitute the purpose behind the form. We have the ability to mentally construct a happening, and see it through to completion. This is the will-to-good. The desire of one to create a loving scenario of 'goodwill' is another but related action. The will-to-good is always an education process where the recipients are left with the freedom of choice to receive the idea or not. The responsibility for expanding the amount of goodwill in the world lies directly on the shoulders of the intelligentsia of the world.

In the goodwill process it is the creative, idea or problem solving individuals who are directly responsible for creating goodwill. The 'rank and file' of humanity simply does not yet possess the mental capacity to evoke the process, even though many are able to participate in the process. This knowledge should fill the responsible group with a greater amount of hope and assurance, because they have the power to generate goodwill in their every day routine solving of problems.

An initiate said: 'When the majority of the inhabitants of the earth are being rapidly oriented towards good, towards righteousness, and the bulk of human beings are inclined towards goodwill, then ill health will persistently, even if only gradually, disappear and die out and finally become non-existent. Slowly, very slowly this is already happening.

## 111

## The Law of Grace

Karma when properly discharged leads to a total release of obligation. This law of Grace can waive the law of Karma. When applied, this law allows a person to receive more than one deserves or works for, provided it is in the highest good for all concerned. When called upon, this law allows the person to send another a healing, to do soul talk or to use divine decree, and not suffer the consequences of karma interference with the receiver's soul plan. The wording to insert in the request is 'under the law of Grace…'

Another aspect of this law is to be of higher vibration to consistently live in grace. i.e. A loving person who works diligently sending world healing to 'mother earth' and all life on her body, and focusing so much on this activity, will find that life will run more smoothly than otherwise, due to the law of Grace. This condition, however, cannot be taken for granted nor abused or it will leave one.

The law of Grace states that any divine being can apply the law of Mercy to grant a pardon to one who has made a mistake, so that the Karma my be set aside. But such an act of pardon is entirely at the discretion of the divine being, and though individuals may request and seek, or beg, they have no right to demand grace, mercy or forgiveness, when other karmic justice is their due.

The Grace of God does not descend upon us, i.e. does not come to us for no reason. We first have to earn it. We have to lift ourselves up to God and then the Grace of God will meet us and lift us further up. The less selfish life you live, the more you are aware and in union with the Divine, nature and humanity, the more you will activate this law.

# 112

## The Law of Gratitude

Although the Creator allows us to create through the absolute principle of Grace, gratitude is a function of free will. Compliance with this law does increase our heart's desire and heals old patterns. The law of Gratitude is that sense of satisfaction in knowing that energy, which has been given, receives its certain reward according to its nature. Energy that is given moves out on that curved and unequal line and when extended far enough, can only return to its source bearing its appropriate gifts. It governs the process of petal unfoldment and so it demonstrates a triple law, the law of Solar Heat, the law of Solar Light and the law of Solar Fire.

You have heard it many times that an attitude of gratitude has the power to get you realizing your dreams at record speed. Why? Because gratitude completes the cycle of knowing. Remember, you cannot know what is without knowing what is not. What you like and what you hate are two ends of the same thing. For example, if you like being with your spouse and hate being separated from them, realize that you are working within the same essence, which is your spouse. It is because of the moments of absence that you appreciate and recognize the moments of presence. When you are grateful for both what you like and what you don't like, you complete the knowingness and you are released from having to experience what you don't like. This cannot be explained logically, but some very significant shifts occur in your mind and soul—and you can feel this releasing shift—whenever you are genuinely grateful for all things, even the ones you don't like.

Gratitude will speed you through your growth and success more than any amount of hard work ever can. Gratitude completes the lesson, and as a statement of completion rings that tone of success, pulling to you the end result desired. Another way to put it is that you cannot leave a situation permanently unless you appreciate the gifts it brings you, and all situations bring a gift, no matter how terrible the situation may appear to be. This law ensures that you will always complete your knowing and embrace all that is, before moving on.

The way to put this law into practice is to be constantly grateful and thankful for what you have, never to complain when the going gets rough, but to genuinely show gratitude at all times.

Develop a habit of counting your blessings each morning when you wake up and each night before you go to sleep. Focus on your blessings in life rather than on the negative or what fails or ails you. Having an attitude of gratefulness and being thankful for all the experiences you have in life, both the good and the bad, will surely bring back its rewards.

Refer also to the law of Increase.

# 113

## The Law of Gravitation

The law of Gravitation shows itself in one aspect as the power, and the stronger urge that a more vital life may have upon the lesser, such as the power of the spirit of the earth, the planetary entity, to hold all physical forms to itself, and prevent their scattering. This is due to the heavier vibration, the greater accumulative force, and the aggregated 'tamastic' lives of the body of the planetary entity. This force works upon the negative or the lowest aspect of all physical forms.

The law of Gravity shows itself also in the response of the soul of all things to the greater Soul in which the lesser finds itself. This law affects the two lowest forms of divine life but not the highest. It emanates in the first instance from the physical sun and the heart of the sun. This force works upon the negative or lowest aspect of all physical forms.

There is a popular story that Newton was sitting under an apple tree and an apple fell on his head and so he suddenly discovered the law of Gravitation. It is the law of Gravitation that is responsible for keeping the earth and the other planets in their orbits as they orbit around the sun. It is this law that keeps the moon in its orbit around the earth and for the formation of tides. Without this law of Gravitation life as we know it would not exist.

# 114

## The Law of Group Endeavor

This law defines the multiplying of energy one creates when acting with like minded individuals to form a group effort to pray, to manifest, to do light work, for the good of all concerned, or even to create degrees of control which we define as evil or black magic. Where the efforts of an individual may equal one unit, the efforts of two praying or healing for a common goal with equal energy will affect the energy of twenty units instead of the sum total of two. With three, the resultant energy will explode even further. The longer pure thought, to the exclusion of any other thought, of one's desired goal is held in the mind, the more powerful the result. Holding a pure thought for an increment of time is the beginning lesson of manifestation.

See the law of Manifestation.

# 115

## The Law of Group Life

The law of Group Life comes into expression when one fulfills love family, social, national and global obligations, when one thinks of the wider terms of humanity itself. This is also known as the law of Brotherhood. Brotherhood is a group quality. Questions of self such as, 'will my action tend to the group good?' or, 'will the group suffer or hurt if I do this or that?' should always be foremost in our minds. Abiding by these actions will gradually become part of our human consciousness and our civilization will adjust itself to these new conditions. All aspects of life are interdependent and when one proceeds to full expression then all members of the group (family) benefit.

## 116

## The Law of Group Progress

This law is also known as the law of Elevation. The symbol is the mountain and the goat standing at the summit with the astrological sign of Capricorn. All hard places can be surmounted and the summit reached by the divine goat—a symbol meaning group effort. The ray energy is progressive energy of the seventh ray, the evolving factor.

## 117

## The Law of Growth

Spiritual growth is mandatory and infinite. What attention is placed on a specific thought, a course of action, causes it to grow and to increase. Lack of attention on a specific thought whether positive or negative, causes it to decrease, which, however, is also to be interpreted as growth.

This law makes it clear to us how important it is for us not to dwell on unhealthy thoughts, on fear, worry, failure or violence. If we dwell on a negative thought, in accordance with this law, it will grow to an extent that we run the risk of it manifesting only because we have fed the thought so much energy by giving it our attention. Keep in mind thoughts are things!

Refer also to the law of Paradox and the law of Thought.

# 118

## The Law of Happiness

The law of Happiness states that it is not what you are, what you do, or what you have that determines happiness, but how you feel about who you are, what you do, what you have and more important, what you do with what you have.

Many people spend their entire life chasing after happiness and never find it. Many seek their happiness through other persons or objects in their life, unaware that true happiness comes from within and has much more to do with the attitude you have about yourself, life, your role in life and relationship with life and your fellow humans. When you have arrived to this awareness then you will not need to look for happiness because joy and happiness become a part of you.

The secret of all success and happiness is to manifest in your own behavior whatever you would like to receive from others.

See also the Law of Acceptance.

# 119

# The Law of Harmony

The law of Harmony is an eternally fundamental law of Life. The law of Harmony and Agreement states that efforts to manipulate, to trick or force another to behave in harmony and agreement will only disrupt previously established areas of harmony and agreement. Yet, even between the most hostile enemies, some area of harmony and agreement can be discovered when there is an agreement to discover these areas. Ever increasing harmony and agreement grows from the mutual agreement to discover more areas of agreement. This law is based on discovering rather than on the enforcement of harmony and agreement.

We must first establish this harmony within ourselves. When the thought is held in a harmonious state, we can control our feelings, which are the realm of our sub-conscious. This is the realm within us, which needs to be continually safeguarded against the impacts from the outside world. The outside world makes its impressions upon the conscious mind through the thought, and upon the sub-conscious mind through the feelings, which are controlled by the thought. When we can focus our thought and keep it upon the inner self, it automatically becomes harmonious, controls and harmonizes the feeling.

Irritation, resentment, anger, self-pity, hate, pride, jealousy, selfishness are the feelings that make us resist harmony and, therefore, make us fail in our endeavors in life. When harmony is maintained, we can accomplish anything that we put our mind to.

# 120

# The Law of Healing

The law of Healing concerns the ability of one to channel energy also referred to as Holy Spirit, Prana and Chi, which radiates from the Source, the Higher Power or from whom we call God. The purpose of this channelled energy is to either improve the self or another by removing blockages or instilling the sacred energy that pulsates from the Source. With intent or technique we may send this energy to the past, present or future. Hands on healers who are effective in healing have brain waves at 7.8 Hz—the same as the earth's pulse beat. Their brain waves are in sync with the earth's beat, at the time the healing is performed. Another aspect of this law is the ability of one in the third dimension to heal self by that, which triggers a leap in faith.

All initiates of the Ageless Wisdom are basically healers, though all may not heal the physical body. The reason for this is that all souls that have achieved any measure of true liberation are transmitters of healing energy. Since all disease is the result of inhibited soul life, the art of the healer consists in releasing the soul so that its life can flow freely through the form.

There are three ways in which healing can be brought about, and all three have their value, depending upon the point of evolution of the subject being healed. The first is where the patient is passive and methods are used which gradually cure vitality. All homeopathic schools of healing are included in this method. The second way is that of the modern psychology who seeks to correct the attitude of mind, inhibitions and neurotic complexes that bring about the disease. This is a positive and active method and it is a step in the right direction. The combination of the psychology with the outer physical treatment is sound and right. The third and newest method, however, is that of calling positive activity in the subject's own soul. This is where the true healing is brought about when the life of the soul can flow without any hindrance or obstacles that block it. In this case the soul can vitalize the form with its own power and so eliminate all congestion that causes the disease.

Disease differs in humanity depending on the point of evolution of the individual. The healer must be able to make a distinction and to gauge the point of evolution that has been reached by the patient. Some diseases the healer must deal with through the mind plane, others require a concentration of the emotional energy, and in other cases the healer need only to be the transmitter of pranic energy to the etheric body of the patient via the healer's etheric body. Any man or woman prompted by the incentive to serve who thinks and loves can be a healer. Every initiate is a healer and the more advanced initiates automatically heal whomever is within their aura.

See also the law of Essential Integrity and the law of Thought.

# 121

## The Law of Higher Will

From the perspective of our separate self and smaller will, it is normal for us to act on the basis of our own earthly desires and material preferences. When we can, however, surrender our lower self and will, to the guidance of a higher will and dedicate our actions for the highest good of all (everyone) concerned, we feel an inspired glow at the center of our life. The higher will is from the divine power, the Source of life, the lower will, is the individual personality will.

To surrender our personal will requires us to let go of our ego and our ego demands, to have faith that whatever the outcome is, it is for our own best, and to give the control over to the Higher Will. In the bible it says, 'Thy Will be mine.' That is exactly what it means, Thy higher will is my will, I surrender to Thy higher will. When we are able to surrender, we free ourselves from all worry and fear and we feel total relief, and we accept the outcome whatever it maybe as it is.

## 122

## The Law of Honesty

The law of Honesty requires that we see things as they are, without an attempt to alter that, which is seen, either for purposes of advantage or out of fear. To recognize, to accept and to express our authentic interior reality, lies at the heart of honesty. Only when we are honest with ourselves can we speak or act honestly with anyone else. In the sense of integrity, honesty entails acting in line with higher laws despite negative impulses to the contrary.

We don't need to be punished for breaking spiritual laws or higher laws. The act itself is the punishment and sets into motion subtle forces whose natural consequences we cannot escape, any more than we can escape the force of gravity. When we allow our fear to stop us from expressing our true feelings and needs, we are being dishonest with ourselves and this drains us from our energy and spirit.

The law of Hierarchy is that by which the entire life is founded, that by which the world progresses and that upon which evolution is built. Hierarchy and leadership are affirmed upon the Cosmic Law.

# 123

## The Law of Honor

This law requires us to honour ourselves along with all other life forms. In embracing the law of Honour, we embody 'real love' and we release any remaining co-dependent partners with others based on illusionary love, glitter or glamour. In embracing a state of honour, we choose not to harm another either consciously or unconsciously on any plane of reality. In a state of honour, the vibration of harmlessness is maintained within an initiate's field.

A state of honour recognizes that all aspects of Godliness are equal and that even the unconscious anti-Christ souls are a part of the Creator and honors them as such. It is from the act of self-honour that we do not allow another to harm the self. Through self-honour, we do whatever it takes to cause others to understand that abusive and violent patterns of behavior be they physical, emotional or mental are not acceptable in our presence.

# 124

# The Law of Humility

The opposite of humility is selfish pride. The central feature of pride is enmity. Enmity, or animosity, may be pitted against persons or groups in society. Pride leads to contentions and strife, causes divisions and destroys unity through selfishness, greed and envy. Humility, gratitude and camaraderie serve as primary antidotes to dispel pride. As difficult and as fraught with danger as it is, the spiritual challenge is for man to let go all that he thinks he knows, so that a much deeper wisdom might emerge.

This wisdom is one that is born not of having definite answers, but rather being willing to live with questions that cannot be answered. Out of this shift of perspective, can come a powerful humility and a profound sense of compassion for the struggle of others to find their own answers, an openness to truth in whatever form it happens to come and access to the very core of life's deepest mysteries.

Sometimes humility is confused with lack of self esteem. Humility does not mean the absence of self confidence or the absence of knowledge that each of us has great worth. Humility can be manifested in a meek giant. The very best example of humility is when a powerful king takes on the role of a servant. The attitude of self discipline, strength in meekness and the heart to serve, will make children strong, confident and capable as they meet a hostile world.

## 125

## The Law of Identity

This law pertains to the individual right of all to create one's own beingness. It applies to the time spent between incarnations as well as third dimensions, our dimension, incarnational experiences. When one merges with the Great Central Sun-God, one still may separate to accomplish something and will possess an individual identity.

According to Aristotle, the concept of identity is important because it makes explicit that reality has a definite nature. Since reality has an identity, it is knowable. Since it exists in a particular way, it has no contradictions. Everything that exists has a specific nature. Each entity exists as something in particular and its characteristics that are a part of what it is.

# 126

# The Law of Impartiality

Spirit is divinely unaware of intrinsic difference between each of its thoughts, that which we perceive. Properties of the spirit are equally accessible to all regardless. Each thought is inherently equal and of like value. This statement requires us to contemplate.

Spirit and energy does not differentiate between good and evil. When we are in touch with the spirit and behave in accordance with the laws of the spirit, consciously or subconsciously, we succeed in our endeavors, regardless whether these endeavors are of good intent or bad intent. However, one ought to always keep in mind that one has to take the consequences of one's actions whatever these may be and that with our actions however they may be, we are automatically activating another law.

Here are some religious concepts that include the Law of Impartiality. Hinduism speaks of the 'truth' in the Mahabharata, which entails: Impartiality, self-control, forgiveness, modesty, endurance, goodness, renunciation, contemplation, dignity, fortitude, compassion and abstention from injury to others. Buddhism speaks of seven factors that lead to enlightenment: Clear memory, the exact investigation of things, energy and sympathy, tranquillity, a disposition for concentration and impartiality. Judism, Islam and other religions too all preach impartiality, i.e. treating all rivals and disputants equally, fair and just.

# 127

## The Law of Increase

This law enables you to be lifted up and unconsciously touch the law of Increase and gain from its blessings. What you have created unconsciously or accidentally can be stimulated to increase. Increase can be obtained through praise. The act of praise alone can move mountains. This law is connected to the law of Praise. Praise is complimentary to faith. Whereas faith is wisdom and understanding, praise is the application of that understanding. Faith is the boiler that holds a substance of power, whereas praise is the fuel that generates that power into an active force. Faith without praise is like a cold boiler, an inert mass of machinery. It may be nice to look at or talk about but it has no more value than a conversation piece. Praise is a stimulant of the mind. It magnetizes all the good around you. It transforms that good into usable, visible substances.

    A prime biblical example of this, is the story of Jesus when he had some five thousand hungry souls to feed. He had five loaves of bread and a few fishes, yet he started action by praising the little at hand. You know the story, enough food and wine was suddenly there to feed everyone present at the gathering. It was a miracle. And Jesus said that what he did we could also do. How can it be done? When you learn to take what you have and build on it, not in scorn and condemnation, but with praise and gratitude, you are working the law and the universe will give increasing abundance.

Work with praise and faith and you will benefit from the law of Increase.

The spirit in which you act, for self or for others, is the key to this law. The seed—the spirit, in which you think, speak or act is sown in your inner self and there it grows. Every negative word or thought, such as criticism or doubt, is a weed seed. In some way it is based on fear, distrust or other destructive attitude. Pull these weeds and throw them out! Better still, do not plant them at all in the first place! Your purpose, sincerity and willingness are the three areas to concentrate on to activate the law of Increase. The key to getting in the flow of a universal law is to apply the law. Whatever you want in life, apply that in you thoughts, words and acts toward yourself and others. It will grow and return to you as the 'fruits' of your efforts.

# 128

## The Law of Inertia

This law represents one of the qualities of nature, of prana or of vital etheric energy. Inertia is not only psychological in nature, the qualities of matter or substance are also involved. There are three qualities in nature, these are inertia, activity and rhythm. In Sanskrit these three qualities are known as Tamas, Raja and Sattva.

Inertia is the slowest and lowest aspect of material substance and is called in the eastern philosophy, the quality of tamas. The idea is to transmute this state of inertia into a higher energy quality, the activity of the rajastic quality that leads later on to the highest quality of rhythm or sattva.

Sattva is the rhythm of life, under which the Hierarchy operate, and which vibrate in harmony with human need and hierarchical response.

Inertia is not a desirable state to be in because it is not in harmony with life. Other words for inertia are sluggishness, idleness, passiveness, laziness, inactivity and listlessness, all of which are of the lowest vibration level and are undesirable because they hinder growth and consciousness unfoldment. Anything that hinders growth and the raising of consciousness is undesirable in nature. everything in nature is meant to grow and unfold.

# 129

## The Law of Infinite Energy

Energy has an ultimate Source. There is an Ultimate Intelligence, Infinite Consciousness, Universal Energy, the 'All There Is,'—God—which is totally infused with, and whose sole purpose is the exercise of Love, Wisdom and Power. This is known as the 'Universal Quint Essence.' And we are, each one of us, a conduit of the Source. The degree to which we are aligned with the 'Universal Quint Essence' determines the quality of our life. The more we are aligned to the Source and the more we use these three energies of Love, Wisdom and Power, the higher the quality of our life.

Modern exoteric science has proved that there is nothing in the whole of the manifested universe but energies, in some relationship, each vibrating at particular frequency. The esoteric science acknowledges seven streams of energy, whose interaction, at every conceivable frequency, creates the solar systems, galaxies and universes. The movement of these seven rays of energy, in spiralling cycles, draws all being into and out of manifestation and colors and immerses it with their own individual qualities and character. This is the case be it a grain of sand, human being or solar system. The rays are of particular types of energy, the emphasis being on the quality, which each type of energy demonstrates. There are, therefore, seven ray types of people. The three primary rays of aspect are: First ray of Power, Will or Purpose. The second ray is the ray of Love and Wisdom, the third is of Active Creative

Intelligence. The secondary rays of attribute are, the fourth ray of Harmony through Conflict or Beauty and Art, the fifth ray of Scientific Knowledge, the sixth of Idealism or Devotion and the seventh ray is that of Ceremonial Order or Magic Ritual and Organization.

All of us are basically governed by a total of five ray forces. The ray of the soul, which remains the same for countless incarnations, the personality ray which varies from life to life until all the qualities are developed, the ray governing the astral-emotional body, the ray of the physical body including the brain, and the ray of the mind. These vary cyclically. Each ray works through one chakra and together they determine the physical structure and appearance, the emotional nature and the quality of the mental body. Our attitudes of mind, our strengths and weaknesses are in accordance with our ray types. For the greater part of our evolutionary experience on this earth the rays of the personality control our life, but when we are two thirds of the way along the path, the soul ray begins to dominate and express itself through the being. Knowledge of one's rays provides insight to one's weaknesses and strengths, bridges and barriers between oneself and others. Those on similar rays have the same outlook and approach to life while those on different rays find it difficult to understand one another. The more one acquires the positive attributes of all rays the easier one can communicate with others regardless of the differences in ray energies.

## 130

## The Law of Infinity

This law states that the Creator is limitless, therefore, so are we. The abilities of the Creator are limitless and therefore, our abilities are limitless too. As there exists a spark of the Creator in each one of us, the Creator manifests on the physical level through each one of us.

The mastery over unconscious thoughts will provide understanding of the dimensions of Infinity. Limitless is the stream of thoughts. Accept in spirit the concept of Infinity. Affirm Infinity in your consciousness and apply all your thoughts on a broad scale. People are often perplexed as to what lies beyond consciousness. Of course, in our human understanding the concept of consciousness is limited because of our acceptance of the material world only. Knowledge remains confined within physical limits if the boundaries of visibility are not broadened. Limitation of knowledge is like a grave. Limitation of consciousness is death to the spirit. Look, therefore, beyond the boundaries of human consciousness and human knowledge, penetrate *space*, allow your thoughts to explore the vast horizon, to gain cosmic understanding. Through communion with Infinity new treasures are discovered.

This law needs some digestion and quiet reflection on our part. It states simply and clearly that each one of us is capable of doing and achieving anything that we put our mind to. Regardless!

See also the Law of Creativity and the Law of Manifestation.

## 131

## The Law of Information

The law of Information is that law which states that all information is energy, and carries energy, and that all energy is information and carries information.

The understanding of this law explains the principles of the paranormal situations. Some people are able to access information from the etheric field. All information is stored in the akasha, the etheric field. With special training one can learn to tune in to this field of energy to gain knowledge and to have access to information. This is available to anyone without discrimination. One has to be trained, or one has to be a highly evolved being, in order to have access to the field of universal knowledge. Over the centuries it has been known that some beings have been given glimpses of the akashic records. Many mystics have written about this in detail.

# 132

## The Law of Initiation

The law of Initiation is an expansion of consciousness that leads to a growing recognition of inner realities. It is equally the recognition of a renewal sense of the need for change and the wise engineering of these needed changes, so that real progress can be made. In the initiation process the consciousness is expanded to become more generously and divinely inclusive, at the same time there is a fresh and more potent control by the soul as it increasingly assumes the direction of the life of the individual, of a nation and of the world.

Initiation is when the human being has passed out of the human kingdom into the spiritual kingdom and has entered upon the life of the spirit. Each initiation marks the passing of a pupil in the Hall of Wisdom into a higher stage, the shining through of the inner fire, and the realization of the increasing unity with all that lives. It is a growing capacity to see and to hear on all planes. Initiation is when vision becomes possible of the eternal now, where past, present and future exist as one. Initiation gives a human being the key to all information in graduated sequence and it leads from one state of consciousness into another until expansion reaches a point where the self embraces all selves.

The initiate will know when the event occurs and needs no one to tell him or her of it. It is quite possible for one to be functioning on the physical plane actively with world service with no recollection of having gone through an initiation process in a previous life. The mark of an initiate is his lack of interest in himself and his personal fate.

Since the fact of initiation has been grasped by many, it has been possible today to reveal that initiation is a group event as it is the nature of the soul to be group conscious, with no individual ambitions or interests. Every step upon the path of initiation increases group recognition. As the initiate proceeds from one initiation to another and penetrates deeper into the heart of the mysteries of life, in company with those who are working with him or her towards the same point of evolution and goal, the more s/he is aware that s/he is not alone and that it is a joint effort that is being made.

No one is admitted into an Ashram of Christ or the Hierarchy until such times that one thinks and lives in terms of group relationships and activities. This should not be misunderstood to mean that one should form little groups, as was the case in the Piscean age. Ashrams exist with disciples and initiates at all points of evolutionary development and degrees, and all work together in unison within their differentiated ranks, for each degree stands alone and yet united with all the others.

The initiatory process is the result of the activity of three energies. The energy that is generated by the disciple as s/he seeks to serve humanity, the energy made available to the disciple as s/he succeeds in building the bridge of light, *the antahkarana,* and the energy of the hierarchical Ashram into which s/he is being integrated. The path of initiation includes long periods of search, detachment, pain and of revelations producing tension, fusion and energy projection.

Initiation is not given to any one person, it is the recognition of the lighted way that indicates readiness for initiation. The initiated enters into the light, which penetrates his nature according to his or her development at any one point of time or space and enables him or her to see the unseen on the basis of the newly acquired knowledge. Each initiation dims the light already acquired and immerses the initiate in a higher light. Each initiation enables one to perceive an area of divine consciousness so far unknown.

Initiation is a process of excessive hard work, a graded series of liberation allowing the initiate greater freedom to proceed further on the Way, learning to work behind the scenes, unrecognized, unknown, unclaimed and receiving no rewards and sacrificing the individual identity in the identity of the Ashram. The ashram referred to here is on a higher level, a spiritual level with the various hierarchy, and does not refer to ashrams or schools on the physical level. More often than not higher spiritual ashram and group work is experienced during sleep i.e. while the physical body sleeps.

# 133

## The Law of Initiative

All action occurs as a direct result and in direct proportion to the initiative of each soul. Initiation cannot be given nor forced on any one person. The energy initiative brings about evolution, i.e. it is through the initiative of the particular soul that the soul evolves.

See also the Law of Initiation.

# 134

## The Law of Integration

This law represents the integration of the soul and the personality in the human. Through the use of the mind the personality makes contact with the soul and so become integrated in the three worlds. The personality is the integration of the physical, the emotional and the mental worlds in one.

Integration of the soul with the personality is achieved through the building of what is known in Sanskrit as the Antahkarana bridge, also known as the Rainbow bridge, to connect with the soul, the plane of intuition and the spiritual world.

The goal of all development is integration—integration of the individual as a personality; integration of the personality with the individual soul; integration of the human with the Hierarchy; integration with the Whole, until complete unity and identification has been achieved.

# 135

## The Law of Intelligence

All intelligence is divine. To increase our intelligence level depends solely on our personal connection with the Creator. The nearer we are to the higher realms of Spirit, the higher the level of our intelligence, as we connect with the Divine intelligence of the Cosmos that has all knowledge.

## 136

# The Law of Intention

When one's intention is held in the mind and action of the physical effort does not follow, people create false impressions of the Self. One thinks Self is good or better than actions prove. Energy must follow intention for that which is perceived as good to happen. When an act of kindness is performed and intention is such that one wishes to be recognized for goodness, or has underlying motivation, which is not of the higher order, higher rewards will not be forthcoming.

Both intention and effort must be of the higher vibration to gain or create spiritual accomplishment and reward. If a person gives a promise to another to do something and has an intention to do so, but does not follow through with action, this becomes a lie, a breaking of one's word violates the law and creates karma. In other words it is not enough to think of doing good and to leave it at that. Action must follow the thought, the intent, for it to hold good.

In short, this law requires us to be aware of our thoughts, feelings and our intentions. It requires us to be truthful with ourselves of our intention in whatever we do, and then to follow up on any good intentions that we may have by taking action accordingly.

## 137

## The Law of Interdependence

Inter-dependence is a basic law of our Cosmos. Nothing exists independent of anything or anyone else. When we enter into a consciousness of interdependence, a consciousness of equality of being, we are in harmony with this law.

Meister Eckhart said: 'One creature sustains another and enriches the other and that is why all creatures are interdependent.' Physicists like Fritjof Capra, biologists like Lewis Thomas and ecologists like Jacques Cousteau all recognize inter-dependence as a basic law of our cosmos. 'Two persons who sit together in the same room are exchanging water and vapor within thirty minutes. This is interdependence.' To take a deep breath is to breathe in some of the breath that our ancestors breathed be it, Jesus, Leonardo da Vinci or Mozart. Scientist Brian Swimme confirms this. 'This is interdependece. Every square mile of soil on our earth contains particles from every other square mile of soil on our earth,' says biologist John Storer. 'This is interdependence. Compassion and interdependence is already in the universe, we do not have to invent it new.'

In mutual dependence there can be no conflict or contradiction. The conflict arises because the principle of co-existence is forgotten. Pairs of opposites can subsist together. Ignoring this law the individual then looks at things from one, exclusive point of view, failing to grasp the doctrine of contraries or the possibility of co-existence of two opposite truths. Those who understand this doctrine are able to see the essence of the vision, that every voice serves as a support for another voice, as a support for another voice, i.e. one object supports another. Conflict is not the law of nature but is an imposition.

For us to understand and to practice interdependency ourselves, we first need to learn to be independent beings. We need first to learn not to live our life being dependent on others nor dependent on circumstances.

## 138

## The Law of Intuition

The intuition is on the fourth dimension, which is the plane of the soul. The more one integrates the soul in one's life and activities the more constant and active is the intuition. We can only get in touch with our own source of intuition and wisdom when we no longer depend on the opinion of others for our sense of identity or worth. Do we value and trust our own intuition, or do we value and transfer authority to the opinions of others over our own inner feelings? Our intention becomes more profound when we claim our own sacred identity.

Sometimes instinct or inner voices originating from the lower astral level are mistaken for intuition and caution is advisable here. Many of us have experienced contact with our intuition sporadically or accidentally, but we can, through the practice of regular meditation, solitude and silence, establish a permanent contact so that we are constantly guided by our intuition that has universal knowledge and can, therefore, never be wrong.

Once we have consciously made contact with our intuition through soul culture, we will be able to better differentiate between instinct and other inner voices and the intuition.

# 139

## The Law of Isolation/Limitation

In this law we are given the clue to that which will ultimately sweep disease from the earth. When one is sick it is important to remember that one is not enduring alone and in isolation but that one is sharing the fate of the majority of humans. A right handling of ill health is major factor in breaking down separateness and a sense of aloneness and isolation. That is why the effects of bad health, when rightly handled, lead to a sweetening of the disposition and a broadening of the sympathies.

Sharing and a sense of general participation have usually to be learnt the hard way—such is the law. When the majority of the inhabitants of the earth are being rapidly oriented towards good, towards righteousness and all are inclined toward goodwill, then ill health will persistently even if only gradually disappear and finally become non-existent.

# 140

## The Law of Inverse Proportions

Also known as the law of Longevity. One need not die if the pranic life force is not lost but increased and drawn from the Cosmic Source, conquering death and fate.

The span of life is related to the rate of breathing. If the span of life is 120 years and the normal person breathed 21,600 times per day, that is 15 respirations per minute. If the rate of breathing is 18 per minute, however, the span of life will be about 96 years. If because of poor living habits and needless expenditure of energy the average rate of breathing is 30 per minute, the life span will be only 60 years. If the rate is slowed through yogi practices and self control to an average of only 5 respirations per minute the life span will be 360 years. If it is one breath per minute the life span will be increased to 1800 years. If the rate of breathing is reduced to zero, the life span becomes infinity. The secret of longevity lies in the technique of diverting the breathing to the subtle channels and centers.

See also the law of Respiration.

# 141

## The Law of Justice

Also known as the law of Exchange. The law of Justice is likened unto scales in balance in which, that which is heavy on one side, must be balanced by that which is equally heavy on the other side. Thus, when one human violates another, the heavier the violation is, the heavier must be the balancing weight. This is related unto the law of Karma.

All things in time come into balance. When one puts on a heavy karma, one may help remove that karma by lightening the load of another who has been violated by that karma, if possible, or by lightening the load of someone who has an equally heavy load. It is simply a matter of weights and measures and this is the cosmic law of Balance, Justice and karmic accounts. This law also gives us the sense for the existence of fairness in the world. No deed goes unnoticed, whether good or bad. Everything comes to a balance in one way or another in spite of the fact that this might not be visible to us or apparent at any one time.

On the spiritual level justice consists in taking one thing and giving something of equal value in exchange. The most valuable thing that we have to give is our life. If we give our life, our love and our attention, we can get anything we want from the cosmos. We work on the physical level and get money as compensation. The same is true on the spiritual level. As an example, let's say I want to help someone but it turns out wrong and I hurt this person instead of helping. I would be punished on the physical level for that according to human laws, the higher powers cannot interfere on the physical level, but on a spiritual level I would be rewarded generously because of my good intentions and efforts. Actions and motivations of the soul are under two different jurisdictions. If my intentions are evil in character and my actions on the physical level give the impression of being good, I may well be rewarded by human laws, on the physical level. However, on a higher spiritual level I will be called to justice and I will have to make good, in one way or another, for the imbalance that I have caused.

Refer also to the law of Karma.

# 142

## The Sirian Law of Karma

This law is the synthesis of the system of Sirius and predicates the effect of the Sirian system has on our solar system. Each of the two systems is independent in time and space and manifestation. We have no effect on our parent system but very definite effects are felt in our system through causes arising in Sirius. These causes when experienced as effects are called by us, the law of Karma, the law controls our Logos.

The law of Karma is also referred to as the law of Cause and Effect and is basically known to us as stated in the Bible, as 'what you sow is what you will reap.' This is an important law for us to understand that makes it clear that there is a cause for every effect. Nothing happens of its own accord. There is always something or someone to make something happen. According to this law put very simply, if I hurt someone it would be presumptuous of me to think that I could get away without being penalized for my ill deed no matter how trivial. The penalty is not necessarily from the same person or at the same time nor in the same way, but eventually, I will get the same energy back as I gave it out.

Karma is a learning tool of spirit, and manifests through physical circumstances. That which one places into the universe, one receives back, ten-fold. Karma does not discriminate. This is the natural principle of cause and effect. Every cause has its effect and every effect has its cause. Everything happens according to law. When we think something happens by chance it is only because we do not recognize the law. Nothing escapes the law of Karma. It is ever at work with chains of causes and effects that govern all of life and manifested matter. It has its beginnings and endings in the non-material realm, the realm of spirit. It affects the rock slide that is caused by rain or wind, the snow avalanche or the throwing of dice or a card on a gambling table. The law itself is illusive and cannot be proven other than observed with the mind and is used to determine the causes and effects of any event.

When this law is used with conscious effort, desired results can be produced in a person's life by steering him or herself along definite paths of causation. When the law is used in an unconscious and haphazard mind, the effects could become potentially disastrous for the individual or group of individuals. Many so-called 'accidents' could occur without warning to individuals who toil through life without awareness.

We are responsible for the very thoughts we produce and the final result for our own mental alchemy. Fear is one of the most dangerous mental causes that prevents a person from thinking and acting as the 'Higher Self' would prefer. The cause of fear is the result of a lack of knowledge about the unknown God, that would be the most important educational journey in a person's life. The causes of fear can only be removed through knowledge, wisdom and understanding of universal laws. The greatest evil under the sun, according to Hermes/Thoth is not knowing God. In every minute thought, action and deed that is performed, a person sets into motion unseen chains of causes and effects which will vibrate from the mental plane throughout the entire cellular structure of the body, into the environment, and finally into the Cosmos. Eventually the vibratory energy returns to its originator upon the return swing of the pendulum.

This law is mechanically or mathematically operative and men and women of divine wisdom can scientifically manipulate its workings. The karmic law requires that every human wish finds ultimate fulfillment. Therefore, desire is the chain that binds man to the re-incarnation wheel. Karma is attracted only where the magnet of the personal ego still exists. An understanding of karma and the law of Justice underlying life's inequalities serve to free the human mind from resentment against God and man. The law of Karma is that law wherein entities arrange within themselves, on any level, to make just payment for any action committed that affects the welfare of oneself or another. The law of Karma is irrevocable and may be depended upon to bring those who stray from the law of Unity back into balance through the divine justice of the universe.

The law of Cause and Effect encompasses several sub-laws. For example like begets like. You cannot get a pear out of an orange tree. This law determines what you get according to what you do or give. If you project hate you get hate in return. If you project love you get love in return. The law works both ways for negative and positive thoughts, feelings and actions. We always receive the fruits of our actions. The universe gives you back what you project to the universe. What we send forth into the universe comes back to us. We reap positive rewards for our good deeds and negative consequences of our misdeeds. Ancient scriptures state: 'All that we are is the result of what we have thought, it is founded on thought, it is made up of our thoughts. If a man acts or speaks with evil thoughts, pain follows him as the wheel follows the foot of the ox that draws the chariot.'

## 143

## The Law of Knowledge

This law concerns the fact that all knowledge concerns energy, its application, and its right use or misuse. Much esoteric information is withheld until one is a disciple, and still more until one is a pledged initiate. Information is not as necessary to the training of the disciple or initiate as is the proper use of thought energy, which is full mindfulness. Knowledge is the right apprehension of the laws of energy, of the conservation of force, of the sources of energy, of its qualities, its types and its vibrations. Knowledge should be understood not only formally but in its entire multiformity.

Certain aspects of knowledge are esoteric and other aspects are exoteric. Some knowledge deals with the subjective side of life and the other type of knowledge is concerned with energy and force, and with that which is being energized. We are told that the goal of evolution is for humankind to acquire full consciousness on all planes, and the human race in general has so far only the physical plane somewhat under control.

Information and knowledge of the life evolving through the physical forms is considered, therefore, esoteric knowledge as also the laws governing energy on the astral and mental planes are. Exoteric knowledge is all that can be acquired by instinct and by the use of the concrete or lower mind functioning through the physical brain.

As one evolves and activates the higher abstract mind and intuition, and as certain centers in the head begin to function, more esoteric knowledge will be acquired. The point that is emphasized here is the fact that all 'knowers' must endeavor to attract others who are, ready for expansion of consciousness to join the group soul on the upward arc of evolution.

There are risks involved in having too much knowledge because too much knowledge brings responsibility and power. When one uses knowledge wisely, is discrete, reserved and is able to discriminate, one increases one's capacity to receive the hidden wisdom.

See also the law of Initiation.

# 144

## The Law of Least Effort

Nature's intelligence functions carefree with effortless ease, with harmony and love. When we harness the forces of harmony, joy and love we create success and good fortune with effortless ease. This we do by practicing acceptance. Accept people, situations, circumstances and events as they occur. Know that this moment is as it should be because the whole universe is as it should be. To struggle against this moment is to struggle against the whole universe. Accept things as they are and not as you wish they were. Once you have accepted circumstances as they are, learn to take responsibility for situations and events that you perceive as being problems. Taking responsibility means not blaming anyone or anything. Recognize that every problem is an opportunity in disguise allowing you to transform into a greater benefit. Give up the need to defend your point of view. Remain open to all points of view and not be rigidly attached to any one of them.

There is a wonderful word in the German language that illustrates someone who acts as explained above, acting with least effort, it is to be 'gelassen.' I guess the nearest English equivalent is to be relaxed, to be 'cool.' To be cool is to be easy about things in general, i.e. not rebelling, fighting or arguing, criticizing or insisting on one's own point of view. Most of us know people like that, people who just seem to float through life, winning all the way, effortlessly. This law demonstrates why it is so. Whether they are aware of it or not they are quite obviously flowing in harmony with the energies of this law.

Go on, give it a try, relax, accept things as they are, watch how you will feel more relaxed about life in general, and how your life will turn to one pleasant experience after another.

See also the law of Acceptance.

## 145

## The Law of Leverage

This awareness indicates that the future is never fixed. The future depends on what is occurring in the present, and a change in consciousness at present will effect a change in future experiences. This is related to the law of Leverage wherein a small amount of energy exerted to change the course of events at a present time, at the right moment, can move mountains in the future. This law reiterates the importance of the awareness of living in the moment.

# 146

## The Law of Liability

The law of Liability states that one is held liable for the use or abuse of whatever rights one has, and one is held liable for using or neglecting to use those rights. Even where it is clearly one person's fault, the action of making that person a scapegoat for misdeeds is seldom in itself a proper solution. For the main reason for finding the case of a mishap is to be able to prevent the mishap from recurring.

# 147

## The Law of Liberation

This law is activated through right thinking to correct an undesirable situation leading to the right attitude. For example, disease is a fact of nature. When this is accepted, one begins to work with the law of Liberation, with right thought, leading to right attitude and orientation and with the principle of non-resistance.

Of this non-resistance, the overpowering willingness to die, which is so frequently a characteristic of the final stage immediately preceding death is the lowest manifestation. It is non-resistance that psychologically governs coma.

This is generally recognized today in the medical field. It is the will power of the patient to overcome a disease and in worst cases a coma, to accelerate the path of recovery. It is known that if the patient has given up all hope for recovery and wishes to die then help is useless. This is the act of non-resistance and goes against this law of liberation. This is the case also with some cases of cancer. It has been known that through change of attitude and positive thinking one can heal oneself in the early stages of the disease.

# 148

## The Law of Life

In accordance with the law of Life the spiritual and the psychic coordinate and balance one another in the world of the spirit and material. On this plane the soul must serve time until perfection is achieved before returning back to the Source. In accordance with this law one changes and grows constantly with each additional impression and experience of life. Issues in life are not determined by outward conditions but by one's own consciousness.

The law of Life on earth requires that we human kind must acknowledge and give credit where its due, namely, to our Creator. We must feel gratitude and only then can we lift ourselves out of the world of limitations where we have put ourselves in of our own free will.

This law requires us to understand that the human body as it is has no power and no intelligence in its actions. We need to recognize that there is a Spirit guiding our thoughts, emotions, movements, actions, behavior and so on. The 'I', the Spirit determines everything we do and our physical body follows this guidance. The Creator gave us consciousness and it is this consciousness that is the creative sustaining and maintaining principle. We are given dominion through our consciousness. Life is the intelligent direction within. Think of your body as your radio, and your consciousness is the director of your radio. You can tune into or out of any activity or condition as you wish. You can change the program of your life if you do not like it and make it better.

*Cosmic and Universal Laws*

The law of Life says that the only way to expand is to give of one's self. The more you give of yourself the more you and your world will expand. Life is the greatest of all mysteries. The truth of life is to be found in respiration, in breathing.

See the law of Respiration. See also the law of Synthesis.

# 149

# The Law of Light

Cosmic Light is Spirit, is God, is All that is.

Light cannot be perceived without darkness. However, light being of the highest vibration always prevails. Light is absolute. Enlightenment is an outcome of light. First we need to realize that everywhere about us there exists a universal substance that we call Cosmic Light. The Bible refers to this as Spirit. This is the One Pure Primal Essence—out of which emanates all Creation. It is the 'Pure Life Substance' of the First Cause, God. This is infinite and we may draw upon it at any time, for anything that we require, by the power of concentration. This 'Pure Electronic Light' is the great limitless storehouse of the Universe. In it is all perfection and out of it comes all that is.

We are presently witnessing the earth as it is passing through the throes of a tremendous new birth, and will continue to be in a transition period in the few years ahead. It is changing now in a cosmic way, from the attitude of war into that of peace, in accordance with the new age of Aquarius. We will witness changes such as hatred to love, selfishness to unselfishness and into full recognition that in the future, we the human family must exert strength enough to live according to the law of Love.

We have arrived at a certain time in the process of evolution of our planet and we humanity must express the full peace, harmony, perfection and the divine plan of the system to which we belong. When the time comes we humanity either move forward in fulfillment of God's plan or those of us who will not come into alignment with the new vibrations, will move on to another school room of the Universe, until those personalities learn obedience to life.

The law of Life is heaven, peace, harmony and love to every created thing. Even the ethers of infinite space express this harmony everywhere. We human beings are the only creators of hell. Each one of us carries our own heaven or hell with us every moment of our life, for these are but the results of our own mental and emotional states, which we have created because of our own attitude. All misery, darkness and ignorance exist only because of lack of love. The Light does not receive disharmony into itself. As students we enter the light, to become all light, hence all perfection. To have disharmony drop away from our body or our affairs, we must let go of all thought, feeling and words about imperfection. It is forgiveness that fills all with Light's perfection.

See also the law of Balance.

# 150

## The Law of Lotus

This is the name given to the influence from the cosmic law of Attraction that linked the two poles of spirit and matter producing upon the plane of mind the egoic lotus or the 'Flower of the Self.' It is the law that enables the lotus to draw from the lower water and matter aspect the moisture and heat needed for its unfoldment. It governs the process of petal unfoldment and, therefore, itself demonstrates as a triple law:

The law of Solar Heat – Knowledge petals
The law of Solar Light – Love petals
The law of Solar Fire – Sacrifice petals

There are several energy centers distributed all over the human body through which the human connects with the universe. These energy centers are known as chakras. Chakra is Sanskrit for the 'wheel of life.' As the human develops in consciousness the charkas unfold. The symbol for each chakra is a lotus with a certain number of petals.

As the individual progresses on the path of evolution each chakra opens and flows and the lotus of knowledge unfolds its petals. All of this occurs on the psychic level. The symbol of the root chakra is a four petal lotus and for the hip chakra is a six petal lotus. The solar plexus is represented by a ten petal lotus. A twelve petal lotus is the symbol for the heart chakra and a sixteen petal lotus for the throat chakra. For the third eye chakra the lotus symbol has ninety six petals and for the crown chakra on top of the head it is a thousand petal lotus. As the individual expands in consciousness the lotus petals open to allow universal energies to flow through the human. When all petals are open then the individual has reached divinity.

# 151

## The Law of Love

Love is the key to the mystery of life. The law of Love is one of the seven laws of the solar system and is the law of the astral plane, the plane of emotions. This law aims at the transmutation of the desire nature and links it up with the greater magnetism of the love aspect on the Buddhic plane. On the astral plane, the home of our desires, originate the feelings which we call personal love, in its lowest form it shows itself as animal passion. In the highest form it manifests as pure love. We are unfailingly responsible to act with love in every thought, word, deed, intent, motive and action.

The stages of love in the personality develops with a simple and selfish love for the self, then expands to love of family and friends and to more people, until it arrives at the stage of group love consciousness, which is the characteristic of the soul. At this level one is a master of compassion, loves, suffers with and is loyal to his kind. This love gradually develops from love for humanity, to love of the universe and all forms of divine manifestation. The first love in the personality is love for the three worlds, the second love in the soul is for the solar system and the third, which is love of the Monad, demonstrates Cosmic Love. Love was the primary motive for manifestation, loves bears all on the path of return and love eventually perfects all.

When one is aware of divine love as more than just an abstract principle, then one will realize that one can generate it at will, and direct it consciously, to accomplish whatever one decrees. Divine love for the Ascended Masters is a Presence, an Intelligence, a principle of Light, a Power, an Activity and a Substance. Love is magical. When we refer to that great Love of Life, it is the Scepter of Power. It is the law of all that is perfect. It is the illuminating power of all wisdom, and it is energy without limit to produce whatever manifestation we command to appear in action. We are required to live our life with love. Love is the key and the motor of life and when you live your life with love you cannot go wrong.

The law of Love is that law which places the welfare, the concern and feeling for others above the self. The law of Love is that close affinity with all forces that you associate with as good and it is a force that denies the existence of evil in the world that resists not. For love follows the course of least resistance. The greatest gift that an entity can give to another is that portion of the self, which is given with love, which no strings attached and no expectations. In giving yourself, unconditionally, the spiritual self moves in communion between you and the other.

Love is the building block of all things. Love is energy. The energy which is the actual building material of all things. It is an actual substance; in fact it is the only substance that exists, taking on the appearance of many forms. Love is also acceptance. It is the acknowledgment that All Things Are One. The law of Love ensures that you see this truth. You cannot leave an experience permanently unless you exit it with love and acceptance. That is why people tend to keep repeating the same type of experiences until the day they stop hating and fighting the experience and instead, embrace it with love, see what the situation holds for them, and heal it with love. This could be a money issue, a health or a relationship issue. It doesn't matter. You cannot leave a situation permanently until you exit it with love. You cannot permanently get rid of what you hate, you can only leave it or transform it through love. This law ensures that you recognize the truth of unity and drop the illusions of separation.

Do you now clearly see how these laws work and how your life could be so much more effortless and prosperous simply by flowing with the laws? Why resist what you cannot break or change? Just flow with it! Resistance creates time and friction, acceptance creates miracles. Look at this again and you will see how time and effort are the creations of resistance against these unbreakable laws. Flow with the laws and allow them to carry you where you wish to go effortlessly. They have to, they can never fail. You were not meant to struggle through life. Most people learn most, unfortunately, through suffering. There is no way to escape the consequences of your actions, remember—you cannot escape from *yourself*. Our freedom of choice though is not compromised in any way, we have feedback when we make mistakes so that we can learn the lessons we need to learn. The universal laws actually give us a self-correcting mechanism. *Isn't it just magnificent?*

In giving we attain. In giving we acquire. In giving, love becomes the fulfillment of desire, guided and directed in a way that brings more perfect knowledge of self as related to the universal, all powerful, all guiding, all divine influence in life. Love IS life. As we merge with the God Source, in some infinitesimal but profound way, we expand the mind of God. Our God and Higher Self always points to the best and most perfect way and it is our choice to listen and choose or reject what we hear. God does not blame, but patiently tries again to show the perfect way, the loving way. All of creation pushes ever forth. We are ever becoming!

The energy of love has the highest frequency vibration and is the best cure for healing. The feeling of love produces certain chemical reactions as well as hormonal effects in the body that create an emotional high unmatched by any other means of healing. Only the few realize that you need not depend on anyone or anything else to experience the feeling of love. You can at any time develop love from within you for yourself and for all life.

## 152

## The Law of Macrocosm and Microcosm

The law of Macrocosm and Microcosm is the first law of Infinity. This law indicates that the whole is equal, more or less to the sum of its parts, depending on the ordering of those parts. In each living thing, in everything that exists there is within it some part of the whole. The whole is the grouping together of each of its parts in a certain order.

An analogy is the sea or ocean in comparison with a drop of dew on the petal of a flower.

# 153

## The Law of Magic

The law of Magic is the law that creates change. Physical change comes about through the change of consciousness. Consciousness changes in response to anticipation. Anticipation results from imagery and preparation, fears and desires based on fallacies or facts. Preparation for change changes consciousness, which results in physical change.

The quality and quantity of description and imagery, the intensity and consistency of attitudes and actions, the collective or disruptive energies of others, all work together in unison to influence the direction and course of the change.

Every one to some degree, for good or ill, is both victim and master of the law of Magic. The law of Magic is an extension of the law of Unity.

See also the law of Miracles.

# 154

## The Law of Magnetic Control

This law is one of the seven laws of our solar system under the three major laws. It is through this law that the spiritual nature of the human governs the personality through the soul nature. This is the law on the Buddhic plane. It is the law of Love that holds all together and that draws all upward. It is also a demonstration of the law of Attraction. It is this law that holds the atoms together. It is the law where sex expression as we know it is transmuted and elevated. This holds predominantly on the Buddhic plane, and in the development of the control of this, lies hid the control of the personality by the Monad via the egoic body.

A second description on a very physical level, is that every thought we have creates a match that comes back to us like a boomerang. This law teaches us to control or ever thought, for example if we think of doing harm to someone else, we are doing harm unto ourselves as the energy colored by the quality of our wicked thought will eventually come back to haunt us.

## 155

## The Law of Magnetic Impulse

Also known as the first step towards marriage or the law of the polar union. It results in an eventual union between the man or atom and the group that produces harmonious group relations. It is also known as the law of the polar union, and the symbol is two fiery balls united by a triangle of fire, this picturing the triple interplay between all atomic structures.

# 156

## The Law of Magnetism

This law produces the unifying of the personality, the physical, the emotional and the mental bodies and is of a much higher order than the law of physical sex. This law is concerned with the body of the human in the final three stages of the path of evolution. The stage of high intellectual or artistic attainment, the stage of discipleship, and the stage of threading the path of return, i.e. the fifth, sixth and seventh stages in the evolution of the human being.

# 157

## The Law of Manifestation

The law of Divine Manifestation requires one to believe in the principle that whatever is needed for one's growth and fruition, will be supplied by the universe, for whatever price one truly believes is fair. But one must believe he or she truly has the right to receive the manifestation, at the price of energy cost, the entity believes is fair. If it is a worthy request, and one believes it is allotted at the time of asking, it will come. A worthy request expressed through prayer, imaging, ritual or whatever method, is anything that harms no one, but benefits all involved. It is a win-win relationship. Any thought or action that harms another, either in the process or outcome of manifestation is not of the Divine and will carry 'a karmic debt.' The spirit is manifested in the flesh. Only through this manifestation can one come to know oneself.

Spirit manifests its thoughts through the readiness and willingness of its soul. Souls manifest their thoughts through the readiness and willingness of their intentions. Manifestation of the spiritual leads to manifestation in the physical. Only thought exists, therefore, it is important to know that everything that exists on the physical plane is a result of pure thought.

Decide what you want, state it as clearly as possible in every minute detail, let it go and assume that it is already done. Do not doubt. It is usually our internal sabotage patterns, disbelief and doubt that stop manifestation of our innermost dreams and desires.

## Cosmic and Universal Laws

When we are in alignment with the Divine Will, our ability to manifest is guaranteed provided we have unwavering faith.

Desire for material things is an endless part of human existence and in the teachings of Buddha we are told to let go of desire. To progress on this path you need to be aware of what it is exactly that you desire to manifest, whether that what you desire is superficial in nature, whether it is really worth it for you to have, whether you need that what you desire for your spiritual growth, and that it is not just a temporary whim that needs to be satisfied. If your desire is indeed genuine, comes from the heart and is beneficial for you own spiritual evolution, allow that desire to take shape and ask the Universe for it. A request to achieve the highest purpose of human life will surely be heard by the Universe. The Universe is also apt to acknowledge and grant an unselfish request that will be for the greater good and of benefit to others, besides your self. The Universe does not appreciate nor is likely to hear prayers or desires from someone who is lazy, selfish or greedy. Ask yourself if you deserve what you are asking for. Ask yourself if you have done your part and what is required of you on the physical level to manifest what you want. Once you have determined what you want, ask yourself, are you actually doing what it takes to achieve the goal? Have you given yourself with your full passion towards achieving your goal? Sitting and desiring, praying and waiting or demanding, does not do it. That is not how this law of manifestation works. The secret to manifestation lies within the gap between the breaths. As you breathe in, you pause before you breathe out. In this state of timeless consciousness there is no thought, there is only silence, a stillness where truth is found. It is a state where the infinite, the eternal and the fire of your Higher Intelligence is encountered. Be aware that, although the Universe is generous and accommodating when you do your part always in harmony with the law, there is, nevertheless always a price to pay. Read the above again about 'karmic debt'. Keep that in mind and be aware as you work in harmony with the law.

See also the law of Attraction and the law of Creativity.

# 158

# The Law of Mantras

In accordance with this law there exists a secret knowledge that is based on the study of sounds and of the differences of vibration levels. These sounds and vibrations vary in accordance with the state of consciousness of each human being and all life on earth. The basic sounds that have the power of establishing communication with the spiritual world are known as mantras.

Mantras are the most powerful media to free the practices from illusion or ignorance. From the explosion caused by the training of mantras, extremely small power waves or vibrations result that take the practicing person to his or her goal. Through the mantra itself, a practicing person, mingles his own existence with the eternal power. There are three types of mantra reciting: verbal recitation, recitation in a low voice or murmuring, and recitation of mantras without voice, in other words, mental recitation.

Each mantra is a combination of sounds and words and is a linkage to a certain aspect of the absolute, a certain manifestation of Divinity. In true mantra practice, one forgets the fact that the self is chanting, becomes the mantra itself, and attains the state where nothing but the mantra exists. One's being then connects with the Higher Being. The mantra connects with the Higher Being, if it is the name of a Master, or connects with the ray of Light emanating from God, if it is a sound such—Aum, Om, Hu, Alleujah, Allah, Jesus, Mary, St. Jude, etc. The practice of chanting mantras is profoundly beneficial in raising the vibration of self. Sound, like color, has a powerful affect on the human system.

The wrong mantras or sounds can be detrimental. A combination of certain sounds can at a lower level of consciousness, put one in relation with the corresponding forces to obtain certain powers. There are mantras that can kill and mantras that can heal. This kind of magic is achieved by consciously manipulating the lower vibrations. There is also a higher magic that deals with vibrations on a higher plane of consciousness. This can be words, poetry or music. On this level the mantra serves to connect with one higher force or being.

In ancient days this art was well known as wizards and witches used such mantras constantly to create miracles, both good, or evil. This method is still used today by those who have this secret knowledge.

# 159

## The Law of Meditation

This law is defined as a current of unified thought. It is a continuum of mental effort to assimilate the object of meditation, free from any other effort to assimilate other objects. When meditating on God, the most profound happening will bring a merging of the two, the personality and the divine within, or 'enlightenment' as Easterners call this occurrence. The very least that may happen is the calming of self. Technically speaking, meditation is the process where the head center is awakened and is brought under control and used. When this happens, the soul and the personality are coordinated and fused, and 'oneness with the Divine' is experienced. This experience produces in the human a tremendous inflow of spiritual energy, galvanizing the whole being into activity and bringing to the surface not only the dormant good, but also the evil.

The Creator has built-in special instruments in the human body for man to develop in order to receive and transmit certain cosmic energies. Through meditation we can develop these organs and the inner strength so that we can receive and transmit the sound waves from the cosmos, which are of a much higher vibration level, without suffering any damage to our body. These built-in instruments are found in the chakras, the solar plexus and in certain centers in the brain, for example the pineal gland and the pituitary gland, commonly referred to as the third eye. Without them we are incapable of receiving or understanding the cosmic signals that are constantly arriving from the universe. As a person meditates regularly and begins to receive the cosmic waves, something inside develops which enables one to stand up to the greater tension. This stage cannot be achieved in a hurry nor can it be forced by artificial methods. It needs patience and regularity and constant meditation until the organism has a chance to grow gradually stronger and is able to stand up to the strains as cosmic energies are received.

When one is advanced enough one can with concentration and an intensive thought, reach someone across the world anywhere by just thinking about them. This is what we call telepathy. One is just as easily able to obtain any element from the universe, minerals for example, if one's body needs that instead of actually taking tablets. One can also acquire any quality that one desires from any entity, as an example, an artist concentrates on a great long gone favorite artist and calls forth those qualities from the universe. Distance makes no difference and you don't even have to know the whereabouts. All this is possible, however, it is not as easy as it sounds. It requires many years of diligent practice, the development of the higher mind and abstract thought, and above all the spiritual faculties. This can only be developed over several life times. Through reincarnation, all work physical and spiritual that is done and whatever faculties are developed during any one life time, are carried over to the next life span.

Meditation involves the living of a one-pointed life at all times every day. When meditation is carried out systematically with years of effort, supplemented by meditative living and at one-pointed service, this will eventually arouse the entire system and bring the lower man under the influence and control of the spiritual man. It will awaken the centers in the etheric body through the chakras and stimulate the kundalini fire, that mysterious stream of energy that lies dormant at the base of the spine. When this process is carried out with care and under direction over a long period of time, the awakening will take place normally and under the law of Being itself.

See also the law of Reincarnation, the law of Prayer and Meditation, the law of Telepathy and the law of Being.

# 160

## The Law of Meekness

'Blessed be the meek' may seem literally to support those kindly timid souls who are an easy prey for the more aggressive souls. What it refers to, however, is to the one who is able to follow the law of Non Resistance to the point of inheriting the earth and all things thereof. To be meek does not mean to be an easy mark, not to be a doormat for anyone to walk over, nor does it mean to be submissive to the conditions of discord and disorder. We are meek only to the natural laws of the universal. Meekness is, therefore, strength acquired when we do not argue, when we do not become proud and boastful, when we do not insist on being right in any argument. Meekness is the steel of one's nature and is enduring. Meekness is the strength by which we win an argument in refusing to argue. The spirit of meekness is recognized as being cooperative, persistent application, accurate computation and perfect harmony.

See also the law of Non-Resistance.

# 161

## The Law of Mentalism

This law gives us the opportunity to learn from both our mistakes and successes. This means that we can learn more from our mistakes, which are usually painful experiences and the next time, we will usually make changes to correct that particular situation, then we learn from our successes. This would need us to take the time to reflect on ourselves, on our life, and not only to reflect on all our mistakes but also on all our accomplishments.

# 162

## The Law of Mercy

The law of Mercy is that law which allows us to forgive all error; to forgive equally those who err against us as we err against them. This law requires us to be merciful. To be merciful is akin to the law of Love, and if we obey the law of Mercy there can be no error in the world.

# 163

## The Law of Miracles

Life is a miracle and we all create miracles every day. This law can be activated by any person who has realized that the 'Essence' of creation Is 'Light.' A master is able to employ his or her divine knowledge of light phenomena to project instantly into perceptible manifestation the flawless light atoms. The actual form of the projection whatever it is, for example, water into wine, is determined by the master's wish and by his powers of will and visualization.

All events in our precisely adjusted universe are lawfully wrought and lawfully explicable. The so-called miraculous powers of a great master are a natural accompaniment to his or her exact understanding of subtle laws that operate in the inner cosmos of consciousness. Nothing is a miracle except in the profound sense that everything is a miracle. Is anything more miraculous than that each of us is encased in an intricately organized body, and is set upon on earth whirling through space among the stars?

You are a miracle and you have been given the power to create miracles in your life. Once you have understood and accepted this fact you have taken the first step towards creating a life for yourself that is full of miracles.

# 164

## The Law of Moderation

This natural law states that anything in extreme is as harmful as insufficiency. The Indian scriptures, the Baghavad Gita warn us to be always moderate in our approach and not to go to extremes in our pursuit of spirituality and in our search for God, as exaggeration can have negative and undesirable effects. Moderation is a greater virtue than over indulgence or total abstinence.

The practice of yoga for example is a moderation of conduct and internal adjustment. Moderation is to know when one has arrived at the point that once crossed, can bring destruction. In practicality, for example, a cook needs to use just the right amount of salt or spices in the food, a few grains too many and the food would be inedible, too salty or too spicy to eat. An artist knows intuitively when the work at hand is complete and perfect, one stroke too many could ruin the whole artwork. We can love someone dearly but if we love too much love and are too possessive, we can smother and suffocate the loved one to such an extent that he or she will want to run away from us.

Too many rules and regulations are confining, on the other hand, total freedom without any guidelines or limitations can lead to disaster. Moderation is to recognize that certain perfect level or point and to know when to stop. To be able to do that, we need to be fully aware and to have total control over our faculties. Buddha taught to walk the middle way. It is that golden middle line that we want to stay on.

# 165

## The Law of Monadic Return

This law concerns the force of evolution and is the sum total of three influences.

The strength of vibrations from the seven stars of the Great Bear depend upon the closeness of the connection and the accuracy of the alignment between any particular heavenly man and his prototype. Second is the seven sisters or the Pleiades. Third is the sun Sirius.

It is the appearance or the disappearance of these waves of life force which sweeps into incarnation the divine pilgrims, and which brings about the cyclic manifestation of such great lives as the 'silent watcher' and the great 'sacrifice.'

Within limits, the human is the controller of his destiny, wielding forces and energies, manipulating lesser lives and controlling lesser centers of energy and as time passes his radius of control becomes even more extensive.

# 166

## The Law of Money

The law of Money states that money is but an artificially created symbol used as a substitute to store energies borrowed, earned, spent, owed, claimed or exchanged.

To be 'good' money the symbol must be acceptable to others in a society who are willing to part with valuables or energies in exchange for the money symbol. Each society may further define its own money and the use thereof.

On a practical tone, money comes to those who love and respect money and it stays with those who use it wisely. Just as energy begets energy, money begets money. Some esoteric people wrongly believe that money is dirty or unimportant so naturally because of their negative thoughts about money, they do not attract money to them.

Money is manifested energy or solidified spirit and should circulate widely and wisely. Hoarding money is a violation of this law as it is blocking of the circulation of energy in its solidified form.

# 167

## The Law of Music

The law of Music is working throughout the universe, which can also be called the law of Life or the law of Harmony. It is the law that brings about balance, the law which is hidden behind all aspects of life, which holds this universe intact and works out the destiny of the whole universe, to fulfill its purpose.

What we know as music in our everyday life, is only a miniature of the music or harmony of the whole universe which is working behind everything and which is in itself the source and origin of nature. The wise of all ages know this that is why music is looked upon as a sacred art. In music we can see a picture of the whole universe, and it is the wise, who can interpret the secret in the realm of music.

All religions have taught that the origin of the whole of creation is sound and there is music in the depth of our very being. A great Sufi Poet, Hafiz of Persia, said: 'the truth in life itself is music.' Music gives us pleasure because it corresponds with the rhythm and tone keeping the mechanism of our whole being intact. We feel good when we are with nature because nature's music is perfect. It gives us a sense of exaltation to be in the woods, to stand near a running stream, which has its own rhythm, its tone and harmony. The swinging of branches in the wind, the rise and fall of the waves in the ocean, all that is music and when we can relax and become one with nature we can open our hearts to its music.

## Cosmic and Universal Laws

The movement of stars and planets move according to the law of Vibration and Rhythm, perfect and unchanging. Even the cosmic system works to the law of Music and when there is a disharmony, according to the proportion of the disharmony, disasters come to earth in the form of forces destroying nature. One who receives the key to the working of life, is the one who becomes intuitive and has inspiration. To such a person revelations manifest and his language become music that inspires others.

Being at the one-moment-with God, is being in tune with the Infinite, in harmony with the whole universe, it is being a receptacle of the music of the whole universe. Everyone should feel harmony and disharmony according to how open he or she is to the music of the universe. The more one is open to all that is beautiful and harmonious, the more one's life is tuned to the universal harmony and the more one will show a friendly attitude towards every other person one meets. The whole being of such a person will create music around him.

When famous and unique composer Stockhausen was interviewed about his work 'Sirius' and what it is that designates a Sirius spirit, he replied : 'Extreme musicality and extreme openness for unknown musical forms, and what is more important is that the musical forms must always be related to natural, organic events on this planet, which means to the elements—the four elements – to the movements that we can experiene in nature, to the rhythms and to the harmonic principles that one should study, the ecology of this planet and human bodies ; the rhythms of the organs of the human body, so this is a typical sign that the spirit tries to relate music to the natural laws of musical parameters ; melody, harmony, rhythm in particular.'

See also the law of Sound and the law of Rhythm.

## 168

### The Law of New Being

The law of New Being lessens polarities and reconciles oppositions. The law of New Being reconciles the yes and no, right and wrong, good and evil, and brings the concepts of God and Satan together in harmonious resolution, integrated totally under the law of One. The law of New being acknowledges the return of Lucifer to the Godhead or Source of All Being and realizes there is no longer a force of evil in the world, that there is only the echo, the memory of the fear of evil remaining and that these are also fading from consciousness. Those who follow the law of New Being are beings who may transcend matter, or any situation that appears to matter, and may move into new states of being with greater freedom and energies of a New Being.

# 169

# The Law of Non-intervention

This law concerns the individual right of people and society situations to serve self rather than live in the vibration of service to others. This law prevents physical beings and non-physical beings from intervening or correcting what they see as wrong or harmful. If this law is violated, there is great karma incurring.

Another aspect of this law is that spirit is not permitted to channel material to a recipient that would force a change in the evolution of the person. There is exception when the channeler is willing to undergo a trance, and the consciousness leaves the body for another consciousness to enter and impart knowledge that was previously unknown to the individual.

# 170

# The Law of Non-Judgment

The universal Spirit is non-judgmental. Judgments are human inventions, a means to compare, contrast and control as we judge ourselves against artificial and often idealistic standards of perfection, morality or truth.

Under the law of Equalities our judgments attract judgment to us in equal measure. The life karmic review conducted by you after death is a conditional living in the third dimension of duality.

In a practical sense, this law requires us to live our life without judging others if we want to live a happy life. Not judging others or situations, is a soul quality.

# 171

## The Law of Non-Resistance

True harmony cannot come from disharmony, nor peace from discord. It seems contrary to the natural reaction of a body, for when we meet with opposition it seems natural to steel our energies and collect our wits, and use whatever means we have to outwit and break down the opposition.

Yet as contrary as it may seem in one sense, a meek and non-resistant position taken is the more powerful and easier way to utilize the forces of nature. When we are working to gain success and to bring forth an increase of supply or material wealth and we sometimes get into the habit of talking and fearing hard times, we may talk about our neighbor or criticize the method he used to get ahead. We may fear business conditions and when we see the graph take a downward swing, we fear for our investments or our job. When we do these things we are acting foolishly, for such an act is resistance of thought. Thought action is just as substantial as physical action, therefore, it is wise to realize, monitor, and modify our thoughts as much as we do our physical actions. Thoughts are matter and have a major effect on the flow of circumstances in our lives.

When we meet an obstacle we may stop our progress to collect forces and put up a fight to remove it. This resistance causes friction. Friction causes irritation and an inflammation. For this reason, our life becomes hard and exacting. It is like machinery that is resisted upon. The machine breaks down and wears out. It is not the movement of the machine but the friction that causes the breakdown and difficulties. Friction is opposition and resistance. If we go through life, fighting, opposing, resisting, arguing, we are bound to meet with many obstacles and are likely to become so occupied fighting them that we lose sight of our real goal. If we strive to make little of the obstacle and keep our minds on the objective or desire we set out to gain, we will ultimately win.

In the beginning we have many obstacles and trials to strive past. The wise one will not fight these obstacles, but bless them and go on. As we go on with faith and assurance, we grow stronger and become more momentous in our progress towards our goal. The less we resist the better opportunity we have to build a stronger momentum in our progress.

'Blessed are the Meek' may seem literally to support those kindly timid souls who are an easy prey for their more aggressive brothers. Rather it refers to the one who is able to follow the law of Non-Resistance to the point of inheriting the earth and all things thereof. To be meek does not mean to be an easy mark, nor does it mean to be a doormat for anyone to walk over. To be meek does not mean that we are submissive to the conditions of discord and disorder. We are meek only to the natural laws of the universe.

Meekness is, therefore, strength acquired when you do not argue, when you do not become angry or boastful and proud, when you do not insist upon having your rights in a quarrelsome manner. Meekness is the steel of one's nature. It is enduring. Meekness is the strength by which you win an argument in refusing to argue. In science we recognize the spirit of meekness as cooperative, persistent application, accurate computation, perfect harmony and symmetry of design and color.

When we integrate the law of Non-Resistance into our lives, letting go of every worried thought, every fear, doubt, complaint, argument, and angry thought, we tend to shorten the time for our goal to be reached. Remove and dissolve every obstacle by blessing it and be willing to understand it. Turn your obstacles into stepping stones of progress leading to your highest good.

See also the law of Meekness.

# 172

# The Law of Number Measure and Weight

It is written in the Sepher Yetzirah, the Book of Creation, one of the oldest Jewish texts that God designed, that is, engraved, carved, weighed, permuted and transformed, the 22 letters of the Hebrew Alphabet to form the foundation of his creation and how He combined these letters to generate the words by which 'He depicted all that was formed and all that would be formed.'

The text states that 'God placed them in a circle.' The word circle, which can also be translated as 'sphere' or 'cycle' used to denote the cycle events in the world. The Book of Creation also states that God weighed the letters, which refers to the 'weight' of their numerical values. Mathematicians use this natural metaphor with phrases such as 'weighted sum' and 'weighted average.'

The values of each letter may be seen in the Jewish Alphabet Table. Aleph 'A' is the lightest having a weight of Unity and Tav 'T' the cross, is the heaviest with a weight of 400 in number. The primary significance of many alphanumeric relations is often immediately obvious, as with identities such as Wheel which equals the number 66 and Alpha Omega which equals 801 The Creator.

A proper understanding is required with a great deal of study, experience and patience with heavy emphasis on virtue and respect. The alphanumeric relations encode the deepest mysteries of life.

# 173

## The Law of One

All that is exists as part of God Oneness. This awareness indicates all is one and all reside within the law of One. All souls are cells of the body of this awareness, and when awareness of the law of One is present, one has no need to struggle or to compete, as one would be fighting with oneself within one body.

All who understand this law of One realize that all that appears to be separate is an illusion. There is only one Power in existence, only one Creator and One God.

Nothing exists outside of the Creator. 'I' and 'me' do not exist only 'we' and 'us.' Even we and us are temporary perceptions as all that is, is ONE. Separation from God exists only as a misperception and, therefore, does not exist at all. Perhaps we will witness a time in the future when awareness of the meaning of this law will grow. When educators can teach this law to children at a young age we will see a new generation of peace loving people grow.

Indigo children and angelic humans were created specifically with precise organic abilities to assist in the healing processes as embodied within the original divine blueprint.

All who have studied metaphysics and understand somewhat the action of the mind recognize that there is one underlying law and that through this law all things come into expression; also that there is one Universal Mind, which is the source and sole origin of all real intelligence. First there is the mind, then the mind expresses itself in ideas, and then the ideas manifest on the physical level. This is a metaphysical statement of the Divine Trinity, the expression of Mind, and the manifestations of Mind are found in simple numbers and complex combinations everywhere.

See also the law of Three.

# 174

# The Law of Opportunity

Under this law opportunities or choices are unlimited and always lead to success. That which is needed is available when needed. What is mandatory is that we recognize and act as the opportunity presents itself to us.

As it says in the Bible 'ask and it shall be given unto you.' And 'knock and it shall be opened unto you.' You have got to take the initiative and move to act. Opportunities and choices are presented to us daily according to our needs, it is up to us to be aware and to see these for what they are and to make our choices.

Many opportunities in life are lost because one is either too blind to see them or too afraid to take action.

## 175

## The Law of Order and Creation

That which is destined to be appears in Divine Order. Any attempt to place anything out of order is a violation of the universal law of Balance. Confusion does not exist.

Divine Plan always enfolds in a precise and predetermined manner. The beginning of law carried all the way through. And that which comes or begins first is conceived in spirit, grows in the mental and finally manifests in the material.

# 176

## The Law of Paradox

The law of Paradox is the law that recognizes the movement of energies in four dimensions simultaneously. This awareness indicates the law of Paradox as that which combines the law of Cause and Effect along with the law of Inertia, the law of Microcosm and Macrocosm, and the law of Vibration. This awareness indicates that the law of Paradox relates to that which is the focus of attention, whereby energies do come together in a collision at a certain point and whereby that point does create a relationship using the law of Relativity as a type of, or as part of itself, whereby this point in relationship does reflect that which is the microcosms and macrocosm, does relate to movements occurring at a certain momentum. This as the law of Inertia whereby an equal and opposite reaction does occur which moves entities into another dimension on this macrocosmic level and on those vibrations in between. This is relating to the echoing effect of an action.

The law of Paradox when seen in a flat plane, would be likened unto a stone dropped in a stream and watching the ripples move out. The law of Paradox seen in a cube of space would create vibrations in all directions, whereby that stone was emanating an energy, though not being dripped, but simply vibration, and that energy would be felt in various places within that cube of space. When the law is in the fourth dimensional level as that which occurs in all places simultaneously on certain vibratory rates likened unto the ringing of a bell that vibrates every particle of energy within its periphery. The law of Paradox touches into such high levels of vibration and such dense levels of vibration simultaneously that the entire area appears to be alive, and whatever is said about one level can also hold true about the next, yet can also appear to be untrue.

Everything is relative to the ability for measuring by the eye of the beholder. We discover what appears to be an immanent paradox in all our findings and postulates. This tends to deter most minds from coming to a positive stand on many matters. The paradox, while disquieting, is often for the thinker, the first real hint that there is an impermanence about the observable physical world that will always elude his or her enquiries.

All spiritual answers are found in the opposite perception than that which manifests in the physical. In other words, this material world is all about 'control' whereas, the spiritual world answer in comparison, is about 'surrender.' To be near the Divine we need to give up control e.g. to sacrifice the ego and to surrender to the Divine in us. Sacrificing the ego does not mean to give up the ego or to kill it. An ego well developed is mandatory to spiritual growth, but the ego must recognize Divinity at some point and be willing to surrender.

# 177

# The Law of Patience

The law of Patience states that all things must have their time and their season whereby they may work their action to proper fruition.

Patience involves spiritual, mental and physical thought and action. Through this law we get to know our self, to test and measure our ideals, to have faith and to seek understanding through all the other virtues. Patience allows all other virtues to manifest more profoundly. Patiently we realize that any fault we see in another is one we have personal knowledge of from prior experiences. Patiently we seek true understanding, not just knowledge, as we realize that every soul is totally unique and will come to its enlightenment in its own time.

Patience strengthens the will and it makes attainment possible. One of the things that can prevent us from attaining our wish is lack of patience. Lack of patience is detrimental to the soul. Patience is needed in all relations of life, be that with your partner, your children, your neighbor, your co-worker, with your friends. Patience and hope go together for as long as there is hope, there is patience. It is when hope is gone that patience disappears. Hope is also needed in all things. We live on hope, in our friendships and love affairs, in all our undertakings on every level.

There is a beautiful story that comes from the East, it says that Brahma extracted honey from all flowers and this was hope. That means, God, Brahma, extracted the essence from all things in the world and the essence is wisdom. The flowers are all the objects in the world that attract us, they attract us by hope and hope is life for without hope there is no life. To one who is patient all things will eventually come. Patience is a virtue and is a quality of the soul.

# 178

## The Law of Patterns

This law states that any pattern or habit, whether it is good or bad, tends to reassert itself overtime, unless we break the pattern by doing something different.

If we have a good habit we can reinforce the pattern with small self rewards. We have the power of spontaneous action and the power of the imagination to do old things in new ways to change and to restructure our life and our behavior pattern. Some of our change ability is influenced by the ways we have learned in our youth and through conditioning. We learned to make sense of the world by observing patterns in order to survive. When we find the patterns dysfunctional or destructive, however, this law allows us to do something different that will give sufficient impact to interrupt the old pattern and replace it with a new and better one.

Most of us tend to be slaves of our habits. With self awareness we can reassess our habits periodically and we can make the effort to change them, when we find them to be detrimental to our well being and growth.

Character is built by habit and by whatever habit one forms from childhood, as the habit stays with one so the character is molded. This could be a habit of being curious, or sarcastic, gentle, humble, modest or adventurous and daring, it could be a characteristic of being conceited, boastful or shy and thoughtful. It is according to these habits that a character is made. Everyone has brought with him on earth a certain nature and it is not always easy to rid oneself of this. We also inherit patterns from our parents, grand parents or great parents, and these are just as hard to get rid of. Habits can be our friends or our enemies and it is this law that gives us the possibility to shed our bad habits when we are ready to do so. The main purpose of life is to refine the character. Some people who are interested and wish to build, change or improve their character have a conflict if their nature is so strong that it opposes this imposed change to be something different to what it is. As an example let's take a man who is by nature coarse and inconsiderate, and this man has gone to great lengths to learn to be polite. We might find that he can be very polite for a while, but if we spent a longer time with him he will eventually slip, the barriers will drop and his coarse nature will inevitably come through. This is because the rough nature is stronger than the character, the outer cover. It is futile to change the nature of a person if the person does not wish it. This will only result in total confusion.

The character of young people can be molded for the better, but it is not advisable to change them completely by deviating far away from their essence, their nature, what they really are. One can be scientific the other creative, one can have a quiet nature the other a lively one and every virtue can become a vice when exaggerated or neglected. It is easy to help and to mold children to acquire habits but it is most difficult to help adults. The change would have to be desired by the person, only then can one build one's own character and make the effort to change it. The one who does not care to change will never change.

Personality is the finishing of character. As long as the personality is not developed, no matter how good or virtuous the person is, they remain as a diamond in the rough. Personality is the harmony of nature and character. When the nature is in harmony with the character, when there is no conflict between the two, a personality is born. But the power constantly working from within can no doubt change the nature to anything, positive or negative.

The building of the character and the developing of the personality is an art. The art of improving on nature, it is through art that

God completes His creation. This is the very purpose of life. The Divine in the human is there to be developed, only then can such a personality create beauty and spread harmony, peace and love as is meant to be.

Christ said: 'Make your personality as it ought to be, that you may no more be the slave of the nature which you have brought with you, nor of the character which you have made in your life, but that you may show in your life the divine personality, that you may fulfill on this earth the purpose for which you have come.'

# 179

## The Law of Peace

The law of Peace states that peace comes from within and is related to the concept of surrender. But peaceful surrender cannot be to that which is divisive, causing disagreement, and polarized or greater conflict will follow. Under this law we are warned that any compromise with forces that divide instead of unify, that oppress instead of liberate, that harm instead of benefit, will inevitably lead to greater conflict. This law allows surrender only to that which brings a total unit by reconciling the yes and no and other oppositions.

Peace is not only found in harmony, but may also be found in conflict when that conflict is essential for the harmony, welfare and liberty of everyone involved. It also suggests that inner peace nourishes external harmony, and grows by increments and degrees even as yes or no are merged into maybe, even as you and I are brought together into we. With inner peace, one can witness harmony even in the midst of conflict. Through this law of Peace a soft response will often put a wrathful tongue to rest. It is through the maintenance of an inner state of peace and harmony that initiates allow all others their unique truth and their unique creation upon the earth plane. Acceptance of all that is means that one must embrace the dance and rhythm of earth as it currently is, unconditionally, even though it is full of pain, fear, judgement and deficiency. Unconditional acceptance does not mean that an initiate must partake in the dance of pain, fear, judgement or deficiency but that they must allow others to dance in such a way if they choose to do so.

'Being in the world but not of it' is only accomplished as one separates their thought form from mass conscious experiences. In order to retain an inner state of peace, harmony and centeredness, our channels have learned not to listen to the news or any form of media including the radio. They also do not read the newspapers or magazines nor do they maintain contact with those who perpetuate abusive or judgemental patterns. To embody a state of harmlessness, initiates must take full conscious responsibility for every thought and every action that they participate in.

Peace is a transcendent condition. It is not a product of our thoughts or our speech, it is rather an essential quality of Love Divine. It is not possible to find peace by thinking or talking, we can find it only through direct experience. Inayat Khan says: But to what does the love of God lead? It leads to that peace and stillness, which can be seen in the life of the tree, which bears fruit and flowers for others and expects no returns, not even thanks. It serves and cares for nothing else, not even for appreciation. That is the attribute of the Godly.'

A prayer offers us the insight that we are able to rise above the petty differences that divide us. The differences will never cease to exist, it is we who must change and the nature of change is to rise above all the differences that separate us. This is not a task for the rational logical mind. This is far beyond mind. Here lies the key to peace, to go to that still, quiet, eternal place within. This inner stillness must be experienced. We cannot find peace outside of ourselves.

## 180

## The Law of Penetration

The law of Penetration states that anything that is looked at with great attention and focus, with a great quality of consciousness penetrates directly to the heart, and then emanates into all of consciousness.

This awareness suggests that when a healing is given to someone, that the healer also gives the suggestion. This awareness indicates this in particular to these who find it difficult to accept a healing for any particular length of time or a permanent healing. Another awareness also suggests that when a healer gives you a healing and states that this healing appears to be good for an 'x' number of months, or more, then other forces within your own psyche are capable of taking over and to continue with the healing process for the stated time.

This is connected with the law of Suggestion.

## 181

## The Law of Perception

Perception reveals perception e.g. we see things not as they are, but as we are according to our perceptions of our experiences of life. Each Soul's ability to discern highest truth is in direct proportion to its initiative to achieve it.

Our thought, ideas and desires differ as much as we differ in our looks from each other. If ten people look at the same scene or hear the same story, they will give ten different interpretations based on each individual perception. How we see, hear and perceive depends on the conditioning that we have had, from what we have experienced in our lives, past and present.

There are three ways of perception. The first way is to perceive with the intellect, with a definite form, line and color, this is more on the surface. This type of person lives in the mind. The second way of perception is with the feeling it is more in depth than perception with the intellect. The more the heart quality is awakened in a person the deeper the perception is of the feelings of others. This would be a sensitive person because the thoughts and feelings of others are clearly perceived. Here the person lives life with feeling and heart. The third way of perception is that experienced through the deepest depths of the heart, combined with the faculty of intuition, the sixth sense. It is the highest perception, crystal clear, it belongs to the light, it is the voice of the spirit.

In order to study life fully, these three perceptions must be developed. Only then are we able to understand life.

# 182

## The Law of Perfection

This law concerns the absolute perfection of the process of our unfolding. From a transcendental perspective, everyone and everything is unconditionally perfect. From a conventional viewpoint, perfection does not exist. Excellence is the best we can achieve and achieving takes time and practice. When we understand the larger picture, we understand our role and responsibility in helping the world we live in to become more loving, more giving, kinder and gentler. When we live up to this responsibility, we expand into the perfection of our higher selves. Spirit is perfect. Consciousness is perfect. Perfection is an absolute. Perfection, like truth, has many aspects, but also like truth, it is of the highest vibration. Nothing exists which is not perfect.

Life can be looked at as a line with two ends. At one end is the limitation, and at the other end is perfection. As long as one looks at and focuses on the end that represents limitation, however good, virtuous, righteous, religious one is, one has not touched what may be called perfection. Worshippers of Deity are found among the simple people and among the intellectuals and the educated of this world, but do they all arrive at perfection before leaving this earth by their belief and worship? Many have studied much, attended countless seminars, followed gurus, read hundreds of books or written books themselves, yet remain themselves stuck in the same place where they started because they are focused on the end of the line where limitation is. One cannot arrive to the end where perfection is found unless one turns around, faces the end with perfection and walks towards it.

The possibility exists to attain perfection by not depending on outside things but to shift focus on one's own inner being. This is not attained but discovered and it is in this discovery and satisfaction that perfection is attained and the purpose of life is fulfilled. Perfection can be defined as the expansion of consciousness. One becomes naturally unselfish. One has discovered the silence within where one can forget the limitations of the self and be in touch with the part of one's inner being which is perfection itself. It is in this perfection that genuine peace is experienced.

Life is a journey from one end of the line to the other, and the perfection of the conscious life is the final destiny of the imperfect life. Every aspect of life in this world of variety gradually evolves from imperfection to perfection.

# 183

## The Law of Periodicity

Training for the aspirant will be cyclic and will have its ebb and flow, as everything else in nature. Times of activity succeed times of 'pralaya' or rest, and periods of registered contact alternate with periods of apparent silence.

If the student develops as desired, each paralayic period is succeeded by one of greater activities and of more potent achievement. Rhythm, ebb and flow, and the measured beat of the pulsating life are ever the law of the Universe. In learning to respond to the vibration of the high places, the rhythmic periodicity must be borne in the mind.

# 184

## The Law of Permanence

An entity attains permanence when it remains integrated without the vessel that holds it, *the soul within the form.* The earthly body is simply the vessel that embraces the soul while on the earth plane. When we transition back to our energy state, and after a period of time with our soul mates, we reincarnate into new vessels.

## 185

## The Law of Perspective

This law means determining what is more important to you and what will produce soul growth. Activating this law starts with some deep reflection. What is life to you? Why do you approach it? What produces the greatest satisfaction and security for you? If you would die to morrow what would you want to have accomplished and produced with your life? With these questions in mind you can begin to decide what to do first. What desires will you need to accomplish first, second, third and so on.

This is a very important law because you can fulfill many desires in your life only when you put them in order. Without order, you become scattered and unfocused. With proper perspective you can learn planning and you can also learn to use your time and your energy most efficiently.

# 186

## The Law of Planetary Affinity

This law is in connection with the interaction of the planets with each other and their eventual union. The term planetary affinity is used in the occult teaching specifically in connection with the interaction of the planets with each other and their eventual unity. As we know, the planetary schemes, the seven sacred planets, will eventually synthesize, or absorb the life of the planets which are not termed sacred and the numerous planetoids, as far as the four kingdoms of nature are concerned. The absorption of the spirit aspect proceeds under the law of Synthesis. The four minor planetary schemes become first the two and then the one. This process is repeated until the final one is eventually merged in the sun, producing one flaming ball of fire.

The seven sacred planets are the Vulcan, Mercury, Venus, Jupiter, Saturn, Neptune and Uranus. Mars, Earth, Pluto, the Moon veiling a hidden planet, and the Sun also veiling a planet are considered in the occult science as non sacred planets. Some understanding is here necessary as to the relation between the human being and the planets. The seven major force centers, known as chakras in the etheric body are the distributing agencies and electrical batteries that provide the dynamic force and energy to the human, they produce definite effects upon the outer physical manifestation. Through this constant activity the qualities of the human appear, the ray tendencies appear and the point of progress on the ladder of evolution is thus clearly indicated.

## Cosmic and Universal Laws

The planetary influences completely condition and control the unevolved human being with no soul experience. The moment that one becomes aware of one's own soul and begins to control one's own path in life, the influences of the planets begin to weaken gradually. One begins to gain control over the forces flowing through one and one becomes receptive to the subtler and higher energies of the solar system and the twelve governing constellations.

When soul and body, consciousness and form are blended then the disciple brings about this relationship within one's little system and the planetary Logos on a far larger scale within one's range of influence and control. This blending or fusion produces transfiguration, the third initiation. In this process one carries all the four kingdoms in nature: mineral, plant, animal and human. The five non sacred planets correspond to the system of the human being: the first is the physical outer shell of the body, the etheric or vital body, the astral body, and the mental body, plus a fusion of all four, to make the fifth which is the personality, i.e. the conscious individual, the four kingdoms in nature plus the kingdom of God.

# 187

## The Law of Planning

Planning is a function of divine intelligence nothing happens by accident in God's universe. Planning is mandatory. Even failure to plan is temporary and is a function of the divine plan.

There are planetary influences that we as humans have no control of. Each one of us is an individual planet and as one planet is related to another, so in the same way all planets are related to mankind. The changing of the condition of a planet, what is produced by it and what effect is produced by the planet have an effect upon a human being's life. Outwardly man is so small as to be a drop in the ocean. If the cosmos with its planets is an ocean then the individual is a drop. But inwardly the planet is a drop in the ocean of the man's heart. A Sufi philosopher once said, when ignorance vanishes the heart will open and the whole universe will become a bubble in the ocean of the heart. Smallness and imperfection are the outcome of ignorance and relate to limitation. The day the heart is open the whole universe will be in it, and the source of destiny, its secret and its mystery will reveal itself to the man.

We might wonder whether a plan is laid out so that every occurrence in life must be according to a plan that is laid out for us individually before birth. And if this is the case, on what ground and who has laid it out? If it is not God but our own actions to what degree are we responsible? But this is life's mystery, yet to be solved. Most often than not we have our own preconceived ideas, and whatever ideas these are we keep these like a wall in front of us, content with what we know and do not even try to inquire any further. No doubt, each human is born with a plan to be accomplished in life, not only with instincts, with merits of gifts but with the whole plan of how each individual life is to be. There is a saying in the East that one can read the life of an infant from looking at its feet, even the little feet of the infant show the sign of the plan that the infant is to follow through life.

Man is born with certain obligations which willingly or unwillingly the man must fulfill. No matter how powerful and how the great the person may seem, when there is a difficulty it cannot be changed, the difficulty will be there. Then again in spite of all things lacking, a way is open, the person does not do much yet the way is open and smooth. This shows that there is a plan. It is not only qualifications and cleverness that makes one successful, but a plan is to be accomplished. There are times when you are meant to have an easy life, success and all you wish, and other times when you are meant to have difficulties and problems to solve. The question is, is this plan given to a person at birth or is the effect of a person's actions? The answer is it is a combination of both.

A man has two aspects in him. One aspect is that he is a mechanical being where he is but a machine controlled by conditions, his impressions, his actions, by outer and cosmic influences. He is but a tool of influences. The more this aspect is pronounced in man, the less evolved he is. The other aspect in man is his creativity, here he shows the sign of a being representative of the Creator, he shows that he is not only linked with God but is a part of God, i.e. his innermost self is Godly. This Godly spark is within every living soul, it is this Godly power that makes it possible for man to change conditions by his free will, but only when he is aware of this. It is the absence of this awareness that makes a man a machine.

Whether we have success or failure in life, if it is individual in the end it is failure. But in the case of a godly purpose, whether it is failure or success, it is success in the end. It cannot be anything else, it is only gain that is there. When the life of a man is directed by godly power and inspiration, whether he has difficulties or ease, the man who keeps close to God and draws his power and inspiration from God, his way is always smooth and the end is what it ought to be.

# 188

## The Law of Polarity

For everything in life there is an opposite that is equal. Everything is dual. Like and unlike are the same. Opposites are identical in nature but different in degree. All paradoxes may be reconciled. The evidence of this principle is observed in the polarity of planets and the various celestial bodies that includes our earth, solar system and galaxy. Without the law of polarity light, gravity and electricity would not be possible.

On the mental plane, this principle manifests itself in the heart center of each person as the enlightened or the dark mind. The principle of polarity makes possible the choices we make on the scale of life between good and evil, right and wrong, generosity and greed, love and fear, truth and lies.

The law of Cause and Effect is closely connected to polarity and holds us true to the choices and actions we make by returning to us what we have measured out to others. Like the swing of the pendulum, it always returns where it began. 'Do unto others, as you would have them do to you.' This principle establishes the paradox or the dual aspects of reality.

Everything that is, has its double. Positive and negative, light and darkness, hot and cold, love and fear, morality and immorality all are two extremes of the same pole.

From higher dimensional levels of existence, however, polarity is just an illusion. Unity is all there is, there is just one Spirit that moves through everything. All that ever occurs is occurring because of the one God. On our level of existence we interpret things differently, we see things in terms of good and evil, whereas in fact there is no such thing, we only perceive it to be so because we are living in the third dimension in the midst of polarity consciousness. Evil can sometimes be harsh and disgusting but at the level of polarity consciousness these are mere lessons.

Everything actually has three components—the holy trinity and no matter what polarity you think of there will be a third element to it, for example, with hot and cold there is warm, with up and down there is middle, etc. We think we see good and evil but in fact what is really going on is timing. The forces of polarity are necessary for the proper functioning of the universe. The dark forces do everything they can to hinder growth of consciousness, be it on a planetary or an individual level. The light forces in their turn, do everything they can to encourage consciousness expansion and awareness. The opposition causes consciousness to move upwards at exactly the right pace. So we need to see good and evil and be aware of them, but we also need to recognize that the presence of God is in every situation and that there is a reason for everything that happens. We need to understand that everything is whole and perfect and that there is nothing wrong no matter how bad or how good it may seem to us, that life engenders a deep conscious aspect that is everywhere. In our state of mind we tend to think that we are separate from everything out there, and that our own thoughts and feelings have no impact on the world around us. This is far from the truth. Everything we think, feel and do is creating our whole world around us. We are creating everything in every moment more so than we could ever imagine.

# 189

## The Law of Poverty

The law of Poverty states that to the degrees one withholds one's productivity and energy in the hope that someone else will offer theirs instead, to that same degree, an entity earns and experiences poverty.

When you take you become poorer. When you give you become richer because giving triggers stagnant forces, imbedded in your being and as soon as you share with others, these forces begin to flow abundantly, making you richer.

Poverty does not refer to monetary poverty only but also to physical, emotional, mental and spiritual. We experienced for example in the last century a poverty of spirituality in the western hemisphere. So according to this universal law, if you have a wealth of money, health, love or talent and you do not share this with fellow humans, to inspire them, to spread joy around you, you inevitably experience poverty of the spirit.

According to the Sufis the beauty of all creation is that creation has worked in two ways. In one way it has expressed and in the other way it has made itself a responsive mold. For instance, there is a substance, matter to touch, and there is a sense to feel and to touch. There is a sound and at the same time there are ears which can hear sound. There is light, there is form and there are colors, at the same time there are eyes to see and appreciate. What man calls beauty is the harmony of all that one experiences. What we call music is the harmony of the audible notes, but in reality there is also music in color, there is music in nature where there is a variety of trees and plants and the way they correspond with each other. The more you observe nature, the more it appeals to your soul, because there is music there. The wider your outlook on life is the deeper your understanding, the more music you can listen to which puts you in touch with the whole universe.

For the one whose heart is wide open, this music can be heard also in the midst of a crowd of people. Human ideas, creativities, personalities and human nature is as varied as a piano with thousands of octaves. People agree and disagree, some become friends instantly others take time or cannot become friends at all ever. Ever human soul has its own tone pitch, each voice its own octave. The more you study the harmony of music, and study human nature, the attraction and the repulsion, the more you will see that it is all music. The more you are aware of this the richer your life will be.

# 190

## The Law of Practice

We are all familiar with this law and the saying 'practice makes perfect.' To become proficient in any field we need to practice. There is no accomplishment of any goal without practice. The more intelligent the practice is the greater the proficiency and the sooner the goal is attained. This holds true for aboslutely everything, whether it is learning a language or learning to sing or dance. It is the same if we want to learn to swim, skate or fly an aeroplane, cook or drive a car. The more we practice the better we get. Intelligent practice is the secret of attainment.

What counts most is self-discipline without which our practice cannot produce great results. In the path of truth for example, if we study the lives of sages, we learn that they all have practiced self-discipline. No soul in the world has ever arrived to the realization of truth without practice. Everyone who has ever successfully attained a specific goal, no matter in what field practices self-discipline, be that the field of an artist, composer, housewife, student or an executive. There are many ways to practice self-discipline.

One way is the physical way. One may be able to stand or sit in the position for a long time, without feeling any discomfort, but as soon as one becomes conscious of the fact and wants to practice standing or sitting in the same posture for a long time, it will become very difficult and will require long practice. With this practice one develops self-discipline. Another way to practice is be aware of what one eats and drinks, avoiding certain foods that one particularly enjoys, or maybe even practice fasting. When one succeeds in this practice, one develops self-discipline. Another aspect of developing self-discipline is to practice the habit of thinking and forgetting. We usually find it very difficult to hold one thought, leaving out all other thoughts. With practice we can focus and be in control of our thought patterns, we can check our thoughts to eliminate those of depression, prejudice, hatred, anger or agitation. When we can practice this to its fullest this gives us moral discipline, we become the master of our mind.

The highest aspect of self-discipline to be practiced is to be able to feel tranquility and inner peace even in the midst of a crowd or in the midst of the greatest turmoil. This is achieved by practicing solitude. A person who is engaged entirely with whatever is at hand that is of great interest to one, is not disturbed by the environment. Poets, writers, artists, inventors, scientists for example when absorbed in their work are not even aware of their bodies or self for that moment. It is this experience of pure consciousness, freedom of the soul, what is known as nirvana. At this stage one does not think of oneself, of others or surroundings. Spiritual development is being able to raise one's consciousness above all else, above the self and above one's environment. Often we think or complain 'no one is listening to me.' When we can practice to reach this level of consciousness, we begin to realize that in reality it is myself who is not listening to me. It was the self who was not listening. With practice of self-discipline one has power over the self, one begins to feel a mastery over one's own kingdom and life and living slowly begin to flow easily.

This law demands that you practice and to practice at length, whatever it is that you want to master in life.

# 191

## The Law of Praise

This law is connected with the law of Increase. Praise is faith in action, without faith you have nothing to build upon. When you energize your desires with faith and praise you work within universal laws and the power of the mind is used properly and efficiently. Learn to render praise, and always to be thankful for the good at hand. 'As you sow, so shall you reap' is a basic, organic law that works in nature. Equally important is the fact that this law applies in our lives as well as in nature. You sow the seeds by your spoken words, by acts towards others, and by the very thoughts you hold in your mind. What happens in your life is the fruit springing from those seeds. In other words, you yourself sow the seeds of your own experience. The law does not judge what you should or should not do. The law will reproduce exactly as you sow. Once you have planted a good seed, like a farmer, you wait. Do not dig it up to see if it is growing. Be patient with the law, it always works. Praise the creator in all things, good and bad. Giving praise to divinity exalts us.

Praise is an avenue of prayer and desire through which the spiritual law expresses itself. When you offer praise you lift the consciousness to a higher realm and become a greater channel to receive the good that is ever waiting to come to you. Praise opens a little door in your mind that enables you to draw closer to the universe and to be attuned to the Divine forces within and about you. Praise expands and opens the mind upward, while it's opposite, condemnation, contracts and restricts. You have noticed how a child responds to praise, with a glow and gladness, as does the universe, reflecting joy and rejoicing at the act of praise. When we sing and praise in the face of adversity, the adversity will soon disappear. This is not a promise or idle talk. This is a universal law.

# 192

## The Law of Prayer

Prayer is a conscious concrete effort to communicate with the consciousness of life and its Creator and so we speak to God. Prayer is also an aligning cleansing process opening up our inner selves to the source of all life and demonstrating that we are anxious for enlightenment and guidance. In prayer we speak to God, to the higher Power, but more often than not, unfortunately, we do not wait long enough to hear a reply. It has been known that a community joined in intense prayer has produced miracles. Prayer is the forerunner to meditation.

Meditation is the freeing and emptying of ourselves of obstacles that hinder communication and allow us to channel the life force, spiritually, mentally and physically. Meditation is the attunement of our physical, emotional and mental bodies to the spiritual source. In meditation, correctly aligned and unobstructed, the creative forces of God can rise along both the spiritual and physical channels in our bodies, and are disseminated through our sensitive spiritual chakras. It is in meditation that we can meet the Divine within the temple of our own body.

It is only through the practice of meditation that one can get to know oneself, to gain control of the self, to develop virtues and spiritual qualities. There are certain conditions that have to be met before one can begin to meditate. One must be inwardly calm and free which means, the mind must be free of all mundane daily occupation. Certain preparations are also necessary, for example allocating a certain place and a specific time for the meditation. Lighting incense or a candle helps to cleanse and to focus the energy to make it easier for one to relax in preparation. It helps when this meditation corner, if possible at all, is reserved specifically for the purpose of meditation so that energies remain pure and accumulate to enhance the meditation process.

Preparing yourself for meditation you relax and free yourself in body mind and emotions until you have achieved the feeling of having escaped from the prison of every day life. As you free yourself, in time you begin to feel something inside you growing, expanding and the divine flow rising within you. When you have felt this you will begin to be convinced that the soul is a reality, that the divine world exists and countless creatures inhabit this world. When you can achieve this stage then you begin to feel your faculties obeying you. It feels as if every cell of your body is ready to conform. This is precisely the goal of an initiate, to win obedience of his inner world. If we want to meditate we have to understand the nature of the psychic world. Meditation is a psychological and philosophical question. Spiritual work is not achieved through the intellect alone. Every single cell of your whole body should be involved as well as your emotional and mental body. Meditation should be enjoyed, it should not be a duty nor forced. Meditation must become a need in you, in your mind, in your heart as well as in your will. You should look forward to those moments when you can immerse yourself in eternity and drink the elixir of immortal life.

See also the law of Meditation.

## 193

## The Law of the Present Moment

Time does not exist. What we know as past and future have no reality except in our own mental fabrication. The idea of time is a convention of thought and language, a human social agreement. The truth is we have only this one present moment. The *now* moment.

We keep the past alive when we hold a regret with our thoughts and feelings. We keep it alive when we cannot detach ourselves from an unpleasant past experience. We keep the past alive with our memories. The same is with the future. When we feel anxiety about the future and make it come alive through our imagination. We imagine what could and would happen if this or that happened, none of which is real. Time is an abstract concept.

In practicing remembrance that the here and now is all we have our present moments improve and become moments of quality.

It is very easy to become preoccupied, in the rush of our daily life, with our opinions and desires that we forget to pay attention to what is really important. Our awareness of the magnificence of the present moment is often given very little attention as we chase after our ambitions and goals and the pursuit is never ending, as our ego is never satisfied. Of course we must have concern for ourselves and our material needs; of course we must have plans and set goals but when the ego becomes obsessed with desires that we loose sight of what is important to us, losing our true nature in the process, then we have lost our awareness of the Divine Presence.

Most human beings live mostly unaware of the privilege of life and therefore are unthankful to the Giver of life. To see the grace of God we must open our eyes and raise our heads from our little world, then we will see, to the right and left, above and below, before us and behind us, the Grace of God reaching us in abundance from all around us. As long as we remain buried in our own little world full of problems or pleasures we remain blind to the abundance of the universe.

Many things in life are intoxicating, but if we are in touch with the nature of life we realize that there is nothing more intoxicating than our life itself. We can see the truth of this when we think of our life yesterday or last year and compare with today. All our happiness and unhappiness, our riches and poverty in the past are like a dream, only today counts. And our future itself depends on what we do and how live this moment now. When we spend the many 'now' moments lamenting, being angry or negative we are sowing unhappy seeds for our future. With every moment we live 'now' we are creating our future.

# 194

# The Law of Privacy

This is a divine law that states that every person old and young, black, yellow or white, king or beggar is entitled to the sanctity of their own privacy. It is against this law to infringe on this right of individual privacy. Included in this infringement would be such things as mind reading without the person's consent or questioning their motives or thoughts concerning their personal lives without their consent.

Just think how often this law is violated individually and collectively and just how many individuals both young and old are robbed of their sense for privacy. Privacy is a part of becoming an independent person. When personal space, private thoughts and feelings are infringed upon personal freedom and progress is denied to the individual.

# 195

## The Law of Process

This law is about our individual awareness that we have things to accomplish in our life. If we wish to reach a certain goal, we must set a direction and create order, prepare well and proceed in small but sure steps. Any achievement can be managed in addition. This law brings to our attention that skipping a single step or taking a short cut often results in failure. Also included in this law is the knowing to appreciate the accomplishment of a step toward a goal.

We all experience the process of life in many ways. Some of us are so focused on accomplishing that we are too busy to take time off for vacations or rest, and we have so much to do that we have no time to spend with family or friends. Some of us accomplish and make a point of taking time off to relax and take a vacation before we go on with the process to achieve another goal. Some others are more in touch with their intuition and accomplish goals that their feminine intuitive side has communicated and they implement this vision in the physical world by taking action with their masculine energy. They are usually supported by family and friends with whom they are more than happy to share their joy.

The way we process life to achieve is as different as we all differ in character. What is more important is how we process when we meet with disillusionment, discouragement, frustration and failures. It is at such times that it is important for us to keep going, not to feel discouraged and not to give up.

*Cosmic and Universal Laws*

Those who are able to keep their faith, who have understanding and patience with themselves, and who honor the process they are in, who are persistent to continue until they have reached their goal, are those who become shining examples and inspire everyone around them.

# 196

## The Law of Productivity

This law states that turning the energy of our thoughts and of our work into a physical product is the process of productivity. Productivity brings growth and rewards. We take steps in our life to manifest our thoughts towards our goals. When we take those steps the universe will always take many more steps, to meet us. The universal energy does not like idleness. The more effort we make, the more productive we are, the more the universe will be on our side to help us in the process.

## 197

### The Law of Progress

Everything in nature is either progressing or regressing. Nothing stands still. It is the basis of the phenomenon of sensation, which is the key to this solar system of love, our system being a 'son of necessity' or 'desire.'

This law is the working out into manifestation of the informing consciousness of a part of the Deva kingdom and of certain pranic energies. This law governs both the vegetable kingdom and the Deva kingdom. It is the basis of the phenomenon of sensation, which is the key to this solar system of love our system being that of desire.

In practical terms, there are two methods of progress, one is the right one and the other is wrong. The wrong way is when a man, unhappy by present conditions, desiring to bring down everyone to his own level, pulls down any other who seems to be a threat to him, by being famous or superior in his profession. This is a wrong idea of equality. Imagine a piano with all the keys sounding the same note, it would be impossible to play a tune.

The tendency in our times is to try to pull down another who is on a higher level instead of rising to the place where the other is. It takes a long time to create, to construct, to build, but it takes only a moment to destroy. It is the rising high that is difficult, to climb a mountain for example, the walking down the slope is the easiest part. Most people seem to seek the path of least resistance, they have no desire or will power, no patience or perseverance to strive

*Cosmic and Universal Laws*

to rise to higher achievements, so out of resentment and envy, or in order to feel better about themselves, they seek to pull down others down to their own level, under the banner of equality.

The right way is to give equal opportunity to each individual to rise and progress to his or her own highest ideal, whatever that may be, the best way they can.

# 198

# The Law of Projection

The law of Projection states that the film that projects, depicts and creates the events of one's life story, is stored within one's consciousness, and can only be changed from within.

The intimate conversations, attitudes and the relationship one has within one's own consciousness, is reflected in experiences on the outer screen of life; one is both the camera and projector of his life story. Those who wish to see a world premier of new and joyous experiences instead of reruns, trash films, soap operas, tragedies, illness and hostilities, must refuse to bring or to allow such films, concepts or images to enter their theatres or be filled into their storage banks. Those who seek out, allow, enjoy filming such trash do surely fill their cameras with the material that may eventually become part of their outward life.

Those who allow only the highest, clearest and the best thoughts, ideas, words, experiences and images to enter their studio shall create and project films that show a life of joy and art. This law gives us something to reflect on. As environment and experiences influence our consciousness level, this law reminds us to be aware of what we expose ourselves to and what we allow to enter into our consciousness.

# 199

## The Law of Prophecy

The only true future that exists is the desire or will of the Source of all Creation that none shall be lost and that the future is happening, unfolding in the 'I AM' now.

Sacred geometry is an aspect, a manifestation of God's love. People who are able to tune into the Akashic records and into the Universal Consciousness are sometimes using sacred geometry to draw a line from the supposed past, present and to the future. The ability to use sacred geometry comes with the raising of vibration Akasha for the good of another or self. When reading the energy going to the future of people on earth, one must keep in mind that this energy changes from moment to moment.

While those powerful prophets of old were correct in their time and some of what they said has held to present day, much of the prophecies have lost relevancy. Just by hearing prediction, we change the outcome to some degree.

Spiritual Prophets appeared and taught for whatever community or group of people they were born into, and prophesied the coming of the next Teacher, to continue with the Message until its fulfillment. Prophets did not come to give different messages but to correct the corruption and the misinterpretations made of the messages given in the past by its followers, also to revive principles in order to suit the evolution of the period. Man has ignorantly quarreled about the names and forms of Masters, Prophets, traditions, principles, forgetting that they are one in that which unites them. Their messages differ from one another in their outer appearance only, as each message is given in accordance with the age of man's evolution, to suit the country where the message was given, the climate, the customs, language, manners and requirements of the area and its people.

## 200

## The Law of Prosperity

The law of Prosperity states that one prospers in direct proportion to the enjoyment one receives in seeing the prosperity of oneself and others. And that one's prosperity is denied in direct proportion to one's feeling of guilt for being prosperous, or at the envy and hostility one feels on witnessing other's prosperity.

This law states that when one prospers all may prosper. The law of Prosperity works for those who hold images, feelings, actions, dialogue and attitudes associated with beauty, joy, love and prosperity. It works against those who hold images, feelings, actions, dialogues and attitudes associated with ugliness, self-pity, complaints, envy and hostility toward oneself or any other person, group, race, or class.

Those who think, feel, act and speak of themselves as being poor and needy must spend three times the energy for the same prosperity received by those who think, feel, act and speak of themselves as being wealthy and prosperous. An attitude that dwells in depression leads to the way of physical, spiritual, mental, social and financial depression. Those who maintain prosperous attitudes, even in states of poverty, are foreign to such states and will not be allowed to remain out of place in those poverty situations, but will instead be deported to those prosperous states where such prosperous attitudes belong.

What we desire manifests only when we release any thoughts, words, deeds, intent, motive and actions to the contrary. Prosperity is our birthright and needs no justification. Additionally we may keep in prosperity only that which we are willing to surrender and are assisting others to manifest also.

The mind may be likened to a garden, it can be intelligently cultivated or neglected to run wild, whether intelligent or wild it will and it must give fruit. If no useful seeds [thoughts] are sown, then it will produce an abundance of useless weeds [results]. Just as a gardener tends to his garden, keeping it free from weeds, so must a man tend to his mind, cultivate it, to keep it from useless, negative and impure thoughts. Every person is where he is by the law of his being, and by his thoughts, which have developed his character and have brought him to where he is. In the arrangement of his life there is no element of chance. Everything is the result of a law, which cannot err. This is just as true of those who feel out of harmony with their life and surroundings as of those who are happy and content with where they are. The soul attracts that which it secretly harbors, that which it loves, and also that which it fears.

Every thought seed that is allowed to enter and to take root in our mind produces sooner or later its own blossoms with acts. Good thoughts bear good fruits and bad thoughts produce bad fruits. The outer world of circumstances shapes itself to the inner world of our own thoughts. We do not attract to us that what we want, but that which we are. We cannot improve our circumstances if we are not willing to improve ourselves. We cannot directly choose our circumstances, but we can choose our thoughts. When we are prepared to alter our thoughts, we will be astonished at the rapid transformation in the materials conditions of our life.

## 201

## The Law of Purification

This is about purifying the self to gain contact to the higher spiritual world. A clean radiant aura is essential to draw those helpful godly elements near to you. Purifying your emotional body of all irritation, anger, fear and all other such negative lower emotional traits, developing soul qualities instead such as love, generosity, courage, integrity, patience, etc. Purifying the mental body of all the negative dark thoughts such as revenge, criticism, envy, hate, jealousy, etc. which keep you chained down to the lower plane, and instead observing and being aware of the quality of your thoughts, your speech and your actions. Purifying the physical body by leading a healthy lifestyle, keeping a nourishing fresh diet of fruits, vegetables, grains and nuts rather than meat and dead food, purifying your environment by being aware of your surroundings and of the company you keep.

Music and in particular singing gives us the conditions most conducive to the purification and embellishment of our physical, emotional and mental bodies.

Every spiritual journey inevitably begins with a self- purification process. The real purity is keeping the heart pure from feelings that disturb the rhythm of the mind and thus upset the spirit. Feelings have a greater power than thoughts. Life rightly and honestly lived has inner struggles, but by adding to it feelings that disturb life's tranquility one only adds to one's trouble in life, which then become endless. The main thing to remember is that the soul is pure and it cannot bear the lack of purity without feeling restless. The spirit has a tune and rhythm and when it is out of tune and rhythm, one becomes miserable. No riches in the world can compensate for the peace that the soul seeks. Without peace life is worthless. The eyes are the mirrors of the soul, they say, and focused in the center of the heart. The heart bears impressions, beautiful or ugly, this is mirrored upon the center of the head, and so it is reflected accordingly in the face, especially in the eyes. Purity of the heart causes it to expand, and the lack of purity makes it narrow. The pure hearted may seem to think or do simple things, and yet there is beauty and charm in everything that they do because there is nothing more attractive than life itself. For the pure at heart all is pure, therefore, their presence makes all pure.

See also the law of Sound.

## 202

## The Law of Radiation

This law comes into activity in connection with the highest specimens of the various kingdoms and governs the radioactivity of minerals, the radiation of the vegetable kingdom and perfumes. Smell is the highest of the purely physical senses. It is the outer effect produced by all forms in all kingdoms when their internal activity has reached such a stage of vibratory activity that the confining walls of the form no longer form a prison, but permit the liberation of the subjective essence.

Liberations means the ability of any conscious atom to pass out of one sphere of energized influence into another of a higher vibration of a larger and wider expanse of conscious realization.

## 203

## The Law of Reality

The law of Reality is that law which is measured by empirical formulae, which are set up in relation to dimension. If an object can be seen, can be heard, can be measured, can be felt, then this object is said to have reality. This is a measurable idea, something in the dimension of time as well as the dimension of energy and the dimension of form.

# 204

## The Law of Rebirth

The law of Rebirth is a natural law on our planet and is a process of progressive development enabling the human to move forward to spiritual perfection and intelligent perception to become a member of the kingdom of God.

This law is established and carried forward under the law if Evolution and is related to and conditioned by the law of Cause and Effect. It accounts for the differences among men and in connection with Karma it accounts for the differences in attitudes and circumstances of life. The law of Rebirth comes into activity upon the soul plane and incarnation is motivated and directed from the soul level, upon the mental plane.

It is under the law of Rebirth that man slowly develops the mind to control the emotions to reveal the soul, at which point the man begins to thread the Path of Return and orients himself gradually, after many lives, to the Kingdom of God. when the man has a state where he has a development mentality, wisdom, practical service, understanding and has learned to ask nothing for the separated self and renounces desire for life in the three worlds he is freed from the law of Rebirth. At this point he is group conscious. All souls incarnate and re-incarnate under the law of Rebirth.

This law, when understood correctly, will do much to solve the problems of sex and marriage and other relationships. It will create a person who treads more carefully on the path of life as each life is an assuming of ancient obligations. Each life is not only a summary of life experience, but also the unfolding of awareness, a recovery of old relations, an opportunity for the paying of old indebtedness, a chance to make restitution and progress, an awakening of deep seated qualities and recognition of old friends and enemies. Each life is the solution of revolting injustices and the explanation of that which conditions man and woman and makes them what they are.

It is possible for the man to break the wheel of rebirth consciously to bring about his own liberation.

According to ancient scriptures it is our desires that keep us chained to the Wheel of Rebirth. It is our cravings that make us drown in the sea of rebirth. For us to rise above and liberate ourselves from the cycle of rebirth we need to develop our higher awareness, to develop our higher minds and attain wisdom. Some souls who have managed to attain this freedom volunteer of their own accord to be reborn to return to our world in order to help humanity. These brave souls have courage and compassion choose to willingly suffer the cycle of rebirth to work toward the salvation of all beings.

See also the law of Consciousness.

## 205

## The Law of Rebound

The law of Rebound concerns the right of one to come out of a negative situation stronger and bolder and with more soul growth than previously experienced. This has been used as an example in stories since the beginning of mankind. Traumatic situations create the need for rebound, and the soul then often seeks these negative occurrences to give self a leap in faith. This law works in this way too. If we take a ball and throw it against the wall and if we do not step aside it will bounce back and hit us.

This law is closely related to the law of Karma. Karma is a natural law of the mind, just as gravity is a law of matter. Karma is not fate, for man acts with free will, creating his own destiny. Karma literally means 'deed or act' and more broadly names the universal principle of cause and effect, action and reaction, which governs all life on earth. Karma refers to the totality of our actions and reactions in this life and in previous lives, all of which determine our future. The conquest of karma lies in intelligent action and impartial reaction. Not all karmas rebound immediately. Some accumulate and return unexpectedly in this or other future births.

# 206

## The Law of Receiving

It is said, 'It is more blessed to give than to receive' and 'as you freely give you freely receive.' This law cannot proceed to supply our needs without a pattern to work with. Many would say, 'well, after I get, then I will give.' But the law works differently. If you want to receive good you must first give some good to build upon. You give and according to what you give you receive back. Some people say, 'well, I do give and sometimes until it hurts, but I seldom see any sign of return.' There is a right way and wrong way to give. There is careless impulsive giving and there is careful, scientific giving.

When we give impulsively we are retarding progress, we are wasting our substance. Where we give to one who doesn't put forth the effort to help himself we need not expect a good return. Nature does not support a parasite or a loafer, but she gives her energy to the ones who are struggling forward. Nature lets the parasite and the loafer see that she will help if they put forth the effort to help themselves. But with us, if we support a loafer in what he is in, how can we expect any good returns? It is more likely that the loafer becomes more arrogant and demanding for more and more relief, until we wonder where and when it will end.

After we give, our next step is to prepare to receive the response or results of our giving and to receive, as the law states, 'good measure, pressed down, shaken together, and running over.' This is the exciting part, because our preparation shows our active faith.

*Cosmic and Universal Laws*

Instead of rocking and waiting, we are prepared and working. This in turn, enlarges our view. It stimulates our interest; it disperses our doubt and fear, and energizes our power of reception. The key to this law is that we are continually drawing into life what we give and expect. Therefore our actions and intent whether well thought out or careless will have an effect on what we receive.

# 207

# The Law of Reconciliation

The law of Reconciliation allow those things which are normally in conflict to become harmonious in relationship to one another. The law of Reconciliation is that which finds in different qualities unifying similarities that allow these differences to be brought together; to accept the unifying qualities and diminish the differences, so that the differences in the qualities become less clashing and conflicting and the unifying qualities become more binding.

This is to reconcile, to find common denominators in things that are normally seen as separate, and to emphasize and exaggerate and promote those common denominators, thus allowing the differences to fade away, or fall into proper alignment. We can apply this law in our daily personal and professional relationships, by making it your custom to look for the common denominator, to find common interests so that you can get along with someone, rather than to concentrate on the differences that exist. It is all a matter of changing your perspective.

Open another window to look out from to get a different point of view of the world.

# 208

## The Law of Reflection

'As above, so below.' Like a mirror the universe reflects back that which shines forth into it. On a practical level this also manifests in all our relationships. If we meet someone who reflects to us characteristics that we think we have or would like to have then we approve of this person. If the person reflects to us characteristics that we have that we dislike in ourselves or pretend not to have, then we feel an immediate dislike to the person. So next time you feel an immediate like or dislike reflect on why you feel that way.

On another level, we can also think of this law as the world reflecting back to us like a mirror, the energies and the images that we send to the world.

# 209

## The Law of Reincarnation

Reincarnation once agreed upon must play out to its natural conclusion unless one submits to the universal law of Planning to change its course. Reincarnation is not mandatory but the optional process once begun, will run its course.

This law applies to the greatest majority of those of us in the physical world. In other words, the soul chooses the situation to be born into, and the parents, in accordance with the lessons the soul has to learn. One of the reasons why a soul re-incarnates is to continue the perfection process upon the earth, another is to satisfy some unfulfilled desire. But the most important reason is the will and knowledge of the Plan. The main incentive is sacrifice and service, to those lesser lives that are dependent upon the higher inspiration of the spiritual soul. Contrary to general belief, it is usually group rebirth that is taking place all the time and incarnation of the individual is occasional in comparison.

In eastern religions the concept of reincarnation dates back to beyond antiquity. The ancient Egyptian religion believed in transmigration of the soul, which is the reason why they embalmed the body. Hindus and the Druids believed in reincarnation. Both Plato and Pythagoras thought the soul to be immortal and merely resides in the body, survives physical death and goes through a series of rebirth. Christ spoke of reincarnation and early Christianity embraced reincarnation for three hundred years. In Saint Gregory's words, Bishop of Nyssa: 'It is absolutely necessary that the soul

## Cosmic and Universal Laws

shall be healed and purified, and if it doesn't take place in one life on earth, it must be accomplished in future earthly lives.' When the Roman Emperor Constantine recognized the Church, reincarnation was repudiated because of the eschatological teachings of death and judgement which were established as orthodox Christian doctrine, i.e. that man has just one life in which to merit his eternal reward or damnation. Such a doctrine gave more power to the Church over the believers. To many, reincarnation is taught by nature herself. Just as the earth is renewed so is the spirit or soul, which knows no death.

See also the law of Cyclic Returns, the law of Rebirth, the law of Karma and the law of the Soul.

# 210

## The Law of Relativity

This awareness indicates that the law of Relativity is but the relationship of all things understood by the particular viewpoint from which they are seen. As the experience continues, greater awareness and the desire for more understanding increases. The entity, the force, the man then begins to probe into the nature of those forces outside of its own control and understanding. As this occurs, this awareness indicates, the quality of reason, the rational approach begins to develop.

This awareness also indicates as the viewpoint shifts, the relative relationship of those things also becomes different. As an example a train moving at a particular rate of speed, in relation to an entity standing beside the tracks, is somewhat different from the rate of speed of another train passing in the opposite direction, or of an automobile travelling in the same direction as the train. It all depends, on where we stand in life and from which window we are looking through, and how we feel at that particular moment. Each viewpoint is relative, and each is accurate, and yet the description will be totally different.

In the same sense the law of Absolute tells us that there is only love in the universe. Nothing else exists but love. There is no evil. But in order to know and experience love we humans on this planet have created evil. We created evil so that we can have a comparison between good and evil in order for us to experience love.

## 211

## The Law of Relaxation

In many cases the laws of mind are the reverse of the laws of matter. On the physical plane usually the more effort we make the more we achieve, for example the harder we hit a nail the quicker it will go into a piece of wood. It does not work like that on the mental plane. The moment you force something on the mental plane you create tension and when tense the mind cannot be creative. On the physical plane the quicker you walk or run the quicker you reach your destination. On the mental plane the more effort you make the less your result will have. You cannot force your mind to work faster because you will only create a mental block. You stop the creative energies flowing. You need to relax to let the energies flow freely so your mind can be creative. The idea is that you need to be relaxed but alert in all your mental work, unhurried and quiet, but focused, because effort defeats itself. All creative people are aware of this law and the way it operates.

In the same way this law of relaxation applies for meditation and spiritual work. Without learning the art of relaxation it is impossible to meditate and to grow spiritually.

# 212

## The Law of Release

You are bound to that which you do not release and let go. Release that which is holding you down, let it go. Release it to the Higher Power to be released in minute, benign particles disseminating into the infinite universe.

Release of useless desires opens the way for greater love. The more we give love the more love we will receive. The release of love to others leads to a tenfold increase of love in our lives. This law of Release states that we cannot keep it unless we give it away, no matter what 'it' is. All that is, belongs to all who are. Personal possessions is a myth. One of the hardest things for us to do is to let go. Let go of old relationships or situations when they have stagnated and served their purpose.

The juggler in a circus is a good example of how to let go. Without having the confidence and the trust of letting go, being flexible, creating a balanced rhythm, it would be impossible for him to juggle three, four or ten balls or rings. This law demands that we learn to let go, to give, to reach of ourselves into and to interact with our fellow humans and environment.

See also the law of Affinity.

# 213

## The Law of Repetition

Everything created repeats itself every large cycle includes in its earlier stages, all the lesser, and repeats the earlier procedure. One good example is the human physical body. The foetus reproduces all earlier stages and forms until the human is achieved. Everything in life repeats itself. This is a law of nature.

On another level, the mystics teach that in repetition lies the secret of power. Great importance is given by the mystics, to the number of repetitions, for numbers are a science and every number of repetitions has a certain value. One repetition means one thing and a few more mean something quite different, as in medicine one grain of a drug may heal and ten may destroy life. These words are given by saints, sages and prophets who have come inspirationally from God. In them when repeated, is all blessing and the mystery of how to acquire all that the soul desires in life.

# 214

## The Law of Repulse

This is also known as the law of all destroying angels, and its symbol is an angel with a flaming sword, turning in all directions. It is the angel guarding the treasure, driving man forth in search of another way of entrance, thus forcing him through the cycle of rebirth until he finds the portal of initiation.

# 215

## The Law of Repulsion

In a similar manner, the law of repulsion can be stated this way. As you seek, you repel, at the same time you are repelled by that which does not fulfill your search. You have created whatever exists in your life or is happening to you at this time. Through the laws of attraction and repulsion, coupled with your deep desires, you have brought that creation into your life to fulfill your present needs and desires, consciously or subconsciously.

# 216

## The Law of Respect

The Law of Respect is that principle of looking twice, or more precisely, looking twice as deeply for respect goes far beyond the surface appearance and superficial glances to discover a deeper meaning, purpose or basis for discovery.

Without the principle of respect, the 'Book of Love' will never be read, the 'Tree of Life' will never be seen in full bloom, and the thousands of rainbows of the 'Land of Essence' will never be viewed. But with the law of Respect in action, the mysteries of the universe, or any part, will open layer after layer, like the unfolding of a thousand petal lotus.

This law demands that we live with respect for life itself, respect for our own self and every other being, for all of God's creations, for mother earth and all nature.

In the Bible it says, love ye one another, with that is meant you show respect for those with whom you come in contact with. You cannot love if you do not respect. The higher civilization and the culture of people, the greater degree of consideration, courtesy and politeness is shown by its people to one another. Some people wrongly believe that to be polite and to show courtesy is a sign of servitude whereas the truth is far from this belief. One who is courteous, polite, who shows unprejudiced genuine respect to others, is someone who shows thoughtfulness and concern thereby demonstrating oneself as a highly cultured and civilized human being. Above all this behavior shows that one has respect for the self.

The standards of respect never change, they are constant and international, they know no boundaries of culture, age, gender, race or color.

# 217

## The Law of Respiration

Breath is the beginning and the end. Our life begins with our first breath and ends with our last breath and the mystery of life is to be found in respiration. Respiration is breathing in and out, contraction and expansion. Everything breathes, the Cosmos breathes, our earth breathes, oceans, stars, stones, trees and animals breathe. All breathe in their own way having their own rhythm.

Respiration has a paramount importance in the life of every spiritualist. Ancient Indian Yogis and Sages have studied respiration in detail and state that the rhythm of breath when in harmony with the rhythm of earth can facilitate communication with certain parts of the spiritual world.

Regular breathing exercises will improve your health. Each individual has his own rhythm which he must find by listening to the inner doctor. Breathe slowly and rhythmically, focusing all your attention on the air coming into your lungs. Think of all the elements that it is bringing you for the benefit of your breath. When you draw air into your lungs, you must do so in the conscious conviction that you are receiving divine blessings with every breath you inhale.

Breathing is also very important for the functioning of the brain and you should get into the habit of taking few deep breaths several times a day, to purify your blood which then supplies your brain with the elements it needs to function at its best. As you breathe out think that you are expanding to the very outer limits

*Cosmic and Universal Laws*

of the universe and as you breathe in again you withdraw inwards into the point at the center of an infinite circle. As you expand and contract you will discover the 'ebb and flow' which is the key to all the rhythms of the universe. When you become conscious of this movement within your own being, you enter into the harmony of the cosmos and thus establish a relationship, breathing in elements from space and breathing out a part of your heart and soul into space. The one who knows how to harmonize himself, with the respiration of the cosmos enters into the sphere of divine consciousness.

See also the law of Inverse Proportions.

# 218

## The Law of Responsibility

The law of Responsibility states that one entity or more working in a manner that is responsive to the needs of many does receive energy from those many. The ability to respond to the needs of others allows that responsive entity energy from all those who await that response. This relates to the law of Co-Creation, yet it is somewhat different, for one being who is greatly responsive can have the power of 144 whose energies are simply utilized for their own personal interest.

It was the Creator's idea to separate, to give our soul existence. It was our idea to go away from God into materiality with the original purpose of profound and speedy soul growth. There are some souls who have experienced, to some degree, soul loss. God is responsible for us through love and we are responsible to become or reclaim this Divine Love. Once we establish the limits and boundaries of our responsibility, we can take full charge of that which is our duty and let go of that which is not. We find more enjoyment supporting others as we create more harmonious cooperative relationships by understanding that which falls within our realm of responsibility.

Under this law we understand a person's need to over cooperate to such an extent that one becomes co-dependent—the condition which is obsessive focus on other peoples' lives. This law reminds us to respect our internal values and find our own point

*Cosmic and Universal Laws*

of balance. We are unfailingly responsible for every one of our thoughts, words, deeds, intents, motives and actions.

## 219

### The Law of Revelation

God's divine plan is guaranteed to be revealed to those who have been prepared to and have agreed to receive it. In other words nothing is secret. All is there for us to know, if we want to know.

## 220

## The Law of Rhythm

Everything flows, out and in, in and out and through. Everything has its tides, all things rise and fall, the pendulum swing manifests in everything, the measure of the swing to the right is the measure of the swing to the left. Rhythm compensates. This principle, on the physical plane, is the most visible of all principles and its powers are observed within the forces of nature, which move the waves and tides of our oceans and the continuous changes of the seasons. It is observed in the continuous cycles of life and death and the rebirth of all things, a constant creation and destruction of suns, worlds, and galaxies and in the rise and fall of governments and nations. On the plane of energy it is observed in the behavior of the alternating current wave of electricity, light and heat as it vibrates between the positive and negative pole. Rhythm on the mental plane is experienced, as the wide mood swings displayed in human nature from extremes of happiness or sadness, gentle or violent.

Rhythm is the law of compensation and maintains the equilibrium in all things. It returns to us what we measure out in life. There is no escape from the immutable law. The law holds true whether we believe or not and compensates us accordingly. All of nature follows this law. Rhythm perpetuates the phenomenon of time. There is a time for everything. The pendulum, like swing of the rhythm is immutable, and we can only counteract its backward swing by mentally polarizing ourselves in a desirable position on the scale of life. It requires a dedicated personal commitment to cultivate the unknown within all of us, in order to cause a quantum leap in the evolutionary process of life with all its aches and pains. This is a mental art that is known to hierophats, adepts and masters of all ages.

We will fulfill this law one way or another. We either use the law to our advantage or we become its subject. The door of universal law swings in all directions. The final result depends on what we have chosen to believe and whether or not our belief system allows us to see the truth as it really is. If we do not want to know, or we do not care to make an effort, then we will evolve through the standard process of evolution.

Nothing can, or is allowed to stand still in life. All manifestation is the result of active energy producing certain results, and expenditure of energy in any one direction will necessitate an equal expenditure in an opposite direction. Everything flows in rhythm. Rhythm is a spiritual reality. To observe this law, go to the beach during the change of tides and observe the tide coming in. Observe the waves coming in then out, then in again and out again in perfect rhythm and harmony. In life we need to establish our own rhythm, a time to work and a time to rest. When we don't do that we end up exhausted and with a burn out since every day will be more pushing. Listen to the rhythm of life and the best way to achieve all you want to achieve is to dance with the rhythm of life.

There is a time for everything.

# 221

## The Law of Right Human Relations

This law helps us define limits of our behavior control with others in the third dimension which is the world of illusion. This is a world where we think the unreal is real. Everything is within us. Let no one assume to forcibly teach, counsel or guide another by force. This means, give no advice that is not called for. Uncalled for advice makes the receiving party feel wrong and lousy and that is against our nature of feeling good about ourselves. While each teacher is in a manner a director, the individual person may only be a means not a way of life. A strong action may promote refusal and achieve rejection, or it may encourage one to become dependent on another's will. By not searching for excellence within, one refuses the gifts already there but not recognized or realized. We achieve greater results in our relationships with others by our own fine example and also by listening. People answer their own questions if given enough opportunity. The only real control we ever have and need to have is with the self.

The sufi thinks that man was not created to live the life of an angel nor was he created to live the life an animal. The sufi thinks that the first thing that is necessary for man in life is to prove to his own conscience to what extent he can be human. It is not only a spiritual development, it is the future of humanity, in what relation man stands to his neighbor or friend, to those who depend upon him and those who look up to him; to strangers unknown to him and how he stands with those younger than himself or older people; with those who like him and others who dislike and criticize him. He should feel, think and act throughout life and yet keep on progressing towards the goal, which is the goal for every soul in the world. When a man cannot understand himself, when he cannot understand his own imagination and his own problems deeply, then he cannot understand the problems of others and where there is no understanding there is no communication between one person and another.

The law of Right Human Relations and the principle of goodwill are concerned with the welfare of others and with world peace. The principle of goodwill is the basic intention to do goodwill. We can will good to promote right human relations. We can use a complete thought form built by the balanced fusion of thought, feelings, imagination, visualization and will. There are tools we can use to create a complete thought form, concentration, repetitive affirmations, contemplation, creative visualization and meditation.

# 222

## The Law of Right to One's Space

This is an aspect of the free will but another law of its own. Everyone is entitled to make decisions for one's self, decide the belief system one feels comfortable with and generally create the life that will allow one to fulfill his or her own birth vision.

This is having the right to one's own space, to live one's own life, allowing for parental direction to the developing young person. Over protective or controlling parents, friends and even dictators have impeded this law and right since almost the inception of mankind.

In accordance with this law no one has the right to influence or infringe on someone else's space and life.

# 223

## The Law of Ritual and Ceremony

The law of Ritual has to do with the importance of ceremonial ritual as a protective safeguard to the etheric body. The health of the physical body is dependent on the health of the etheric body. Signs of ill health begin with the etheric body and when this is neglected manifest eventually in the physical body. Medical science does not recognize this fact as yet. Through ceremonial rituals with colors, smells and sound vibrations we can heal and/or maintain the etheric body.

Rituals and ceremonies are an important part of our life as we celebrate all meaningful occurrences and special dates in history, births, marriages, deaths and other. The use of candles, incense, offerings, gifts, prayers, songs, dances, all have their meaning, place and time. We have lost much in our modern times, unfortunately, as we tend to belittle all old rituals and ceremonies as having no meaning and beliefs are taken as superstition.

To mark certain special occasions in one's life through ritual and ceremony shared with loved ones and friends who add to the positive joyful energies activates the elements and entities in the universe to work with us on the psychic level and to bless the event. Throughout the ages rituals and ceremonies have been important to mankind and this continues to be so today.

# 224

# The Law of Sacrifice

The law of Sacrifice is one of the seven laws of the solar system. This law determines the nature of each kingdom. Each kingdom is meant to be a laboratory wherein are prepared the various forms of nutrition which are needed for the building of the more evolved and refined structures. So the plant world feeds from the minerals. Animals feed off the minerals and plants and the humans who are still more refined feed on all three.

For the early stage of human development it was correct and necessary for the human to feed off the animal world. But this is not the case any more. The more refined the human development is, the less need there is to feed off the animal world.

The principle of sacrifice is to be found on every level in the process of evolution. That which is lower is always sacrificed, in order to transform to that which is higher and more refined. In the human family, for example, through death the principle of life is renounced and sacrificed and returns to the reservoir of universal life.

The law of Sacrifice and the law of Compensation are closely associated, but the first to be active and to be recognized in daily living is sacrifice. Compensation comes later. Put more simply something has always to be sacrificed in order to get something else. Once can say there is a price for everything. Or, the compensation we receive is in accordance to the sacrifice we are willing to make. On a practical level for us it works in the same way on all levels. Our sacrifices would be a commitment or an investment of our time, energy and hard work for example in order to achieve a certain goal. Nothing is gained for free. In every day language we say: No pain no gain. The pain would be whatever sacrifice we choose to make.

It is important to understand that 'sacrifice' here has no relation to the word sacrifice, as humans have so far understood it to be, as in blood sacrifices and offerings of killings of humans or animals. The sacrifice meant here has absolutely nothing to do with blood shed, Divinity does not demand blood sacrifices.

See also the law of Compensation.

## 225

## The Law of Sacrifice and Death

Death is the controlling factor on the physical plane. The destruction of the form, in order that evolving life may progress, is one of the fundamental methods of evolution. This law is linked to the law of Disintegration. This controls the gradual disintegration of the form and its sacrifice to evolving life. Everything must end before something else can begin. We die everyday. Our bodily cells are replaced every single day. Every day we become more and more divine than the day before.

See also the law of Sacrifice, and the law of Disintegration.

# 226

## The Law of Schools

This law also known as the law of Love and Light is primarily applicable to all units of divine life who have arrived at, or transcended the stage of self-consciousness. It consequently deals with the human kingdom. It is the law that enables one to unite two of one's aspects, the personal self with the Higher Self. It is the law, which governs the transition of the human atom the physical, into another and a higher kingdom. It is the law of the perfected human that when comprehended enables man to enter into a new cycle.

Mankind is now at a stage where a number of units are ready to come under the specific influence of this law and thus to be transformed out of the Hall of Learning, via the Hall of Wisdom into the fifth Spiritual Kingdom.

This law concerns the great experiment, inaugurated on earth by our planetary Logos in connection with the process of Initiation, and does not concern all members of the human family, some of which will achieve initiation slowly, under the basic law of Evolution. As there are various planetary schemes, each scheme exists in order to teach a specific aspect of consciousness and each planetary school or hierarchy subjects its pupils to this law in diverse manners.

There exist five great planetary school groups: The first planetary group is known as the outer circle of initiates. Of these our earth is one; The second is the sacred planets or the seven divisions of the field of knowledge; The third planetary group is the inner round that is followed by those who have passed through the human stage and have consciously developed the faculty of etheric living and can follow the etheric cycles, functioning consciously on the three higher etheric planes in all parts of the system; The fourth planetary group is the circle of the planetoids. The fifth planetary group is the absorbing Triangles. This term is applied to the evolutionary schools found located in the three major planets of our system—Uranus, Neptune and Saturn. The rulers of these planets, chains and globes are called the Divine Examiners. This group is responsible for the work of transferring men and women from one school to another and for the expanding of the human consciousness. They are the custodians of the Path. They work with men and women who begin on the probationary path of evolution and work with them until the seventh initiation is taken.

## 227

## The Law of Seed

Everyday, we spend our energy sowing some kind of 'seed' and our 'now' sowing will, by a natural universal law, have a 'future' reaping. When we sow to satisfy our material needs to please a wicked nature disregarding the spirit within, we will reap nothing but destruction. When, however, we sow seeds to please the spirit and do good deeds, we are by law bound to reap a good harvest.

This is what we do all day long, we either plant good or bad seeds, not only with our thoughts, words and deeds but even our gestures communicate seeds. From ancient scriptures we learn that the prudent man will consider the consequences of what seed he sows i.e. his actions. He does not only see the road in front of him but also thinks about where the road might lead to. A prudent man sows spiritual seeds by being prudent, by taking precautions, by having patience and by persevering. If you want mercy for example you need to sow the seeds of righteousness.

The Bible is full of quotes about the law of Seed and Harvest. How one seed can multiply and give back thousands of seeds. Take a look at an apple tree, which might have hundreds of apples and each apple giving ten more seeds. How a seed for a flower can produce many more flowers with hundreds more seeds to plant more flowers. Nature is telling us something here. Nature is telling us that life is full of abundance, and that some seeds might never grow. So if you really want to make something happen, try more than once. Your seeds are your treasures given to you at birth, your talents, the Spirit and the Power within you.

As soon as you give back to the world a portion of what was given to you, it will be multiplied. It will be returned to you tenfold. But you need to make an effort first. If you need wisdom, ask and it shall be given freely. But ask in faith, not wavering. Because if you waver and doubt you will be like a wave of the sea driven with the wind and tossed around. Be firm, ask for what you want, do what you need to do in good faith and you can achieve anything. This might mean that you meet a hundred acquaintances to find that one special friend. We might try fifty times to get to where we want to be and still keep on trying until we get there. We might go for thirty interviews before we get that job, or talk to forty people before we sell that house or car or insurance policy. The key is never to give up but to go in good faith, planting good seeds with awareness, at every moment of our life.

# 228

## The Law of Service

The law of Service grows naturally out of the successful application of the sciences of the antahkarana and meditation, and is the governing law of the future. With the linking of soul and personality the light of the soul pours into the brain consciousness, resulting in the subordination of the lower self to the higher self. This identification produces a corresponding activity in the personal life and the activity we call service. There in lies the growth through the service of the human race, and through a cultivated self-forgetfulness.

Service is the true science of creation and is a scientific method of establishing continuity. This is also known as the law of water and of fishes. The symbol is a pitcher on the head of a man who stands in the form of a cross. This law is the governing factor of the age of Acquarius. The ray energy is outgoing energy of the sixth ray, vivifying factor. If the evasion of this law is a conscious action, there are karmic penalties. This work requires so much sacrifice of time and personal interest, requiring deliberate effort, conscious wisdom and the ability to work without attachment.

First there is service of the personality wherein one sacrifices much in the interest of one's own desires. Next comes the stage of service to humanity and finally the service to the plan. Service is the extension of your love. Serve cheerfully at work for example, as your work is your service. We go to university and learn so that we can serve more people. As you give of yourself you shall receive.

See also the law of Sacrifice and the law of Giving and the law of Love.

# 229

## The Law of Sex

This is the term applied to the force which brings about the physical merging of the two poles in connection with the human kingdom and of the animal kingdom, viewing him as responsive to the call of his and her animal nature. It concerns itself with the due guarding of the form in this particular cycle and its perpetuation. This sex force attraction is only powerful during the period of the duality of the sexes and their separation and in the case of the human will be offset by a higher expression of the law when man is again androgynous.

On the physical level, in the same manner that we eat and absorb our physical food, astral food, is absorbed by our psychic body. This means that when two people are in a deep embrace, a process of absorption takes place in the electromagnetic dimension of their beings, in their emanations, a process in which each one absorbs the weaknesses as well as the strengths of the other.

The attraction between things and beings, as well as the attraction between the sexes is all based on the law of attraction. In Sanskrit woman is called Ardhangi, the half body, half of that complete body constituted of male and female. Throughout creation each element attracts to itself its like, as a sage once said 'each element returns in time to the single goal of that element.' This law may be more clearly observed in the attraction that exists between the sexes, and is indeed, the chief reason of the attraction between these two halves, which are derived from each other.

## Cosmic and Universal Laws

Each sex is made of the element of the opposite sex, as a Sufi sage says, the female is born of the seed of the male and the male is molded in the womb of the female.

The spirit possesses the sexes in order to bring them together for its own purpose of manifestation. The harmony that exists between persons of the same sex is also accounted for by this similarity. Many religions and philosophies have considered the sex relationship to be most sacred since it is thus that the spirit manifests itself. For the same reason the sex relationship may become most sinful if this purpose of the spirit is lost to view. To disregard this purpose of the spirit is a defiance of the law of the whole mechanism which inevitably drafts the structure to ruins.

There is no time and space during sexual orgasm. Highly evolved people have no need for sex because they are in a perpetual orgasmic consciousness. An animal cannot watch itself whereas a human being can. It is a rare privilege to be born a human being. We are blessed in the world of illusion. That means we can see the world in whichever way we want it to be. As an example, you want to live a spiritual life and you think to yourself I'll do that in five years from now, then when the five years are up, you can change your mind and not live a spiritual life if you don't want to, you can put it off again till later or not at all. It is your choice.

## 230

## The Law of Silence

The law or principle of Silence is that which allows beings the space, peace and time to rest and recuperate from the noises and chatter. The silence is found within the soul, and is not limited to sound, but relates also to silence in terms of motion, emotions, feelings and inner dialogues.

The law of Silence contains also the chaos that can exist in any moment when that chaos is experienced from levels of non-resistance. There are those who chatter endlessly and sometimes without meaning. Some find it very hard when they have to be silent and so resist. It is when one can be silent and can live within, be at peace with the self that one can listen to the higher divine impressions. One also needs to put a stop to the endless meaningless chatter going on in one's head. To be more in control of one's thoughts and be aware of the quality of the constant inner dialogue that goes on in one's head.

There is a saying that words may be valuable but silence is much more precious. This saying will always prove true. The more we understand its meaning, the more we realize its truth. How many times have we disturbed the peace of our surroundings, without meaning to, by not being silent. How often have we said something that we later deeply regretted. Silence may seem empty but things are never what they seem. Silence can be a profound connection to the Divine. There is great power in silence. From a scientific point of view breath is 'prana' in the Vedanta, which is life. It is said that the breath is the chain that links body, heart and soul together, and we know the breath is of great importance to keep the body alive. It is also said of speaking being the breach of breath, meaning that when one speaks one takes ten breaths in the time, which would otherwise be normal for one breath. When silence is needed and we speak we find that we often make many mistakes and we wish we had kept silent instead.

When the lips are closed then the heart begins to speak, when the heart is silent then the soul blazes up bursting into flame and this illuminates the whole of life. The mystic realizes the power of the word yet at the same time recognizes the splendor of silence. A sincere feeling of respect needs no words, even the silence can speak of one's respectful attitude. The word uttered by the lips can only reach the ears of the hearer, but the thought proceeding from the mind reaches far, shooting from mind to mind. The vibrations of the mind are much stronger than the vibrations of words. One feeling heart can pierce the heart of another, they speak in silence, spreading out into the sphere, so that the atmosphere of a person's presence transmits thoughts and emotions. The vibrations of the soul are the most powerful and far reaching, they are like electric currents that transmit from soul to soul in an instant regardless of distance. Silence is relaxing body and mid, It is repose, a healing. It is when you are in control that you can experience an inner silence, enabling you to hear the voice of Silence, the voice of God and the music of the higher spheres.

See also the Law of Awareness, the law of Vibration, the law of Sound and the law of Breath.

## 231

## The Law of Simplicity

While the perception of complication exists in the lower mind with God all things are simple. Therefore, confusion does not exist. God is most easily understandable and such understanding is available to all.

Humans have made life so complex that whatever we seek after, we want to find it in complexity. Simplicity is the living beauty, it says in the Vedas. All things in life, which have importance, beauty and value, are simple. It is through development and refinement of one's higher faculties that one can understand this simplicity.

## 232

# The Law of Solar Evolution

This law is the sum total of all lesser activities.

When we are too wrapped up in our daily mundane life activities we lose our inner balance and we think that all these trivial activities are our whole reason for being.

The more spiritual you are, the higher your vibration is and the more excited you are and enthusiastic about life itself and so can look above the unimportant trivialities of life.

## 233

## The Law of Solar Union

This is an occult term used when the inter play of the suns is being dealt with from the material aspect and from the consciousness aspect.

The Seven Beings in the Sun are the Seven Holy Ones, Self-born from the inherent power of the matrix of Mother substance. It is they who send the Seven Principal Forces, called Rays, which at the beginning of Pralaya will center into seven new Suns for the next Manvantara.

# 234

## The Law of Soul

Matter is the vehicle for the manifestation of soul on the physical plane of existence, and soul is the vehicle on a higher plane for the manifestation of spirit. Through the use of matter the soul unfolds and finds its climax in the soul of man or woman. The individual soul is created out of spirit with an ability to have free will, to make its own choices, to have its own opinions, intelligence, imagination and creativity. Soul is eternal with no beginning and no end and this means that when a person ceases to exist on this physical level, the soul continues to exist on a higher plane. The soul is the intermediate between the personality and the spirit.

Soul consciousness lives in all that exists on earth in different grades for example, it exists at its lowest form in minerals, and at its highest, in the developed human being. We are eternally related to the souls of all men and women, and we have a definite relationship to those who reincarnate with us, who are learning with us the same lessons, who are experiencing life and experimenting with us. It is the soul in all forms, which reincarnates, choosing and building suitable physical, emotional and mental vehicles through which to learn the next needed lessons. Souls incarnate in groups cyclically under the law and in order to achieve right relations with God and their fellow humans. Progressive unfoldment, under the law of Rebirth, is largely conditioned by the mental principle, for 'as a man thinketh in his heart, so is he.'

*Cosmic and Universal Laws*

The soul is neither spirit nor matter but is the relation between them. It is the mediator and the link between God and His form. The soul is the form building aspect that drives all God's creatures forward along the path of evolution. The qualities, vibrations, colors and characteristics in all kingdoms of nature are soul qualities and these are brought into being through the interplay of the pairs of opposites, spirit and matter and their effect upon each other. The individual self, conscious soul is an integral part of the universal soul and when one has become aware of this fact one can intelligently cooperate with the will of God and work with the plan of evolution.

Humanity is an expression of two aspects of the soul, the animal and the divine, these two fused in the human being make the human soul. It is through a long struggle and the sublimation of the animal soul that the divine soul is liberated. The two qualities of the soul are serenity and joy as the man and woman know that he and she is life itself. The more we think of each other as souls and not as limited human beings, and as our love for humanity increases and love of the self decreases, the nearer we move towards the center of light, towards love and nearer towards God.

See also the law of Reincarnation, the law of Cyclic Returns, the law of Vibration and the Soul's Journey.

# 235

## The Law of Sound

Every living thing in existence has a sound. Through this knowledge changes will be brought about and new forms developed through its medium. The release of energy in the atom is linked to the science of sound. Healing with sound is profoundly effective be it vocal sounds, tuning forks or music. Sound has the power to restore people to their harmonic patterns. Chanting specific sounds and mantrams brings about great healing and raising of vibration and produces virtually unimaginable results when done with group mantric chanting. The most powerful and popular mantra known to present mankind is OM MANI PADME HUM.

Each sound, each vibration, triggers a movement in space and releases certain forces in the human. The sounds we hear produce geometrical figures within us which are real enough even if we cannot see them. The effect of sound, the vibratory energy of the waves it creates, causes myriads of minute particles in us that arrange themselves into geometrical figures. This is why when we listen to inharmonous music or very loud sounds the pre-existent structure and harmony within us, the order that was established by the Creator, is disturbed and eventually shattered causing disharmony, disease and chaos in our life.

It is said in the words of an occult manual on healing: 'He who lives under the sound of the AUM knows himself. He who lives sounding the OM knows his brother. He who knows the SOUND knows all.'

## Cosmic and Universal Laws

Music in particular singing, is a form of nourishment for the soul, which enables us to work on a spiritual level if it is done with awareness. The Logos is pure music, the harmonious sounds that fashioned the universe and sound models matter and gives it form. Under the influence of the Logos the Cherubims who reign on this level, received a divine vibration, which was communicated to all creatures below, all the way to earth. The Cherubims do nothing but sing together in harmony and when humans also try to sing in harmony they create a bond between themselves and the Cherubims, the angelic order of music and heavenly harmony. When you sing, therefore, whether you know it or not, you are establishing contact with the cherubims and the harmony of sounds causes the material particles of your body to vibrate in harmony and heal. Singing is an expression of our desire to embrace the universe, to be attuned to and in harmony with the whole.

From a spiritual Master we learn that four part choral singing is of great significance for the blending of voices and is at the same time a blending of our souls and spirits. It is a reflection of the effort we have to make every day, to bring our spirit, soul, mind and heart into a harmonious unity. The four voices, the bass, tenor, contralto and soprano, correspond to the four strings of a violin, for a violin is also a symbol of man. The G-string represents the heart, the D-string represents the intellect, the A-string represents the soul and the E-string represents the spirit. The violin itself represents the physicl body and the bow represents the 'will' that plays on the four principles—heart, mind, soul and spirit. The harmonious blending of the four voices or tones played, is a reminder that all the four principles in the human must vibrate in harmony within.

With the rhythmic in and out flow of breathing sound is produced. On the basis of this process breathing has been given the name of sound. Scriptures like the Vedas and Puranas are present in the sound and the art of singing is also based on the sound. The pattern of our breathing has a profound importance in our life. No wealth is worth more than sound and no knowledge is superior than the knowledge of the sound. Sound is like a great lamp that lights the soul.

# 236

## The Law of Speech

We are the only species on earth privileged with the Word. There is power in the spoken word. Thought forms, the blueprint for reality, and speaking power into the blueprint brings that thought to materialize into the physical world. To say something is to make it real. One ought to watch every word that one speaks.

Words are sounds and vibrations that are energy sent out in to the world. When you speak you decree to manifest that in to the material world. When we speak in anger, contempt or abuse, we cause more damage than we think because we are sending out these negative energies into the atmosphere that go far beyond our immediate environment. In a way we can pollute the environment with words spoken in anger and with foul abusive language. We all ought to think before we speak.

One spiritual Master said: 'The law of Spiritual Chemistry is the law transmuting all conditions, all vibrations, all darkness into beauty, music and light. One must learn to speak the language of the angels. One must learn to speak from the soul. The one who speaks with the lips chatters, he or she speak with an empty mind and adds confusion to discord. The one who speaks with the full mind feeds the minds of men and women. The one who speaks from the heart wins the confidence of mankind. But the one who speaks from the soul heals the heartbreaks of the world and feeds the hungry, the starving souls of mankind. The one who speaks from the soul brings light for she or he carries the light. The language of the soul is sacred and most beautiful. It is the language of the eternal spheres and the language of the Gods. It is the gift of the spirit known as the 'new tongues.' The power of transmutation is the power to contact the center of the soul through the heart. This method alone holds the power of fulfillment and perfection.'

See also the law of Change.

# 237

# The Law of Spiral Movement

Movement, change, growth succeeds in a spiral motion, souls circle the truth as souls ascend. The chakras, the energy centers in the physical body, extend from the physical body is a spiral movement.

The spiral movement repeats itself throughout creation. In nature the curve can be seen for example in the pinecone and in the cauliflower you can see a center point where the florets are smallest, organized in spirals around this center in both directions. The curve is also named to Fibanacci as the Fibonacci spiral. Pine cones show the Fibonacci spirals clearly. A spiral is a curve that winds itself round a certain point. While not being a circle, the radius will vary along the angle. We see the spiral in nature in the snail shell and the cochlea in the human ear. In the universe some of the star systems have a spiral form.

## 238

## The Law of Spirit

Spirit is the principle of increase. There is always something more to come, one experience to another experience and future conditions grow out of present conditions.

Every human being has this deep instinct within him to seek something better. Spirit is the all-penetrating power, which is the forming power of the universes and the spirit works through souls. Self-mastery simply means that a person has the ability to run his own life according to the laws of Spirit presuming of course, that the person understands the laws. The understanding of these laws comes through the Light and Sound of God as a direct infusion into the soul. The spirit has many sounds, a sound like a rushing wind, or the sound of the flute amongst many others. 'Sound' and 'Light' are twin aspects of spirit, 'the Voice of God.' When we experience the Voice of God it means we have contact with the divinity. God is 'Being' and the 'Spirit' is an extension of this 'Being' into all universes and you are the instrument spirit made flesh.

No immortal art can ever be produced by a human being, without inspiration from the spirit. No one can produce divine works of art that inspire humanity, if one is not inhabited by heavenly beings. All creators of immortal divine art are aware of the spirit that inspires them.

# 239

## The Law of Spiritual Approach

This law depicts the conscious act of a personality to create with its every thought, word and deed the ability to be the reflection of its God self. Every action is a prayer to the Creator of All. When this is done with success, the personality becomes a mirror of reflection of the God self for others to learn from and emulate. This is a walking, talking example of becoming our Higher Self.

# 240

## The Law of Spiritual Awakening

A basic level of self-control and stability is required to maintain the degree of effort required for the awakening of other states of awareness. Because such awakening brings with it higher forms of perception and power, self-centered misuse of the greater perception and power bears proportionately graver karmic consequences. Spiritual awakening brings with it the need for moral impeccability.

# 241

## The Law of Spiritual Chemistry

Transmutation is a subject that from the earliest ages has occupied the attention of students, scientists and alchemists. Transmutation is the passage across from one side of being to another through the agency of fire. The mind of the public turns naturally to the transmutation of metals into gold. The mind of the scientist seeks the universal solvent which will reduce matter to its primordial substance, release energy, and thus reveal the process of evolution.

Conscious transmutation is possible only when a man has transmuted the elements in his own vehicles; then only can he be trusted with the secrets of divine alchemy. When through the latent internal fires of the matter of his own sheaths he has transmuted the chemical and mineral atoms of those sheaths, then can he safely, through affinity of substance, aid the world of mineral transmutation of the first order. Only when the fires of mind in himself dominate, can he work with the transference of life. Only when the Self within, is in control of his threefold personality can he occultly be permitted to be an alchemist of the fourth order, and work in connection with the transmutation of the animal monad into the human kingdom, with all the vast knowledge that is included in that idea.

The whole process of transmutation concerns itself with the two fires, which reach a higher stage of perfection, the fire of the atom and the fire of the mind. Added to that is the fire of the spirit. In the transmutative process the inner fire, which animates the atom

## Cosmic and Universal Laws

form or man is stimulated, fanned and strengthened till it burns up its sheaths, and escapes by radiation from within its ring-pass-not. This is seen in an interesting way as occurring during the process of the final initiations when the causal body is destroyed by fire. The fire within burns up all else, and the electric fire escapes.

# 242

## The Law of Spiritual Non Perfection

According to the law of Non Perfection no one ever becomes a perfect being. There is no such thing as a perfect being because there is always one more step in the plan of conscious evolution. This is all the more true of spiritual things that always seek and never find completion.

## 243

# The Law of the Subconscious Mind

The law of the Subconscious Mind is not able to distinguish fact from fiction. If it is convinced that a false statement is true, it will act as if it were true. If it is convinced a hot ember is cool, it will not experience a burn. If convinced a piece of ice is red hot, it will experience a burn. If convinced you are a failure, it will make sure that you fail. If the subconscious received conflicting data, it will produce conflicting results. If it is convinced that you can do great and near impossible feats, it will act to make these things occur.

The subconscious is truly the 'Genie in the bottle' that grants your wishes according to the 'commands' you give it in the intimate conversations you have with yourself. When you understand this law you will have the power to take the course of your life into your own hands by changing the perceptions and beliefs of your subconscious mind. Now you know why it is quite possible to walk on hot embers and not get burnt.

The subconscious mind uses all the knowledge that you have ever collected and probably have forgotten about to make things come true for you once it has accepted an idea. It mobilizes all your mental powers whether you are conscious of them or not. If used negatively it brings trouble, failure and sickness and if used positively it brings success, healing and freedom. To activate this law in a positive way you will need to learn to control your thoughts and be the master of your emotions.

*Cosmic and Universal Laws*

See also the law of Substitution, the law of Thought, the law of Manifestation, the law of Magic and the law of Attraction.

# 244

## The Law of Substitution

This is an important mental law and has to do with thought control. It means that we can have only one thought at a time and the only way for us to get rid of the one thought is to substitute it by another.

We cannot hold two thoughts in our head at the same time. It is either one or the other. So if we want to get rid of a negative thought the only way for us to do that is to think of something positive. If we want to stop thinking about one thing in particular then we must turn our attention to something else in order to replace the first thought that has occupied our mind.

Sometimes it helps to engage oneself with activities such as sport, a movie, a book or music to take one's mind off the problem or negative thought. Do not say or think 'I don't want to think about this' because that would make it only worse. It works better if you just turn your attention to something else. After you have taken a little distance you will find it easier to deal with the problem effectively. Always focus on what you want rather than what you don't want. It is more effective for you to focus on the solution rather than the problem.

# 245

## The Law of Suggestion

The law of Suggestion states that a statement carries with it an impact associated with the law of Description. When given through certain levels of consciousness and moments of expression and situation of experience, such suggestions may have a terrific impact upon the psyche of oneself or another.

A suggestion given to someone through hypnosis that reach deep can impact the subconscious. Self affirmations work in the same way, repetition of an affirmation over several days, weeks, months, years depending on the affirmation and the person, does impact and change the information of the subconscious. Mantras work in the same way. For example, a child or an adult, who is told constantly that they are worthless, will eventually think and believe that they are worthless. On the other hand, someone who is constantly told they are the most wonderful, the most intelligent will believe that of themselves too.

See also the law of Penetration and the law of Mantras.

## 246

## The Law of Summons

Otherwise known as soul talk, one can learn how to lift the soul from the physical body and summon another soul, to have *'a soul to soul'* talk. This is most powerful because there is no conscious ego present. The message of love and or explanation or plea is received in a most profound manner.

Focus your attention on the person, call the person's name, say 'I love you' then say, 'I forgive you' say what you want to say to the person, and end with 'I bless you.'

## 247

## The Law of Supply

Man is never satisfied, a fact deplored by many. But God did not intend that man should be forever satisfied. The law of his being is perpetual increase, progress and growth; so, when one good is realized, another desire for a greater good will develop and when a higher state is reached, another and more glorious state will unfold his vision and urge him on and on. Hence, the advancing life is the true life, the life that God intended man to live. The law of good is universal, for, are we not all seeking good in some form or another?

Science and logic alike declare that the universe is filled with the essential substance of every imaginable good that man can imagine, and that he is entitled to a full and ever increasing supply of any and every good he may need or desire. We believe, therefore, that it is right and good for man to seek to gratify all pure desires and ambitions. 'What things so ever ye desire, when ye pray, believe that ye receive them and ye shall have them.'

Every person, consciously or unconsciously, is operating this law in one or more of its phases. It works universally and on every plane of life's expression. We are all daily drawing into out lives the things we most desire and expect, and whether we attract good things or bad things, the principle operated is the same. But as we want more of the good things in life and less of the bad, it will be necessary to understand the law more perfectly, and so be able to adapt our thinking to it in a more direct fashion. Thus we secure the greater benefits that accrue from a conscious, intelligent use of its power. The secret of this law lies in our consciousness. Our life consists not in the abundance of the things we possess, but in the consciousness of that which we have.

If we meet with limitations in our life we need not be anxious or worry about it because worry and fear tend to restrict and limit the supply at hand. They tend to close off the outflow of substance, whether that flow is small or large. Instead of lifting us out of limitation and instead of improving our conditions or increasing our supply they drag us deeper into the throes of doubt and fear. Instead of expecting more to follow, we grow tense and anxious, which increases our fear and brings us less and less. Instead of tightening up our thinking, we must relax and be more expanding, to expect, ready to receive and embrace. To be able to do this we need to educate our minds to a larger state of thinking.

When we can think and realize more abundance, we shall receive more abundantly. According to the law of Supply the more man grows in true knowledge and the more he uses his power in constructive ways, the more good he will create in the circle of his expression and in his own little world.

See also the law of Manifestation, the law of Abundance, the law of Creation.

# 248

## The Law of Surrender

Because people so cherish the Self, surrendering is a very frightening experience. A person may experience surrender as a leap into an abyss or as death. This may be perceived by one who has not yet attained a complete trust and faith in God, the complete assurance that once the Self is abandoned, the 'being' automatically merges with a higher stage of existence which is ready and waiting to accept it. There is no chance for the process not to function. At the instant of surrender, the entire being of the individual merges into the specific higher manifestation of reality that its in relation to at that point in its development. God streams into the soul that has managed to negate the Self. This is the surrender of the idea of the 'I' the personality, the EGO.

Often this process of surrendering the ego is misunderstood as killing or annihilating the ego completely. This is not so at all. In fact a developed ego or personality is a requisite and essential, for the spiritual path. The surrender here is nothing but the recognition by the ego of the Higher Self and accepting the Soul to be the inner Master. When this is achieved the human being is then considered to be a Soul person with all the positive soul qualities and attributes.

Children have complete trust. For example when they are with an adult they like or love they will jump trusting that the person will catch them. There are moments in your life when you feel empty, despite all that you own materially and you are searching.

*Cosmic and Universal Laws*

It is said that when the student is ready, the master will appear. This master does not have to be a guru with a beard, it can be in the form of a neighbor, a friend, your own child or a book.

# 249

# The Law of Symbols

Symbols carry the meaning of messages from our guides. Esoteric knowledge was always throughout the ages and worldwide given out in symbols and codes so only the worthy could understand them. Every symbol has a meaning.

Here are some examples: The dot is the basic symbol of the infinitesmal and supreme power. All the subsequent geometrical forms or shapes, are believed to be developed, from the dot. A line is presumed to be a symbol of the power that began creation. The vertical stroke represents the oneness of God, the power descending from above, or the yearning of mankind for higher things. The horizontal stroke represents the earth on which life flows evenly and everything moves on the same plane. The sign of the cross means God and earth are combined in harmony. In occultism the perfect power or the motion of the life element has been explained by a triangle. Three dots the form, and the motion, or power, make up the triangle. A triangle also depicts the entire trio that pertain to creation, three virtues (triguna), trinity (trideva), three elements (tritatva), three words (triloka) three Gods (Devatrayes). The triangle represents a Pythagorean symbol for wisdom, the triple personality in man and it also represents the female element, which is firmly based upon terrestrial matters and yet yearning for higher things. The triangle standing upon its apex, on the other hand, represents the male element, which is by nature celestial and strives after truth.

When we place the two triangles on top of each other to form a six pointed star, it represents the perfect human being who has transformed, evolved and has achieved divinity. The five-pointed star is Solomon's seal representing the five senses and for the Jews it represents also the five Mosaic books. In ancient times it was a magic charm amongst the people of Babylon. The square is the emblem of the world and the four elements in nature. The cube unfolded displays a cross of TAU, or Egyptian form, or the Christian cross form. The symbol of 'Y' or fork, is a Pythagorean emblem of the course of life, in the form of a rising path with fork roads leading to Good and Evil. It is also a sign of the expectant soul gazing aloft with outstretched arms. The same 'Y' sign upside down expresses salvation descending from above and spreading over the world below. The combined dot form of Shiva and Shakti expands to assume the shape of a circle or ring for the sake of creation. The circle without a beginning or an end also represents God or Eternity. A circle with a dot in the middle is the open eye of God and God said 'let there be Light.'

## 250

## The Law of Synthesis

This is one of the three major cosmic laws. Also known as the law of Life. The law of Synthesis is the basic law of the positive pole. We would need to develop Buddhic faculty in order to comprehend this law. This law demonstrates the fact that all things abstract and concrete exists as one; it is the law governing the thought form of that One of the cosmic Logoi in whose consciousness both our system and our greater center, have a part. It is a unit of His thought, a thought form in its entirety, a 'concrete whole' and not the differentiated process that we feel our evolving system to be. It is the sum total, the center and the periphery, and the circle of manifestation regarded as a unit. The motivating urge of God, His outstanding desire is towards union and at-one-moment of soul and matter, soul and spirit. The trend to synthesis is an instinct inherent in the entire universe, to which man is only awakening.

The trend of all evolutionary processes today is guided by the idea of synthesis: Global planning, international relationships, economic fusion, interdependence, the welfare of humanity as a whole, sharing of commodities all of which alleviate separation, isolation and division. You do not have to join a religion to learn about God or to be close to God, as God is in all of us.

See also the law of Life.

## 251

## The Law of Teaching

This law concerns the responsibility people have to pass on the knowledge which they learn, for the continuation of the human race who can benefit by this information, when it is in the higher interest of people to learn the acquired information. However, learning to some extent is passed on through the genes, however, this is a physical materialization of inner knowledge achieved and retained from past lives.

The human being does not erupt with a clean slate into existence at birth and then laboriously begin its first attempt to gain experience. If this were the case, we would still be back in the Stone Age.

Incarnated advanced souls on the physical plane receive training and instructions at night, during sleep, directly from the Masters or from some of the great devas. These classes are usually in small groups or individually on the mental plane. To be able to receive and to interpret the physical impressions a perfect steadiness of inner poise on the part of the advanced soul is imperative. The aspirant must retain peace at all times, inner serenity, free from all daily turmoil, and keep the mind agile. This is a hard and rigorous training and requires the student to practice self-discipline, be free of all criticism, unnecessary questioning or emotional instability. The focus is on the control of the physical instrument, the physical body.

## Cosmic and Universal Laws

The science of meditation and the building of the antahkarana, the bridge of light between the personality and the soul, are the two preliminary stages on the esoteric curriculum. The relation of the individual soul to all souls is taught and the recognition that the long awaited kingdom of God is simply the appearance of soul controlled men and women on earth, in everyday life and at all stages of control on the physical level. When this relationship is recognized and more advanced souls and initiates come into power, the fact of the spiritual hierarchy will be accepted. The realization will be there that the kingdom of God has always been present on earth, but has remained unrecognized, owing to the few people who actually express the divine qualities of the soul.

When this knowledge has spread and is present in the human consciousness everywhere, the presence of the divine soul qualities will then be regarded as normal, and the divine plan of evolution will be recognized.

The teachings and spiritual impressions of spiritual Masters, Krishna, Buddha, Christ and other spiritual world teachers in the past have not been expressed as was hoped for, as mankind in general lacked the self knowledge and the needed self discipline, and the majority were ruled by personal desires and selfish ambitions and motives.

See also the law of Education, the law of the Soul, the law of Reincarnation, the law of Rebirth and the law of Evolution.

## 252

## The Law of Telepathy

The will, projected from the point between the eyebrows, the third eye, the Ajna center, is known as the broadcasting apparatus of thought. When the feeling is calmly concentrated on the heart, it acts as a mental radio and can receive the messages of others from far or near. In telepathy the fine vibrations of thoughts in one person's mind are transmitted through the subtle vibrations of astral ether and then through the earthly ether, creating electrical waves, which then translate themselves into thought waves in the mind of another person. This is normally done instantaneously.

To some, telepathy is a mysterious phenomenon, but to those who understand it, it is as easy and natural as ordinary conversation in our everyday life. Everyone can understand that thoughts have existence, and many scientists nowadays perceive that thoughts are made of vibration which mystics and sages have understood throughout the ages. As the physical body is made up of physical atoms, so our mind is composed of vibrations, every activity of the mind is a thought.

Telepathy actually is in constant operation. Whatever our thoughts are about others and about ourselves they materialize as such in our world. If we expect someone to behave badly then for sure they will. If we see the best in someone then the person will give his best. Our thoughts and feelings are picked up even when unspoken, by the subconscious of whomever they are directed to and will influence their behavior. True telepathy is a direct mental communication from mind to mind and in its more advanced expression is a communication from soul to soul.

Nowadays more and more are having telepathy experiences. Untrained this can be sporadic and uncontrolled but one can be trained to be telepathic through regular concentration meditation.

See also the law of Thought, the law of Meditation and the law of Akasha.

## 253

## The Law of Tenfold Return

The law of Tenfold Return is that universal principle wherein gifts freely given for spiritual use return to the grantor good fortune equal to or greater than ten times the loss.

This law works on the principle that when a vacuum is created it must be filled, When a seed is magically planted, it will bear fruit greater than its weight and original value. This law states that when we give freely from what we have to another, without expecting anything in return, the universe will make sure that we receive ten times what we have given, thus enabling us to give again ten times more. The return to us is not necessarily from the same source.

See also the law of Giving.

## 254

## The Law of Thought

This awareness indicates there is an old occult law, which humans may benefit from understanding. This law states 'energy follows thought.' Through focused mental thought one can manifest things on the physical plane. Every thought no matter how trivial sends out energy into the universe, colored with the quality of that specific thought, and which will eventually manifest in the material world. If we have constructive thoughts, then good will manifest on the physical plane, if however, we have destructive thoughts then only evil can manifest.

Those who wish to energize need only to direct their thoughts toward that target which needs energizing. This requires of course the ability to focus with great concentration power. There is power in the thought and when thoughts remain unharnessed havoc is created in our environment. This shows us how important it is that we are aware of what we think and that our thoughts need to be guided by the soul within. We can gain control of our thought faculty through developing our mind. Through the practice of meditation we can develop the faculties of the mind and establish the union of body mind and soul, to acquire soul qualities so that our thoughts are guided by the soul.

Contrary to general esoteric belief thought power also cannot heal. Thought can be the directing agency of forces and energies, which can disrupt or eliminate disease, but the process must be aided by the power to visualize, by the ability to work with forces and the ability to handle light substance. Thought alone neither cures disease nor causes it.

See also the law of Meditation, the law of Telepathy and the law of Healing.

## 255

## The Law of Three

Every event requires three forces in order to occur. There is a positive or active force, a negative or passive force, and a neutral or reconciling force, also known as first, second and third force respectively. We see this in the simplest circumstances of life.

As an example, imagine yourself lying in bed early morning. Your intellect is saying, 'it's time to get up!' Your instinct is saying, 'just five more minutes.' This tug-of-war may go on for some time with nothing happening. You lie motionless in bed, experiencing the push and pull between the active, first force and the denying, second force. Suddenly you see the time and realize you will be late for work. The emotional center interjects, 'oh my God, I'm going to be late.' You jump out of bed, propelled into action. A third or reconciling force has entered. The first force can be seen as desire, the second force as resistance to that desire. These are readily apparent to us in the play of life. We do not, however, so readily perceive the existence of the third force. It is said we are blind to the third force. It is an aspect of our sleep, as Gurdjeff would say, our existence in the realm of duality, that we are unaware of a Third Force.

In the second state of consciousness, waking sleep, we are incapable of thinking beyond duality. We engage almost completely in form thinking. Remember, this term denotes our tendency to think in twos, yes and no, left or right, this way or that. It also is referring to our inability to see beyond form to grasp the substance the form contains. We become stuck in what seems to be contradictions. We are constantly engaged in the struggle between yes and no and fail to perceive the third alternative that has the power to solve the dilemma.

The vibration of the number of three emanates power and energy. The balance of three physical, mental and spiritual is necessary to proceed with enlightenment. Three is important and constant throughout the universe, for example Divinity, Soul and Spirit, three in one and one in three. This eternal triplicity runs through every department of the manifested world.

Wiccans have a strict belief in the Law of Three, which states that whatever we send out into the world shall return to us threefold either good or bane. Wicca is a modernized nature-based religion surviving from pre-Christian paganism of Europe.

## 256

## The Law of Three Requests

This law simply says that whenever we pray or request a Higher Power to assist us, we bring stronger energy to the effort by repeating our request prayer three times over. This is the Power of Three.

# 257

## The Law of Time

The only moment we have is now. This is where we create, what we have done is done and that moment in history exists only as a record or energy trace in time and space. The consequences of past actions are atoned through karma and can be rewritten to a degree. The future only ever happens in and from the present tense and is built on today's thought dressed by emotion and driven by action. Activity is the key.

Third dimension living has more rigid structure of time than fourth dimension existence. There are those who can slip into 'no time' but these are people who have raised their personal vibration by demonstrating many virtues and have dispensed a great deal of karma and much killing of their ego and accessed the information to create the ability. Third dimension linear time was created for those living under this veil of forgetfulness to center in the moment and perceive a sense of order without the remembrance of burdens of past lives.

If we observe nature, we see the masterful orderliness by which every little detail occurs in relation to all the other details in the various cycles and we can grasp in this phenomenal order, the universal factor of synchronization. This is the synchronic order of time, the order by which everything in the universe occurs simultaneously in a masterful way from moment to moment in an ever changing kaleidoscope of infinite varieties of order and harmony.

# 258

## The Law of Tolerance

The law of Tolerance allows us to recognize the divinity in others even when covered by their masks and armor of demonic imagery and activities; or hidden behind the walls of apparent ignorance, sleep and stupidity; or residing in the bowels of lust, greed and power. The law of Tolerance is that law which allows one to speak through these walls and barriers to the divine God-Cell that lies buried behind those outer layers and awaits liberation from the deep confines and imprisonment at the very center of the self.

This awareness suggests you are all Gods and must in time learn to speak to each other as though you were addressing Gods. Tolerance creates transmutation of negative to positive and through tolerance we can create the transmutation. Tolerance is result of love balance. It is the first lesson of morals, before forgiveness. It is the control of the impulse of resistance by will. A thoughtless person is intolerant, but if a thoughtful person is intolerant it shows a weakness in character with thought as well as in self-control. If one does not develop tolerance, one is always subject to constant disturbances in life. We live in a world of beauty but at the same time there is much that we despise, it all depends on our attitude and what we choose to focus our attention on. By a slight change of attitude and our outlook on life, we can make our world into a heaven or a hell. Tolerance can be learnt with practice, the more we can tolerate the more thoughtful we become. It is through tolerance that we can create transmutation of negative to positive.

The principle behind the process of change is—tolerance and endurance. The capacity for endurance is necessary for bringing about a change. Without forbearance we cannot change for we are forever afraid of what others might think or say. All progress is stopped when we are preoccupied with what people, family, friends or neighbors would think or say. When we are always preoccupied with other people's opinion and concerned about what their reactions might be, we would not be able to accomplish anything. We must, therefore, develop our capacity for tolerance for the heat and the cold in the sentiments of others. The one who has not withstood the pleasant and the unpleasant in his own psyche, remains imperfect and unnerved by the slightest difficulty in life. The immature person is often perplexed and cannot be trusted, whereas a mature person is not so easily disturbed and always dependable. To mature constitutes the process of change, going through the two fires of what is pleasant and also that what is unpleasant, contrary and hostile.

It is possible to transcend these situations and to establish discipline. This is done through regular meditation and controlled breathing. One's breath carries with it many chemical substances, which act as conveyers and factors. Without breath control it is not easy to communicate a thought or to endure anything but when we have learnt how to control our breath and have practiced deep breathing and rhythmic breathing through alternate nostrils, we shall be able to endure all favourable and adverse situations. In an adverse situation we need to endure. When we are confronted with adverse circumstances, the brain gets heated up. We feel excitement and the pineal and the pituitary glands become highly activated. We can therefore greatly benefit with the practice of deep breathing when faced with contrary situations. All strong passions, emotions and lists consume and waste vital energy unless we learn to control it. Through the process of rhythmic breathing we can conserve our energy to become a productive power to be used constructively.

Tolerance is a very great power, which we develop when we bear pain and endure hardships without seeking outside support. We develop this by the medium of the science of living. It can never be achieved through academic education. Only through experiencing life in all its aspects can we awaken our inner powers and refine our personality.

See also the law of Change.

# 259

# The Law of Truth

Truth being a vibration of the highest frequency, always prevails, it can be subverted temporarily, but will always prevail. Truth being absolute, however, does have levels of frequency. We often confuse truth with fact and we often use the word fact for truth. In reality everything is subtle and complex, but nothing is simpler than truth. It is we humans who make things complex and difficult. Truth is simple and plain. It says in the Vedas: 'Simplicity is the living beauty.'

It is more important to find out truth about oneself than to find out truth about heaven or hell or other things that are far away from us. Truth is in the human soul. A Sufi master said: 'the first lesson that the seeker after truth must learn is to be true to himself.'

# 260

## The Law of Unconditional Love

Our true nature is love. Anything else other than love cannot exist, for example, shadow does not exist. If you shine light on the shadow and the shadow disappears. This is a condition as well as a law of third dimension living. Loving ourselves and other people as they are, is honoring self and another's self and soul path. It is loving without judgment or reservation, without any selfish motive, without expecting anything in return, with the awareness that we are all part of God, the All.

When we love without condition or restraint we connect in a profound manner with our own Higher Self. We notice that we say the right things at the right time in our communication with others while loving unconditionally. Life and events seem to flow to us in a more joyous and agreeable manner. Everything seems easy when we live with unconditional love.

Making this information available is, in itself, an act of pure unconditional love. It allows those who use it to reclaim their original God-given birthright of full union with their own Source. This full union implies a regaining of humanity's true stature, as fully sentient, creative and powerful God beings, all within the context of the Law of One and the sacredness of life. Beings who know themselves as directly emanating from and expressing Source do not need to have power over others, nor do they need to give their power to any higher being, because they recognize and live with the principle of divine equality. This leads to a state of Omni Love,

*Cosmic and Universal Laws*

where the divinity of all the creation is not only acknowledged but also lived as a state of being. This state of Omni Love, All Love, combined with the understanding that all living beings take their origin from the same Source, implies that all life is of equal value. The vast differences in consciousness, for example, on our current planetary stage, reflect the level of consciousness which can be embodied in different life forms, since there is an intimate connection between consciousness and biology. All life, regardless of its level of expression, is held in equal love by the Source. This could not be otherwise as Source recognizes itself in all manifestation. It is, however, possible for individual manifestations of source to deny the law of One and therefore act within a paradigm of separation consciousness. A being acting from a stand point of separation has lost some or all of its ability to draw its sustenance from the *Primal Life Force currents of Source*. It, therefore, feels compelled to feed off other life forms, in order to survive.

All creation is governed by law. The principles that operate in the outer universe, discoverable by scientists, are called natural laws. But there are subtler laws that rule the hidden spiritual planes and the inner realm of consciousness. Contained within these laws is the true nature of matter. Knowledge of these laws has an effect upon the mental urges with the *Mind* as the builder. Stay in full mindfulness of the application of Universal Laws as related to self and to others, and know that in love all life is given, in love all things move.

See also the law of Love and the law of One.

## 261

## The Law of Unfulfillment

The law of Eternal Unfulfillment states that there never can be completion or fulfillment in any moment. For if there were, there would be no further movement, and as each moment contains within itself all that is essential for that moment, so also each moment contains within itself, an emptiness, an unfullllment that is essential and necessary to lead into the next moment.

The law of eternal Unfulfillment states that every moment has something missing and is incomplete, and every moment has something that is present, total and complete; and when one accepts this law the greed-creating obsession to be fulfilled will cease to be.

# 262

# The Law of Unity

The law of Unity is a law, which recognizes no separateness, which ignores the appearance and the illusion of separateness in the apparent divisions of polarities, gender, the one and the many; realizing these each as integrated parts of the total picture. This law is about thinking of the whole instead of the parts. The western mind is usually accustomed to think in terms of the parts rather than the whole. Most people think in fragments and are, therefore, unable to detach to step back in order to look at the picture as a whole.

The law of Unity identifies with the over-all viewpoint and does not see for example night and day as separate but as a night-day process. It does not recognize right or wrong as two separate entities but as one process of right and wrong. It does not see pleasure and then pain, but the pleasure-pain process. It does not see the one nor the all, but the at-one-moment process of the ALL One Being, whose cells and souls work together even in the seemingness of division.

The law of Unity acknoweldges such division, but stresses the oneness of the parts. The law of Unity sees loss and gain, life and death as nothing but the spinning wheel of fortune that is based on the law of Change, which is itself a unified process known as the law of Magic.

To apply this law in our daily life, we can each day experience the different natures of our fellow humans and the other forms of life we relate with. We accept these differences as part of the

*Cosmic and Universal Laws*

Creator's universal design. We use our inner feelings to experience the unity that connects all things regardless of their outward appearance and behavior.

## 263

## The Law of Unity and Separation

The law of Unity and Separation is the foundation of all wisdom and knowledge. It reveals the big picture of how the universe is structured and how it operates. Elements unite and elements separate. Once individual particles (matter) came into existence, two basic processes began: Growth, the uniting of individual particles and decay and their separation. These ongoing actions ensure that continuous change is the natural state of the universe.

Eventually life in its present form will cease and the divisions in the universe will no longer exist. At that point the universe will return to its original state of unity. Only our Creator knows whether a new cycle will begin after that. This great pattern of returning to the source or starting point is repeated in cycles of existence throughout the universe. The symbol for this is the circle.

# 264

## The Law of Universal Sympathy

This law concerns a yogi power that allows a yogi, a person who is devoid of the ego, to transfer information or to influence others' minds. Since the yogi is devoid of ego, which would mean having all soul qualities, he would only use this power for the good of all concerned.

To explain this practically, if something happens to one it happens to all. For instance if I break my little toe my whole body is affected in various degrees. The whole is greater than the sum of its parts. My whole body is greater and more useful than just my little toe, yet the little toe doesn't know of other toes nor of the whole. So you cannot hurt someone and say it does not affect you. We are all in One whole.

# 265

# The Law of Vacuum

Nature tolerates no vacuum. This awareness indicates that energies create a vacuum behind them, and this vacuum naturally draws forth other energies to fill it.

When beings move towards the Light, when they move toward higher spiritual dimensions, or move toward higher levels of consciousness, they create a vacuum. This vacuum in turn attracts others to fill the void left behind. In this manner when some progress toward higher levels of awareness, others are drawn toward higher levels of awareness too. This law works on our earth plane, versus the law of Fulfillment, which is for the level of the Hierarchy.

This law works on a practical level in our daily lives as well. If we want something new in our life then we need to create a vacuum of energy to make room for the new that we wish to have. We experience this law in operation when we refuse to let go of an old love that is hopeless, we hang on to a long deteriorated relationship or an unhappy job situation, or refuse to clear out material junk that clutter our surroundings. In order to create the necessary vacuum to allow the new to enter our lives we need to learn to let go.

# 266

## The Law of Vibration

This is the atomic law of the solar system, one of the seven laws of the solar system, also referred to as the law of Fire and is the basic law of evolution. All is rhythm and movement and when all that evolves on each plane attains the vibration of the atomic sub plane the goal is reached. The law of Vibration is the law of progress, of movement and of rotation. On the seventh or lowest plane, the vibration is slow, clogged and lethargic from the standpoint of the first, and it is in learning to vibrate or to rotate more rapidly, that we mount the path of return. It, therefore, involves building a finer matter of the form. All vehicles, the physical and psychic, astral, mental, buddhic and atmic, have all to be purified ad refined.

The aim of the evolution for us is love dominated by intelligence or intelligence dominated by love for the interaction to be complete. The law of Vibration states that any vibration which is sent out for good, for service, increases into higher frequencies as it moves through space, until it returns to its origin, bringing the gifts of those higher frequencies back to the sender. Forces drawing on vibration for selfish purposes such as lust, power, greed, decrease vibrations in their frequency level. When beings send out selfish energies, those energies bring back, as magnets the lower vibrational forces the drawing of energy, decreasing the vibratory rate. On the other hand, radiance, the giving forth of energy and good deeds increase the vibrator rate. When beings radiate good, those energies increase into higher frequencies and bring back good. You can increase your vibration level through purifying your bodies of all negative energies, keeping a positive attitude towards life and by doing good deeds.

The universe is in a dynamic state. All forms vibrate and have energy. The higher the rate of vibration the greater the energy. All objects are composed of different arrangements of the same elementary particles and each has its own frequency and, therefore, its own amount of energy. The higher the energy level of a form the greater is the capacity to participate in higher life activities. Minerals, plants, animals and humans are all made of the same basic particles, the nature and the qualities of their lives differ because of their energy and vibration level.

Atoms always vibrate with such great rapidity that they seem motionless to the physical eye. At the other end of the scale are objects that vibrate so slowly that they also appear to be motionless or non-existent. In between are the various vibrations of living entities that range from consciousness all the way down to the lowly dust particle that plays an important role in the food chain. Still there are things even lower than dust. If we were to follow the scale of life all the way down to the utmost regions of the negative pole (undifferentiated matter), we again would find ourselves in the realm of spirit- the Alpha and the Omega. All that is, begins in spirit and ends in spirit completing a single cycle of evolution that will be repeated countless numbers of times through eternity.

Everything vibrates at a frequency and according to our own vibration level we are connected to receive the same vibratory frequencies. We can change our vibration level if we want to connect to higher frequencies, just like we change our TV channels to connect with and to receive different frequencies. This law is of great importance to us. The more we are able to raise our vibration level the more we are in tune with the natural laws of the cosmos and the more harmony we will experience in our life.

# 267

## The Law of Will of God

The creators of our world carry out their work of form building under this law. God's working has to do with things free from change and movement—things divine. It is God's will that what is human should be divine and therefore all creation pushes forth to the God Light. God is *all good* and it is by reason of the good that all other things exist.

# 268

## The Law of Will Power

This law concerns the individual divine within a soul extension personality projected from the complete entity. The individual developing soul extension differs in degree of will power from its other extensions soul family members. Depending on the conditions of an incarnational experience and the incoming will of this extension, the personality can possess a drive to accomplish something that may seem overwhelming to others in the soul family and/or other incarnational personalities friends. This law depicts the right and condition of each personality or soul extension to generate its own degree of will power

There are two ways in which the will power works, it is either lighted with the light of intelligence, or then it is not and works by itself. In the first we are consciously aware of working our will power with our mind and body, we are conscious of what we are thinking, what we are speaking and what we are doing in proportion to our will power and to the light that is thrown upon it from the light of our intelligence. In the second case we are not aware, meaning we have acted without will power, for example we do something, which we regret later having done, or said something for which we feel sorry. The will power was there but the strength and light of intelligence has not fallen upon it to the extent to which they should.

Both mind and body are governed and controlled by one power. In one aspect we are the controller in the other we are the controlled. We are the masters when the mind works, and the servants when the body works. When the power of the will is not present the mind becomes distorted and so does the body. Therefore, all disappointments, failures and illnesses, are caused by just one thing: weakness of will power. The will power is not a power of thought nor mind but something else behind the mind even.

# 269

## The Law of Wisdom

Wisdom is the science of the spirit just as knowledge is the science of matter. While wisdom is synthetic and subjective, unites and blends knowledge is separative and objective, differentiates and divides. Wisdom is the enlightened application of knowledge through love, to the affairs of humanity. Wisdom has to do with the development and the progress of the spirit within the physical form and the expansion of consciousness through the many life times.

The wisdom of the triad exists for the use of the personality but it is barred by the lower mind. Only when the three meet, through the regulation of the middle fire of the mind can a full light be achieved, and the whole body be full of light. The fire from above, *the higher self*, the fire from the lower self, *the kundalini*, and the fire of the cosmos, *the cosmic fire*. In their union comes the burning away of all that hinders the completed emancipation.

# The Soul's Journey

As the soul decides to take the path of human life it commits itself to leave the spiritual home, that of unity, and to embark on a journey of reincarnations on the physical plane, a world of duality and separateness. Our present reality in physical form on earth is but one phase of our complete human journey. Our purpose here on earth is to develop and strengthen our human qualities under conditions that are not possible on the spiritual plane. The spirit can only manifest itself through the material form. Our life on earth is a school where all souls go through a learning and a training process. The challenge is for us to be completely involved in the material world, at the same time we are supposed to remember. We are meant to remember our spiritual identity, to remember that we are a part of the Universal Soul and to remember our origin. The Sufis call this 'Zikr' as part of their teachings.

On earth our soul is given the use of a temporary form so that we can operate on the physical level. We refer to the physical body as the temple of the soul. Our first responsibility, therefore, is to take care of our physical body in all its aspects. Through our relationships and experiences in each life time, as we go through the wheel of reincarnation, we are meant to acquire, to improve and to refine such positive human qualities as love, tolerance, patience, compassion, understanding, strength, intelligence, generosity, kindness and all other irrefutable soul qualities. In the Sufi tradition the ones who know say, that God, Allah has three thousand names: one thousand he has revealed to His angels; one thousand He has revealed to His prophets; three hundred are to be found in the psalms of David; three hundred are in the Torah; three hundred are in the Gospel; ninety nine are in the Holy Qur'an. One, the

## Cosmic and Universal Laws

name of His Essence, He has kept for Himself and hidden in the Qur'an. These names are also to be found in the qualities of the refined soul.

Life is all about energy and all relationships and interactions are essentially exchanges of energies. Through our physical body we exchange energy with material objects, humans, animals, plants and nature. We exchange energies on the physical level, emotional, mental and psychic level all of which help us to connect and to understand our relationships and interactions as we go through our individual lives. Our interpretations differ and our responses differ according to our human qualities. The test is for us to gain self awareness and our own identity so that we become masters of our lower sensations and feelings. While doing that we are required to constantly remember who we are and the spiritual world that we come from. The more we are able to remember and the more we are able to connect to the Source, the Universal Soul, the Universal Mind, the more infinite knowledge we have and the more inner harmony is experienced. Some of us experience all this without actually being aware of it, i.e. climb the ladder of evolution slowly without awareness. However, to evolve with awareness enables one to achieve greater things.

It is futile to compare or to complain about the injustice and the chaos in our world. We, individually and collectively, create our world every day anew. We, humanity, are each responsible for our thoughts and our actions. In accordance with the unwritten universal laws of life we must accept the consequences, we pay the price according to our follies and we are rewarded when we have learned well and passed the tests that life imposes upon us. The law of Justice sees to that. The rules of 'the game of life' are fair because we are given a possibility to be forgiven and there is mercy, and even 'grace' as an extra bonus. This means we are always given the chance to repent and to make amends if we wish it. By changing our mind, our beliefs and our actions we can lessen the burden that we carry or we can sometimes even clean the slate altogether.

## Cosmic and Universal Laws

In other words, by feeling remorse, we can change or erase our karma completely. The choice is ours to make. One thing is certain that millions of people have made the same experience. We know this because throughout the ages they have written about it and some of us know this to be the truth because we ourselves, have experienced what they are talking about. The moment you decide to repent and to ask for forgiveness, surrendering yourself totally in humbleness to the Higher Power, you feel, as if you have been touched by a fairy wand, flooded with light, you feel immediate relief. You go through major transformation in consciousness and your life takes a turn to the better instantaneously. It makes no difference what belief you have, what status or what religion you belong to or how evil you have been. There are many thousands who have experienced this truth in their lives.

Whether you call this the Higher Power, the Logos, the Absolute, the Essence, Sun, Light, Energy, Allah or God makes absolutely no difference because all are ONE and the same.

# Glossary

**Ascended Masters—**

Also known as Avatars. Masters are beings who have all without exception gone through the incarnation process of life on earth, evolving through many lives with the same experiences of sufferings, joys and all the trials of the physical plane progressing to the highest levels until ascension to the higher planes of existence is achieved. Krishna, Moses, Jesus, Buddha are examples of the more widely known Masters. There are several many more Masters who are less widely known to us.

**Antahkarana—**

We are connected to the universal Source of energy through the energy cord called *Antahkarana*. The Antahkarana is the bridge between the higher and lower manas, the higher and lower self, during our incarnation on earth. It is also known as the *'rainbow bridge.'* The deeper meaning of meditation is a withdrawal of the lower manas and transcending to the higher manas. This is symbolized in the Bhagavad Gita by Sanjaya, the adviser to the blind, king Dhritarasthra (lower manas, the personality). While the king (the personality is blind) it is Sanjaya who is able to see Arjuna (higher manas, the Individuality) and Krishna (the Higher Self, Atma-Buddhi) and thus acts as a link between the higher and the lower.

**Avatars/Masters—**

An Avatar also referred to as Master is a highly evolved Being who is capable of reflecting some cosmic Principle or Divine quality and energy which will produce a desired effect upon humanity evoking a reaction and producing a needed stimulation. This energy is always focused through a manifesting Entity, is called forth by a demand or massed appeal and evokes response and consequent changes. The constant task of an Avatar is to establish nucleus of energy, spiritually positive. This for the Avatar is the anchoring energy. He focuses or anchors a dynamic truth, a potent thought form or a vortex of attractive energy in the three worlds of human living, which as the centuries pass, acts increasingly as a transmitter of divine energy, which produces effects on human civilisation. Christ, for example, anchored, 2000 years ago a nucleus of the energy of love.

**Chohan—**
'Lord,' superior chief, divine or human.

**Hierarchy—**
A body of dedicated liberated units of life (Masters), in the fifth kingdom governed by Sirius, working in group formation with all forms and lives in all kingdoms and with all souls in particular. Its emphasis is on the consciousness aspect of all forms and expresses itself though the minds of all humanitarians, all aspirants, all disciples and all initiates. The Hierarchy can also express itself through the medium of thought currents and through them impose its concepts upon the embryonic minds of the general and average public. It also directs the educational work of all nations, so that the undeveloped masses can become in turn the intelligent general public. Hierarchy has three departments: the Manu, the Christ, the Mahachohan; the race of men, human beings have three expressions: the Monad, the Soul and the Personality. Hierarchy is something that exists throughout nature. Everything in nature is ordered according to a hierarchical scheme.

**I AM Presence—**
A radiant beautiful glorious body of light. Teachings by the Master St. Germaine who also introduced the Violet Consuming

Flame which one can use to purify the physical, emotional and mental bodies. The 'I AM Presence' is the Higher Self and can be contacted at will to protect one or to guide one. A positive attitude toward life, respect and harmlessness to all alike is mandatory.

**Initiate—**

An initiate is an enlightened evolved individual, initiated in the secret knowledge of the universe. An initiate pursues esoteric knowledge and goes through inner transformations with prayers and meditations, studies and practices. An initiate lives through victory over the lower nature and personality. An initiate's weapons are love and light.

**Logos—**

Manifested deity, the living expression of divine thought.

**Man—**

The word 'man' is actually a Sanskrit work meaning 'thinking being' and refers to both male and female. From the 'Hindu-Dharma by Pujyashri Chandrashekharendra Saraswati Swami of Kanchi, the sanskrit word 'man' means to think. Manu was the first of the human race with its power of thinking. Since man's distinctive characteristic is his capacty to think the descendents of Manu came to be called '**man**ushyas'.

**Manvantara—**

A period of manifestation as opposed to Pralaya (dissolution or rest) the term is applied to various cycles, especially to a day of Brahma (4,320,000,000 solar years) and to the reign of Manu (308,448,000) see Secret Doctrine, Vol. II, p.68.) There are many cycles of manvantaras: prakritika manvantara – universal cycle, saurya manvantara – solar system cycle, bhaumika manvantara – terrestrial cycle, paurusha manvantara – the period of activity of man cycle.

## Cosmic and Universal Laws

**Monad—**
I, 'One', 'Unit', Indivisible, spark, divine center of every living being, atomic to cosmic.

**Occult—**
Concealed, obscured by something else as in astronomy. The word occult comes from the Latin word 'occultus'. The dictionary definition is: not divulged, secret, dealing with, knowledgeable in supernatural influences. Many practices are considered occult for example astrology, divination, the act of foretelling the future, magic and medium, a person thought to have powers of communicating with the spirits of the dead. Omen – any phenomenon supposed to predict good or evil. Sorcery, the use of supernatural power over others, witchcraft and wizardry.

Today practicing the occult has grown in acceptance and popularity. Only the names have changed. For example, instead of referring to persons who contact the dead, as a medium, we call them channelers. Instead of using the term 'divination' we use the word 'psychic'. A mystic is someone who has blind faith in the supernatural and an occultist is someone who goes further than belief and studies supernatural energies. An occultist is a truth seeker, adept in hidden wisdom and knowledge.

**Pralaya—**
In Hindu cosmology is a period of time of the cycle of existence of the planets where activity does not occur. The word pralaya appears in the Cyclops chapter of Ulysses – James Joyce's epic Irish literature novel. See also Manvantara.

**Sirius—**
Sirius is known as the 'Dog Star' and is about 8.6 light years from earth. It is over 20 times brighter than our sun and over twice as massive. Even during normal phases of its life, a tremendous amount of electrical energy is created on Sirius, making it the most energized positive point in our little corner of space. In 1862 Sirius

## Cosmic and Universal Laws

was discovered to be a binary star system with a companion star, Sirius B, which is 10'000 times dimmer than the bright primary, Sirius A. Every 49.9 years the 2 stars in the system, Sirius A and B come as close together as their orbits allow, creating huge magnetic storms between them. As they approach each other the stars begin to spin faster generating billions of volts of electricity. This energy is eventually released to flow down the magnetic field lines to the Sun which transmits it like a lens to all the planets. Sirius the 'dog star' stands for the 'spirit of wisdom' in the Zoroastrian tradition. Many reliable psychics and mystics firmly believe in the idea of a special gene, or personalized 'time capsule' programmed with the knowledge of the 'old ones' who came from the Sirius system centuries ago. This gene has been passed down from generation to generation to the present day. From this Sirian genetic strain a new school of magic has emerged.

Sirius was the guardian star of Egypt, its rising greatly affecting the life of everyday folk through the yearly inundation from the Nile. The earliest Egyptians believed Sirius was the home of departed souls. They considered Sirius to be the most important star in the sky, and was astronomically the foundation of their entire religious system. The celestial movements determined the Egyptian calendar. Ancient Egyptians called Sirius the 'dog star', after the god Osiris, whose head in pictograms resembled that of a dog. It is said that Sirians helped build the great pyramids and temples of Egypt. They also helped to build many of the tunnels and pathways of inner earth.

According to one Master Djwal Kuhl, Sirius is one of the more advanced training centers, or universities to which ascended Masters travel. Sirians are a group consciousness of both physical and non-physical nature. The Sirians in their etheric form are now working with many of us on earth giving us hints and conscious understanding of what our purpose is in the transformation of planet earth. The ascention will be a key, opening and integrating the light body with the physical, emotional and mental bodies, allowing each individual greater access to higher dimensions and experiences of oneness with others. Humans were meant to share in this role for caring for the earth and all of life on it, but most humans have been 'asleep' for a very long time now and are rapidly destroying themselves as well as earth and nature. The Sirians along with many others have been and are here to help us change that.

**Spiritus Mundi—**

The universal Spirit all around us, in space and around everything and in every being on earth and space. It permeates all.

**Sufis—**

Sufism, is generally understood to be the inner, mystical or psycho-spiritual dimension of Islam. Today, however, many Muslims and non-Muslim believe that Sufism is outside the sphere of Islam. There are also Christian, Hindu and Jewish Sufis. The essence of Sufi practice is surrender to God, it is the intention to go towards the Truth, by means of love and devotion. The spiritual path or way towards God. The Tao. Sufism encompasses a diverse range of beliefs and practices dedicated to the cultivation of the elements of the Divine within the individual human being. Practitioners of this tradition are known as Sufis. A Sufi is one who is a lover of Truth, who by means of love and devotion moves towards the perfection which all are truly seeking.

**The Noble eightfold Path—**

The noble eightfold path of Buddha: Right view, right aspiration, right speech, right action, right livelihood, right effort, right mindfulness and right concentration. It is about having knowledge of suffering and the path leading to cessation of suffering. It is about understanding that everything physical is temporary. It is having aspiration for harmlessness, refraining from lying, hurtful speech and criticism. It is about refraining from violence, from taking what is not given and recognizing the golden middle line. It is having the right mode of livelihood in simple words doing honest work. It is about putting the right effort generating good deeds. Nothing comes from nothing. It is about being focused and one minded. The eightfold path is about meditating about life and being aloof from the pleasures of the five senses and activating the Divine in you.

**The Seven Major Chakras—**
(1) The crown chakra, top of the head, is the link to the spiritual world, through the pineal gland, energies affect the brain and the rest of the body. (2) The brow chakra or the Ajna chakra, forehead between the eyebrows, is the link to the soul, it oversees all chakras below, balances mind and mental reason. It is linked to the pituitary gland, affects nerves, head, brain, eyes and face. (3) The throat chakra represents the ability to communicate and express oneself. True expression of the soul affects organs and throat, thyroid, parathyroid, glands, neck, nose, mouth, teeth and ears. (4) The heart chakra is the seat of the soul, gives the inner guidance for higher emotions, true love and friendship, compassion linked with the thymus gland, the energies of this chakra effect lungs, chest, upper back and arms. (5) The Solar Plexus chakra energies is the mind and personal will, lower emotions based on fear, anxiety, anger, jealousy, envy, insecurity. Here is the link between mind and emotions created and the energies affect the pancreas, liver, gall bladder and diaphragm. (6) The sacral chakra or hip chakra, is the seat for creativity and sexuality, here is the seat of joy and inner child. This is linked to sex organs, womb, kidneys, lower back and lower digestive organs. (7) The root chakra is the grounding, linked to planet earth. All issues of a physical nature, body, the five senses, sensuality, sex survival, aggression and self defense, affects endrocine glands system, adrenal glands, hips, legs and feet.

**The Seven Rays—**
The seven rays is a metaphysical concept that is used within Theosophy and the ascended Masters Teachings. Originally pre-

sented by H.P. Blavatsky, further developed by C.W.Leadbeater, Alice Bailey, Helena Roerich. The seven rays, which convey divine qualities, and each associated with a different kind of occult energy and with a different color, are seven major types of Light Substance (spirit/matter) that compose the created universes.

**Third Dimension—**

Our physical existence is on the third dimension, the intuition plane is the fourth dimension, and the Ascended Masters are on the fifth dimension.

# Bibliography

I have omitted making detailed footnotes throughout this book, as Cosmic and universal Laws are part of mankind's heritage, belong to everyone who aspires for spiritual and psychic knowledge and cannot be attributed to any one person in particular. This book is the result of almost forty years of extensive research and collecting of information from hundreds of ancient wisdom manuscripts and esoteric books, plus intensive study, observation and personal experiments and life experience. Sometimes, having no choice, I have had to use exact esoteric definitions, more often I have interpreted the law from my point of view to make it understandable and accessible with practical suggestions that one can integrate in daily life. I do not claim that my work completely covers this complex and endless theme. We certainly know much more today, than we did just two decades ago, but there is still much more that we know nothing about and is still to be discovered. Underneath is a detailed list of some of my sources. These laws certainly give you a guideline to follow but I would like to encourage you to make you own personal experiences and only then to make up your own mind.

**Sources—**

*Books by Alice Bailey, Lucis Publishing Company, London, U.K.*
- A Treatise on Cosmic Fire
- The Consciousness of the Atom
- Initiation, Human and Solar
- Letters on Occult Meditation
- The Light of the Soul, Pantajali

*Cosmic and Universal Laws*

- A Treatise on White Magic
- Discipleship in the New Age, Volumes I and II
- The Externalization of the Hierarchy
- A Treatise on the Seven Rays
- Esoteric Psychology, Volumes I, II and III
- Esoteric Healing, Volume IV
- Rays and Initiations, Volume V

*Books by Nicholas and Helena Roerich, Agni Yoga Society Inc., New York, USA*
- Agni Yoga 1929
- Infinity I, 1930
- Infinity II, 1930
- Hierarchy 1931
- Fiery World I, 1933
- Fiery Wrold II, 1934
- Fiery World III, 1935
- AUM 1936

*Books by Omraan Mikhael Aicanhov, Editions Prosveta SA, Cedex, France*
- Toward a solar Civilization
- Man Master of his Destiny
- The Power of Thought
- The Book of Divine Magic
- Looking into the Invisible
- Creation Artistic and Spiritual
- Man's Psychic Life: Elements and Structures
- True Alchemy or the Quest for Perfection
- Geheimnis Mensch Seine feinstofflichen Körper und Zentren
- The Symbolic Language of Geometrical Figures
- The Living Book of Nature
- Die Antwort auf das Böse
- Struktureller Aufbau und Schichten der Psyche
- Yoga der Ernährung

*Eckankar- Mahanta Transcripts, The Spiritual Laws of Eck*
*The Bahai Faith Teachings*
*Hunas traditions Hawaii Teachings*
*Rudolph Steiner Books and Teachings*
*St. Germaine Book Series - Volumes I to XII*

*H. P. Blavatsky, The Theosophical Publishing Co. Ltd. New York, USA.*
- The Secret Doctrines. Volumes I and II
- Isis Unveiled, Volumes I and II
- From the Caves and Jungles of Hindostan, Blavatsky, The— Theosophical Publishing Co. Ltd. New York, USA
- The Mahatma Letters to A.P. Sinnett from the Mahatmas M. and K.H.,—The Theosophical Publishing House, Adyar, Madras, India
- The Bhagavad Gita, The Gospel of the Lord shri Krishna, Shri Purohit Swami, Vintage Books, New York, USA
- The Mahabharata, william Buck, Nal Penguin Inc. New York, USA
- The Kama Sutra of Vatsyayana, Richard Burton, E.P. Dutton & Co. Inc. New York, USA
- Inana Yoga, The Yoga of Knowledge, Swami Vivekananda, Advaita Ashrama, Calcutta, India
- Autobiopgraphy of a Yogi by Paramhansa Yogananda, Crystal and Clarity, Nevada City, California.
- Krishnamurti teachings
- Dattatreya Siva Baba teachings

*The Complete Works of Swami Vivekananda, Volumes I to IX*
*Published by Swami Mumukshananda, Advaita Ashrama, Mayavati, Champawat, Himalayas*
*The Vedas*
*The Upanishads*

*The Teaching of Buddha*, Bukkyo Dendo Kyoki, Kosaido Printing Co. Ltd., Tokyo, Japan
*Lectures on the Sutra, Hobenand Juro Chapters*, Nichiren Shoshu International, Tokyo, Japan

- The Holy Qur'an, Abdullah Yusuf Ali, Amana Corporation, Brentwood, Maryland, USA
- Islam in the World, Malise Ruthven, Penguin Books, London, UK
- The Most Beautiful names, Sheikh Tosun Bayrak al Jarrahi al Halveti, - Threshold Books, Vermont, USA
- Jesus in the Qur'an, Geoffrey Parrinder, One World Publications, Rockport, MA, USA
- The Sufis, Idries Shah, Doubleday Dell Publishing Group Inc. N.Y.
- Beelzebub's Tales to His Grandson, G.I. Gurdjieff, Arakana, London.
- Judaism by Milton Steinberg, A Harvest HBJ Book, London, UK
- YHWH, The Book of Knowledge, The Keys to Enoch, J.J. Hurtak, The Academy of Future Science, Los Gatos, CA, USA
- Die Essener, Qumran, Johannes der Täufer und Jesus, Hartmut Stegemann, Herder, Freiburg.
- Our Religions, Arvind Sharma, Harper Collins, San Francisco, USA
- The Dead Sea Scrolls uncovered, Robert Eisenman and Michael Wise, Element Books Limited, Dorset, UK
- The Holy Bible, Old and New Testament
- Schöpfung im Wort, Friedrich weinreb, Thaurus Verlag, weiler im Allgau, Deutschland. (*Roots of the Bible.*)
- The Egyptian Book of the Dead, E. A. Wallis Budge, Dover Publications Inc., New York, USA
- Tales from the Arabian Nights selected from the Thousand Night and a Night, Richard Burton, Avenel Books, New York, USA

*Cosmic and Universal Laws*

- Make Your Life Worthwhile, by Emmet Fox, Harper & Row, USA
- The Urantia Book, Urantia Foundation, Chicago, Illinois.
- The Book of the Cave of Treasures, translated from the Syriac Text, E. A. Wallis Budge, Kessinger Publishing.
- Kryon Book and tapes, Lee Carroll, Del Mar, California.
- Seth Teachings

The list goes on and on and on...
and I continue to research and explore....

## my vision

I envision a world in which
enlightened women and men
of soul character qualities
are leaders of
nations, governments and institutions

I envision a world in which
all women of the world are free
of the invisible chains imposed upon them
and have equal rights and opportunities
on every level

I envision a world in which
every child born on earth
is guaranteed care, a home, food and education

I envision a world in which
diversity is respected and celebrated
and unity is found within this diversity

I envision a world in which
everyone regardless of status gender race or color
is encouraged to dream
and to have support in the realization of this dream

I envision a world in which
every human being is fully conscious
of the spirit of God present within all living beings
and in which
the energy of love flows freely everywhere

About the Author
Margo Kirtikar Ph.D.

Margo is a global citizen and entrepreneur who has lived, studied and worked in the Middle East, Europe and the United States. She is an avid believer in continued self-transformation and the refinement of the Self. The metaphysical world, spirituality and inner work have always been a very real, natural and integral part of her life. Her origin is both Syrian and Indian. Margo who was born in Baghdad, grew up in Iraq, Syria and India with liberal parents and was since her childhood exposed to many religions and cultures. Her life in the west began at the age of twenty, in the UK and then moved on to Switzerland and the United States.

After pursuing a career in international business for 25 years and earning various degrees in management and leadership, she decided to follow her soul path. She completed her BSc., MSc. and Ph.D. in the philosophy of Metaphysics and for the past two decades Margo has been counselor, coach, lecturer, guide and healer. Her healing method is based on a combination of eastern ancient wisdom and western psychology, with a focus on emotional, mental and soul healing.

Margo, a futurist, visionary, writer and artist, an indigo adult, coaches individuals in the *art of life*. Her goal is to empower people for life in the new world of the 21st century. Her strength lies in her ability to translate complex ancient esoteric knowledge into powerful modern and practical tools for self-transformation. She believes in the unity of head and heart, and that love is the fuel of life that unites one and all.

Today, Margo who has three daughters and two grandsons, lives in Vevey, Switzerland. She can be reached through her website *www.mindempowerment.net* or via e-mail at *margo@mindempowerment.net*.

### Further Books by the author

You and Change
Visions Unusual

ISBN 1425166695

Printed in Great Britain
by Amazon.co.uk, Ltd.,
Marston Gate.